THE AMERICAN WAY OF STRATEGY

THE AMERICAN WAY
OF STRATEGY

MICHAEL LIND

OXFORD
UNIVERSITY PRESS

2006

OXFORD
UNIVERSITY PRESS

Oxford University Press, Inc., publishes works that
further Oxford University's objective of excellence
in research, scholarship, and education.

Oxford New York
Auckland Cape Town Dar es Salaam Hong Kong Karachi
Kuala Lumpur Madrid Melbourne Mexico City Nairobi
New Delhi Shanghai Taipei Toronto

With offices in
Argentina Austria Brazil Chile Czech Republic France Greece
Guatemala Hungary Italy Japan Poland Portugal Singapore
South Korea Switzerland Thailand Turkey Ukraine Vietnam

Published by Oxford University Press, Inc.
198 Madison Avenue, New York, NY 10016
www.oup.com

Oxford is a registered trademark of Oxford University Press

Library of Congress Cataloging-in-Publication Data
Lind, Michael.
The American way of strategy / Michael Lind.
p. cm.
Includes bibliographical references and index.
ISBN-13: 978-0-19-530837-2
ISBN-10: 0-19-530837-9
1. United States—Foreign relations. 2. United States—Military policy.
3. Strategy—History. 4. National characteristics, American. I. Title.
E183.7.L55 2006   327.73—dc22
2006005502

1 3 5 7 9 8 6 4 2
Printed in the United States of America
on acid-free paper

IN MEMORY OF
DANIEL PATRICK MOYNIHAN
1927–2003

Contents

Acknowledgments

I would like to express my gratitude to Ted Halstead, President of the New America Foundation, and to John C. Whitehead for his generous support during my tenure as the Whitehead Senior Fellow at the New America Foundation. I am grateful to Sherle Schwenninger, Steven Clemons, Barry Lynn, Anatol Lieven, and Thomas M. Langston for their helpful criticisms of drafts of this book. I would like to thank the two editors at Oxford University Press who worked with me, Tim Bartlett and Elda Rotor. Finally, I am, as always, indebted to my agent, Kristine Dahl of International Creative Management.

PART I

AMERICA'S PURPOSE

Chapter 1

Defending the American Way of Life

> You know how impossible it is, in short, to have a free
> nation if it is a military nation and under military orders.
>
> —Woodrow Wilson[1]

THEY SAY IT EVERY FOURTH OF JULY and every Memorial Day. They say it, too,
on the anniversaries of battles like D-Day and Gettysburg. "Generations of
American soldiers have given their lives to preserve freedom in America."
That is what the politicians and editorialists and orators say.

But is it true?

In what sense did American soldiers who fell on the beaches at Normandy
die for the liberty of Americans? Even if Hitler had won World War II,
Germany would have lacked the ability to invade and occupy the continental United States. And Imperial Japan was far weaker than Nazi Germany.
It might have been able to hold on to its East Asian empire. It could not
have conquered the United States and taken away the liberty of Americans.
During the Cold War the Soviets could have wiped out many American
cities and military bases had there been an atomic war, but at the price of
losing most or all of their own. But there was never the slightest chance
that the Red Army would roll into Kansas the way it rolled into East Germany in 1953, Hungary in 1956, and Czechoslovakia in 1968. The Soviets
could have killed tens or hundreds of millions of people inside the United
States, but they could not have enslaved a single one.

Is it all propaganda, then? Is the statement that American soldiers died
in foreign wars defending the liberties of Americans nothing more than a
patriotic lie?

The thesis of this book is that the assertion is true. In most, if not all, of
America's foreign wars, as well as in the campaign by the Union forces
during the Civil War, American soldiers have indeed died fighting for the

freedom of their fellow citizens in the United States—not their freedom from foreign governments, but their freedom from the need to make their own government strong enough to protect them by making it too strong for liberty. The purpose of the American way of strategy has always been to defend the American way of life.

The Fundamental Purpose of the United States

In 1950 the senior staff of the National Security Council, under the leadership of Paul Nitze, the head of policy planning in the State Department, submitted a memorandum to President Harry Truman known as NSC-68. The document laid out a strategy of "containment" of the Soviet Union, which the United States adopted and followed from the early 1950s until the end of the Cold War in the mid-1980s.

By the standards of traditional Old World statecraft, NSC-68 is a peculiar document. The paper begins with a statement of "The Fundamental Purpose of the United States." It is hard to imagine a British or French strategic memorandum beginning with "The Fundamental Purpose of Britain" or "The Fundamental Purpose of France." According to NSC-68: "The fundamental purpose of the United States is laid down in the Preamble to the Constitution: '. . . to form a more perfect Union, establish justice, insure domestic Tranquility, provide for the common defence, promote the general Welfare, and secure the Blessings of Liberty to ourselves and our Posterity.' In essence, the fundamental purpose is to assure the integrity and vitality of our free society, which is founded upon the dignity and worth of the individual."

The document continues: "Three realities emerge as a consequence of this purpose: Our determination to maintain the essential elements of individual freedom, as set forth in the Constitution and Bill of Rights; our determination to create conditions under which our free and democratic system can live and prosper; and our determination to fight if necessary to defend our way of life, for which as in the Declaration of Independence, 'with a firm reliance on the protection of Divine Providence, we mutually pledge to each other our lives, our Fortunes, and our sacred Honor.'"

NSC-68 discusses the threat to the American way of life that would result from a U.S. policy that allowed the Soviet Union to dominate Europe and Asia by intimidation or conquest: "As the Soviet Union mobilized the military resources of Eurasia, increased its relative military capabilities, and heightened its threat to our security, some [Americans] would be tempted to accept 'peace' on its terms, while many would seek to defend the United States by creating a regimented system which would permit the assignment of a tremendous part of our resources to defense. Under such a state of affairs our national morale would be corrupted and the integrity and vitality of our system subverted."[2]

For decades, isolationists on the right and left have denounced NSC-68 as a sinister blueprint for a militaristic American empire. But as a reading of the document itself makes clear, the policy of containing the Soviet Union by means of European and Asian alliances, combined with negotiation from a position of military strength, was designed to avoid the need for a grim choice between regimenting American society and making peace with the Soviet Union on Soviet terms. In 1950 the authors of NSC-68 argued that a Cold War policy of containment was less dangerous to the American way of life than the alternatives.

Of Arms and the Republic

President Dwight D. Eisenhower, who succeeded President Truman, agreed. On April 16, 1953, Eisenhower gave an address entitled, "The Chance for Peace," his first formal address to the American people following his inauguration as president. Eisenhower blamed "the amassing of Soviet power" for forcing the United States and other nations "to spend unprecedented money and energy for armaments." Rhetorically he asked: "What can the world, or any nation in it, hope for if no turning is found on this dread road? The worst to be feared and the best to be expected can be simply stated. The worst is atomic war. The best would be this: a life of perpetual fear and tension; a burden of arms draining the wealth and the labor of all peoples; a wasting of strength that defies the American system or the Soviet system or any system to achieve true abundance and happiness for the peoples of this earth."

Eisenhower then uttered words that have been widely quoted: "Every gun that is made, every warship launched, ever rocket fired signifies, in the final sense, a theft from those who hunger and are not fed, those who are cold and are not clothed. This world in arms is not spending money alone. It is spending the sweat of its laborers, the genius of its scientists, the hopes of its children. The cost of one modern heavy bomber is this: a modern brick school in more than 30 cities. It is two electric power plants, each serving a town of 60,000 population. It is two fine, fully equipped hospitals. It is some fifty miles of concrete pavement. We pay for a single fighter plane with a half million bushels of wheat. We pay for a single destroyer with new homes that could have housed more than 8,000 people."

The president concluded: "This is, I repeat, the best way of life to be found on the road the world has been taking. This is not a way of life at all, in any true sense."[3]

Eisenhower returned to the dangers of the militarization of American society in his Farewell Address to the American people on January 17, 1961: "This conjunction of an immense military establishment and a large arms industry is new in the American experience . . . We recognize the imperative need for this development. Yet we must not fail to comprehend its grave implications. Our toil, resources, and livelihood are all involved; so is the very structure of our society."

He then uttered the famous words: "In the councils of government, we must guard against the acquisition of unwarranted influence, whether sought or unsought, by the military-industrial complex . . . We must never let the weight of this combination endanger our liberties or democratic processes. We should take nothing for granted. Only an alert and knowledgeable citizenry can compel the proper meshing of the huge industrial and military machinery of defense with our peaceful methods and goals, so that security and liberty may prosper together."[4]

What Woodrow Wilson Feared

In 1919 President Woodrow Wilson, having returned from the Versailles Peace Conference that followed World War I, was touring the nation by train. At every stop he pleaded with the American people to encourage the U.S. Senate to ratify the treaty that would make the United States a member of the new League of Nations. Wilson believed that if the great powers of the world replaced the "balance of power" with a "community of power" then wars would be far less frequent and the United States and other nations would be secure with a far lower level of military mobilization.

The alternative was an America permanently mobilized for war, Wilson warned an audience in St. Louis on September 5, 1919: "We must be physically ready for anything to come. We must have a great standing army. We must see to it that every man in America is trained to arms. We must see to it that there are munitions and guns enough for an army that means a mobilized nation . . . You have got to think of the President of the United States, not as the chief counselor of the Nation, elected for a little while, but as the man meant constantly and everyday to be the Commander in Chief of the Army and the Navy . . . And you know what the effect of a military government is upon social questions. You know how impossible it is to effect social reform if everybody must be under orders from the government. You know how impossible it is, in short, to have a free nation if it is a military nation and under military orders."[5]

Even now, almost a century later, Wilson's passion is striking. Here was a victorious war leader who hoped to prevent future world wars. Here was a commander-in-chief who, having presided over the mobilization of millions of soldiers and the conscription of America's vast industrial resources, hoped that American men and American factories would never need to be drafted again. Here was a president for whom a nation in arms was not an ideal but a nightmare.[6]

Paul Nitze and his colleagues, Dwight Eisenhower, and Woodrow Wilson argued for different American strategies: Nitze and Eisenhower for different versions of the anti-Soviet policy of containment, Wilson for U.S. participation in the League of Nations. However, they agreed on the test of any American strategy: it must reinforce, rather than undermine, the American way of life.

The American way of life. The phrase may seem quaint—a cliché of political oratory, a cartoon formula like Superman's fight for "truth, justice and the American way." But foreign policy thinkers who dismiss the idea of "the American way of life" and focus on "vital interests" as the basis of U.S. foreign policy are guilty of a profound philosophical and political error. For there is no interest more vital in American foreign policy and no ideal more important than the preservation of the American way of life.

The American Creed

To understand the American way of life, it is necessary to understand the public philosophy of the United States: the American Creed.

The ordinary American, asked what the United States stands for, answers "Freedom," not "Democracy" or "Republicanism." The American people take pride in thinking of their country as the "land of liberty" or "the land of the free," in the words of the U.S. national anthem, not as the home of competitive elections or constitutional checks and balances, as important as are those institutions. In addition, some Americans can still be found who insist that the United States is not a democracy, but a republic. From the eighteenth century until the twentieth, many American statesmen and thinkers took care to describe the United States as a "democratic republic."

They were right to do so. The political ideal of the American Creed is not adequately described by the phrase "liberal democracy." That phrase, in which "democracy" is the noun and "liberal" the modifying adjective, implies that democracy, defined as representative government, is more fundamental and important than liberalism, defined as government based on human rights. This has never been the mainstream American view. Even worse, the phrase "liberal democracy" completely leaves out the important concept of a "republic," which many Americans from the eighteenth century onward have defined as a constitutional government, not necessarily democratic, based on checks and balances among independent branches of government. In his *Defence of the Constitutions of the United States of America* (1787), which influenced the framers of the U.S. Constitution, John Adams, who became the second president of the United States, criticized those who treated the word "republic" as a synonym for "representative democracy."[7]

The American political ideal is not "liberal democracy." It is "democratic republican liberalism." In democratic republican liberalism, the noun is "liberalism," in the sense of government based on individual rights, and the adjective that modifies it is "democratic republican." This hierarchy in grammar reflects the order of importance of these concepts in American thought, which subordinates democratic republicanism to liberalism. The government of the United States is liberal in substance and a democratic republic in form.

In other countries there are political traditions in which the most important value is democracy or republicanism. But in Anglo-American thought, liberalism has always been more fundamental than republicanism, in democratic or other forms. In *The Idea of a Patriot King* (1749), which influenced eighteenth-century liberals in Britain and America, Henry Saint-John Bolingbroke wrote: "The good of the people is the ultimate and true end of government . . . now the greatest good of the people is their liberty . . . "[8] "That to secure these rights, governments are instituted among men" is the theory of Thomas Jefferson's Declaration of Independence. All governments do not have to be republics to be good. But all good governments ought to be liberal.

Americans are not democrats first, or republicans first. Americans are liberals who happen to be republicans and republicans who happen to be democrats. Democratic republicanism is not an end in itself but merely a means to the end of liberal government.

Republican liberalism is the most accurate shorthand description of the American Creed. Before it was American, the American Creed was English. Seventeenth-century English thinkers who influenced the American Founders, like John Locke, united the tradition of republican government, inherited from Greece, Rome, and the Italian Renaissance, with the idea of natural individual rights, a legacy of medieval and Protestant thought. The synthesis that resulted was republican liberalism.[9] In Britain the tradition of republican liberalism has only been one of a number of important schools of political thought, and far from the most important in recent generations. In the British North American colonies that became the United States, republican liberalism in the form of the American Creed became the secular civil religion.[10]

Republican Liberty

What did George Washington mean when he distinguished republican liberty from other kinds of liberty?

The first President of the United States made that distinction in his Farewell Address to the American people in 1796. According to Washington, by maintaining a federal union that allowed them to pool their defense costs, the individual states of the Union "will avoid the necessity of those overgrown military establishments which, under any form of government, are inauspicious to liberty, and which are to be regarded as particularly hostile to republican liberty. In this sense it is that your union ought to be considered as a main prop of your liberty, and that the love of the one ought to endear to you the preservation of the other."

Why did Washington, the former commander-in-chief of the American army, say that "overgrown military establishments . . . under any form of government, are inauspicious to liberty, and . . . are to be regarded as particularly hostile to republican liberty"? How does "republican liberty," in particular, differ from other kinds of liberty? And why is the minimization of defense costs, by means of a common federal military policy, so important that it is not only a "prop" of liberty, but, according to Washington, "a main prop of your liberty"? If all of this sounds more than a little odd to modern ears, it is because the language that General Washington shared with General Eisenhower is in danger of being forgotten. That is the language of republican liberalism.

In his Farewell Address, Washington alluded to the distinction that republican liberals made between individual liberty and republican liberty. By individual liberty, they mean the rights of individuals to freedom of movement, freedom of speech, as well as property rights and civil rights, like the right to due process under law. By republican liberty, they mean the right of an entire community to self-government. Individuals can no more exercise republican liberty than communities can exercise individual liberty.

Republican liberty has two aspects, one external and one internal. The external aspect of republican liberty is self-determination, defined as the independence of a people from control by other political communities. The internal aspect of republican liberty is popular sovereignty, defined as the independence of a people from control by an unaccountable government. When seventeenth- and eighteenth-century British and American thinkers referred to "free states," they were not talking about states that respected the civil liberties and property rights of individuals. They were talking about states that were independent of other states and accountable to their own citizens.

According to republican liberalism, not all liberal states need be republican. Republican liberals acknowledge that some empires have respected the autonomy of their subject peoples, and some autocrats have granted their subjects a high degree of personal freedom. There have been liberal empires, liberal monarchies, and liberal dictatorships.

But such liberalism is a grant from an uncontrolled power to the communities or individuals it rules. Liberty bestowed by an absolute monarch or an empire is a gift, not a right. The grant of liberty may be withdrawn. Yesterday's benevolent empire may become today's oppressive empire; a good king may be succeeded by a tyrannical king. Therefore republican liberals have believed that, while liberty may exist in non-republican regimes, it is secure only in a liberal state that combines political independence in foreign affairs with a republican constitution based on power sharing among several branches or authorities.

The basis for the thesis that republicanism reinforces liberalism is the premise that laws are most likely to be just if those who make the law have to live under the law they make. An imperial official who does not have to live under the laws he makes for a subjugated colonial population is less likely to take the interests of that population into account than their own elected leaders would be. And a monarch, dictator, aristocracy, or oligarchy enjoying an exemption from the rules imposed on the rest of the population is all but certain to abuse the privilege. The ancient ideal of "the rule of law, not men" is most likely to be realized in an independent state with a republican government, according to the tradition of republican liberalism.

The Two Constitutions
of a Democratic Republic

An independent republican liberal state need not be a nation-state; before the nineteenth century, most republics were city-states, not nation-states. It need not even be completely independent; a republican liberal state could be a self-governing city, province, or nation within a larger kingdom, empire, or federation. Nor need a republican liberal state be a democracy; most premodern republics were aristocratic republics, not democratic republics.

The United States was created as a democratic republic, that is, a republic in which the citizenry, whose members possess political as well as legal rights, corresponds to most or all of the adult population. Over the course of two centuries this ideal was realized by the extension of equal rights in practice as well as theory first to all adult white men, regardless of wealth, then to all white adults, including women, and finally to adult citizens of all races.

When Americans have said their country is a democratic republic, they have not meant simply that the government is democratic republican in form, but also that the society and economy are democratic republican in form. Following Aristotle, Machiavelli, the seventeenth-century English republican philosopher James Harrington, and others, Americans beginning with the eighteenth-century Founders have believed that a democratic republic is most likely to flourish where the majority of people belong to a prosperous middle class. In a society divided between a few rich and many poor, republican institutions were unlikely to endure. In Latin America and other regions, there have long been countries whose constitutions were formally democratic republican, but whose societies were aristocratic or oligarchic, not democratic republican in terms of the actual distribution of property, prestige, and power. This was also the case in some of the class-stratified big cities in the Northeast and much of the American South.[11]

John Adams argued in 1776 that "power always follows property." For this reason, Adams proposed "to make the acquisition of land easy to every member of society" or else "to make a division of land into small quantities, so that the multitude may be possessed of landed estates."[12] The United States started out very well, in this regard, outside of the slave South. In mid-eighteenth-century Britain, two-thirds of adult white males were landless and only one-third owned land; in the American colonies, the proportions were exactly the reverse.[13] In his *Letters from an American Farmer* (1782), St. John Crèvecoeur wrote: "Europe contains hardly any other distinctions but lords and tenants; this fair country alone is settled by freeholders, the possessors of the soil they cultivate, members of the government they obey, and the framers of their own laws . . . "[14] As Senator Thomas Hart Benton of Missouri observed in 1826: "The freeholder . . . is the natural supporter of a free government, and it should be the policy of republics to multiply their freeholders, as it is the policy of monarchies to multiply tenants. We are a republic, and we wish to remain so; then multiply the class of freeholders . . . "[15] Franklin Roosevelt agreed in 1936: "In our national life, public and private, the very nature of free government demands that there must be a line of defense held by the yeomanry of business and industry and agriculture. . . . Any elemental policy, economic or political, which tends to eliminate these dependable defenders of democratic institutions, and to concentrate control in the hands of a few small, powerful groups, is directly opposed to the stability of government and to democratic government itself."[16]

The United States, then, is a democratic republic that has two constitutions: a formal constitution of government, based on separation of powers, checks and balances, and frequent elections; and an informal constitution of society, based on the dominance in culture and politics of a free, educated, prosperous middle-class citizenry. The middle-class social constitution complements and reinforces the democratic republican government constitution.

American Nightmares

The American dream is the aspiration of Americans to be free and prosperous citizens of a free and prosperous country, to achieve personal independence in a country that itself is independent of foreign control.

The American nightmare is the antithesis of the American dream. The American nightmare comes in four versions: the Caesarist tyranny, the garrison state, the tributary state, and the castle society.

The United States is unlikely to become a Caesarist tyranny because of a military or presidential coup d'etat.[17] The more plausible and frightening scenario is one in which the American people sacrifice their liberty, their sovereignty, or both to obtain safety from foreign danger. To preserve their safety from foreign threats, the American people might create one of three versions of the American nightmare: the garrison state, the tributary state, or the castle society. In different ways each is incompatible with the American way of life.

The garrison state reduces the liberty and prosperity of citizens directly. It restricts their freedom by law and takes their property to pay for an enormous military and an immense internal security apparatus. A garrison state at its most extreme may draft everyone and socialize the economy.[18]

The tributary state preserves the liberty and prosperity of citizens, if only for a time, by surrendering national sovereignty under the pressure of foreign intimidation. In return for being allowed autonomy in its internal affairs, the nation surrenders its independence in foreign affairs. The danger of this strategy is evident: if the aggressor decided to renege on the bargain and dictate internal as well as external policy, the country might be unarmed and unprepared to resist.

In a castle society liberty and prosperity are not taken away by the state; they simply wither away because of anarchic conditions. Freedom is meaningless to someone who is imprisoned by fear in a house or apartment that has become a barricaded bunker. Citizens who must spend much of their income on personal protection, because the government cannot or will not protect them from terrorism, crime, or other threats, are likely to avoid paying taxes by engaging in black-market transactions. Because informal economies tend to be smaller and cruder than large-scale, regulated national and international markets, the economy in a castle society not only tends to shrink into a number of smaller, local economies, but also tends to regress from a more complex to a cruder form. This is what happened in the Dark Ages in Western Europe, when the Roman Empire was no longer able to control the incursions of barbarian tribes. It can happen in any society, no matter how advanced, when terrorism, crime, or other sources of disruption prevent a central government from policing its territory.

In an American garrison state, reluctantly but rationally, citizens would maintain their collective safety by sacrificing the American way of life to precautionary militarism. In an American tributary state, reluctantly but rationally, citizens would maintain their collective safety by sacrificing the American way of life to precautionary appeasement. In an American castle society, reluctantly but rationally, citizens would try to maintain their individual safety by sacrificing the American way of life to precautionary survivalism.

The Garrison State as a Response to Foreign Threats

The term "garrison state" was coined by the American political scientist Harold Lasswell in 1941 to refer to a regime created voluntarily by a free people who sought safety by surrendering most of their liberty to a government strong enough to protect them.[19] Lasswell and many of his contemporaries feared that the safety of the United States and other nations in the atomic age might require the permanent surrender of personal and economic liberty to garrison states. An American garrison state would not be imposed on the American people, against their will, by a tyrant who had sprung up among them. The garrison state is not to be confused with an illegitimate Caesarist dictatorship. The American garrison state would be a legitimate system that would be constructed reluctantly but voluntarily by Americans who were convinced that the requirements of their basic security required a permanent state of preparation for total war against powerful enemies. Given a choice between survival and liberty, the American people would choose survival.

In demanding independence from Britain, Patrick Henry famously said, "Give me liberty or give me death." But most people would sacrifice liberty in exchange for life, in the hope that liberty might be regained at some point in the future. And their decision would be justified. "Safety from external danger is the most powerful director of national conduct," Alexander Hamilton observed in the Federalist Papers. "Even the ardent love of liberty will, after a time, give way to its dictates. The violent destruction of life and property incident to war—the continual effort and alarm attendant on a state of continual danger, will compel nations the most attached to liberty, to resort for repose and security, to institutions, which have a tendency to destroy their civil and political rights. To be more safe they, at length, become willing to run the risk of being less free."[20]

Properly understood, the American tradition does not hold that republican liberalism is the best form of government in all countries in all circumstances. Republican liberalism is the best form of government when *internal and external conditions permit it to be established and maintained without sacrificing security*. In the words of the nineteenth-century American statesman John C. Calhoun, to the power of government "there must ever be allotted, under all circumstances, a sphere sufficiently large to protect the community against danger from without and violence and anarchy within. The residuum belongs to liberty. More cannot be safely or rightly allotted to it."[21] The limitation of danger is the precondition for the limitation of power that makes liberty possible.

In conditions of imminent foreign danger or internal chaos, an authoritarian regime might well be preferable to a republican liberal regime that cannot cope with the threats to the United States. It would be impossible for America's civilian and democratic institutions to function while atomic bombs were raining down on the country or while terrorists had shut down power grids nationwide. In such extreme national emergencies martial law might be necessary, at least for a time.

But authoritarian government, even if it were rational and adopted with the consent of the people in a brief or prolonged emergency, would be incompatible with America's republican constitution of government and its republican constitution of society alike. In wars and warlike conditions, the system of checks and balances tends not to function, because of the great augmentation of the powers of the president in the role of commander-in-chief. The separation of powers gives way to executive rule.

At the same time, the costs imposed on the economy by an enormous military weaken the middle class, the foundation of the republican social constitution. It is not the rich, but the middle and working classes who are most likely to suffer, when resources are diverted from the civilian economy to the war economy. And it is not the rich, who can find ways to avoid combat, but the middle and working classes who are most likely to be conscripted by a draft. Even in the absence of a draft and even in the absence of actual war, a high degree of mobilization of the economy for military readiness has the potential to turn the United States from a middle-class republic into a bureaucratic garrison state.

The Tributary State:
Purchasing Safety with Appeasement

The tributary state is the opposite of the garrison state. A garrison state retains its sovereign independence from foreign control or intimidation by jettisoning liberty. By contrast, a tributary state retains the liberties of its citizens by sacrificing sovereign independence. The garrison state preserves one half of the republican liberal formula, the freedom of the state from other states or stateless groups, by sacrificing the other half, the relative freedom of the individual from the state. The tributary state does the opposite. The tributary state preserves one half of the republican liberal formula, the relative freedom of the individual from the state, by sacrificing the other half, the freedom of the state from other states or stateless groups.

The tributary state is familiar from history. Many weak countries have averted attack or conquest by bargaining with aggressors. In return for being allowed to preserve its internal autonomy and the way of life of its people, the tributary state may agree to defer to the aggressor in its foreign policy. Finland, during the Cold War, was a tributary state in this sense. Its combination of internal autonomy and external deference to the threatening Soviet Union became known as "Finlandization," another term for coerced appeasement.

A tributary state, as the name suggests, may pay tribute to an aggressor to avoid being attacked. The aggressors engaged in extorting tribute need not be governments. Stateless groups can extort tributary payments as well. In the late eighteenth and early nineteenth centuries, the United States along with the countries of Europe frequently paid ransoms to North African chiefs who kidnapped Western hostages. The line "to the shores of Tripoli" in the United States Marines' Hymn—"From the halls of Montezuma / To the shores of Tripoli"—refers to a raid carried out by the Jefferson administration in 1805 when it broke with the previous U.S. policy of paying ransom to obtain the release of kidnapped Americans.

For a time, avoiding conflict by paying enemies or submitting to their demands in foreign policy may allow a civilian, liberal society to preserve its way of life as an alternative to sacrificing much of its economy and the liberty of its citizens to armed strength. But bargains between the extorted and the extorter are unstable. Success in extortion may lead the aggressor constantly to increase demands on the victim, forcing the choice between armed resistance and total subjugation that the policy of tribute had been adopted to avoid.

As President Franklin Roosevelt told the American people in December 1940: "Is it a negotiated peace if a gang of outlaws surrounds your community and on threat of extermination makes you pay tribute to save your skins? Such a dictated peace would be no peace at all."[22] Roosevelt repeated the point in his address to Congress in January 1941: "No realistic American can expect from a dictator's peace international generosity, or return of true independence, or world disarmament, or freedom of expression, or freedom of religion—or even good business. Such a peace would bring no security for us or for our neighbors. Those who would give up essential liberty to purchase a little temporary safety deserve neither liberty nor safety."[23]

The term "Danegeld" refers to the gold that Anglo-Saxon kingdoms in the Dark Ages paid to Danish Vikings to prevent them from raiding their territories. In his poem "Dane-geld" Rudyard Kipling wrote:

It is wrong to put temptation in the path of any nation,
For fear they should succumb and go astray,
So when you are requested to pay up or be molested,
You will find it better policy to say:

"We never pay any one Dane-geld,
No matter how trifling the cost,
For the end of that game is oppression and shame,
And the nation that plays it is lost!"[24]

The Castle Society

While the garrison state is created by a public decision to sacrifice personal liberty to national sovereignty in the interest of public safety, and the tributary state is created by a public decision to sacrifice national sovereignty to personal liberty in the interest of public safety, the castle society is the result of countless private decisions by citizens to sacrifice both personal liberty and national sovereignty to personal safety.

In a castle society, the majority of the people have lost faith in the ability or willingness of the government to protect them from threats. The threat may be external, like foreign terrorists or invading armies or falling missiles or dangerous illegal immigrants, or the threat may be internal, like criminals or paramilitary gangs.

Examples of castle societies can be found abroad. Brazil and Mexico in many ways are castle societies, where rampant criminality forces those who can afford it to hide in fortress-like homes and pay for private security guards. At the end of the twentieth century Russia metamorphosed from a militarized despotism under communist rule into a castle society warped by high levels of crime. It went from tyranny to anarchy.

Glimpses of the American Nightmare

In 1866 the U.S. Supreme Court, in a famous case called *Ex parte Milligan*, considered a death sentence given in 1864 to a Democratic politician from Ohio who had been found guilty of disloyalty by a military commission during the Civil War. The court overturned the death sentence and, in an opinion written by Justice David Davis, an ally whom Lincoln had appointed to the Supreme Court, repudiated the Lincoln administration's claims of essentially unlimited presidential power during wartime. Davis wrote: "Martial law, established on such a basis, destroys every guarantee of the Constitution . . . Civil liberty and this kind of martial law cannot endure together; the antagonism is irreconcilable; and, in the conflict, one or the other must perish." Justice Davis also rejected the argument that the Constitution was a charter for peaceful times only, and legitimately could be suspended in emergencies: "The Constitution of the United States is a law for rulers and people, equally in war and peace, and covers with the shield of its protection all classes of men, at all times, and under all circumstances.

No doctrine involving more pernicious consequences, was ever invented by the wit of man, than that any of its provisions can be suspended during any of the great exigencies of government."[25]

Unfortunately, Justice Davis may have been too optimistic. American history proves that constitutional safeguards are inadequate to preserve domestic freedom in times of war and international tension. The elaborate safeguards of the federal Constitution and the Bill of Rights did not stop Congress from enacting the repressive Alien and Sedition Acts in the 1790s, when Europe was consumed by war and many Americans feared that the revolutionary regime in France was trying to subvert the U.S. government. During the Civil War, the military arrested thousands of Americans, including some whose only crime was to have criticized the Lincoln administration; one anti-Lincoln member of Congress was deported to the Confederacy. Domestic Red Scares followed the Russian Revolution and the events of the early Cold War in the 1950s; German Americans were persecuted during World War I and Japanese Americans were interned in concentration camps during World War II. Although he was thwarted by the courts, President Truman claimed the power to nationalize the U.S. steel industry as a war measure during the Korean War. The FBI spied on Americans throughout the Cold War. Following the al-Qaeda attacks of September 11, 2001, President George W. Bush violated the law by authorizing officials to spy on U.S. citizens without judicial warrants, established a system of concentration camps in Guantanamo, Cuba, Afghanistan, and Iraq, authorized or permitted the torture not only of suspected terrorists but also of U.S. prisoners of war in Iraq and Afghanistan, and claimed the right to imprison any American citizen defined as an "enemy combatant" indefinitely, try him before a military tribunal rather than a civilian court, and execute him.

In most of these cases, once the initial panic subsided, the American people returned to their senses. The Supreme Court rejected the sweeping claims of the Lincoln administration, following the Civil War, and of the Bush administration in 2004, and decades after their internment Japanese Americans were compensated for their mistreatment. But the fact that this kind of justice is belated proves the point. During a moment of panic, the U.S. Constitution is likely to be no more than a few pieces of paper.

National leaders often share the panic of the public. Lincoln's Secretary of State William Seward, responsible for a time for overseeing the mass imprisonment of dissenters during the Civil War, sincerely believed that the British and the Confederates controlled the opposition Democratic Party in the North. (Even paranoids have real enemies; Seward was injured, and Lincoln was killed, by pro-Southern conspirators.) Franklin Roosevelt feared that Germany and Japan had planted saboteurs and quislings throughout America; he was blind to the fact that two of his top aides, Harry Dexter White and Alger Hiss, had volunteered to be Soviet spies. Most wartime presidents have thought it less risky to do too much to crush potential threats than to do too little. And they have been forgiven. Lincoln and Roosevelt are justly considered to be among the greatest American presidents, notwithstanding the excessive violations of civil liberties they authorized.

James Madison observed, "[T]he fetters imposed on liberty at home have ever been forged out of the weapons provided for the defence against real, pretended, or imaginary dangers from abroad."[26] Note that Madison begins the list of occasions for despotism with real dangers, not pretended or imaginary ones. Dictatorship by default, in a situation of grave danger to the nation, is a greater threat to the American republic than dictatorship by design. Reluctant Caesarism, forced on a president by circumstances and approved by an anxious people, is more to be feared than the seizure of power by an ambitious tyrant.

Nor is the castle society completely foreign to the American experience. Something like a castle society has been created at different times by the lawlessness of the Western frontier—in big cities during the Prohibition era, and in inner cities where groups fought over the drug trade. At the height of the Cold War in the 1950s and early 1960s, some Americans prepared for the possibility of atomic war by building and stocking private bunkers for themselves and their families. In the last third of the twentieth century, a crime wave swept the United States, fed by the Baby Boom–youth bulge and the mass migration of impoverished immigrants to the United States. Many middle-class Americans abandoned the dangerous cities for the safer suburbs, where they sometimes bought guns for self-protection, fortified their homes with bars and burglar alarms, and paid for protection from private security companies. Following the attacks of September 11, physical barriers began to appear around public buildings and office towers, and ordinary citizens—sometimes at the urging of the Bush administration—began to stock up on duct tape for poison gas attacks, emergency kits, food and water, and, in some cases, no doubt, guns. The every-household-for-itself logic of the castle society is far from unknown in the United States.

It is futile to expect freedom and democracy to survive unimpaired, if they survive at all, in prolonged conditions of acute national danger. The only certain way to preserve civil liberties in the United States is to make such moments of peril rare, and that can only be done by promoting a less dangerous international environment.

The American Way of Strategy

The ultimate purpose of U.S. foreign policy is to create conditions favorable to the individualistic American way of life. The first line of defense of the American way of life is the democratic republic itself, with its two constitutions—the constitution of government, based on checks and balances, and the constitution of society, based on a propertied middle-class citizenry that possesses a significant degree of independence from the government.

The health of America's government constitution, no less than the health of its middle-class social constitution, requires conditions of external and internal order that minimize security costs, whether for soldiers or police. If the costs of security are too high, the limited state may give way to an unlimited state—the garrison state—or to a weak state, which engenders a castle society. Either means the end of the American dream and the American way of life.

The major external threats to both the American people and the American way of life are empire and anarchy. An imperial state conquers other states to add their populations, resources, and territories to its own, or accomplishes the same goals by intimidation without conquest. American security costs would be high in a world dominated by one or a few aggressive empires.

An anarchic state cannot govern its own territory and exports chaos to other countries. American security costs would be high in a world disrupted by terrorism, crime, piracy, uncontrolled immigration, cross-border epidemics and pollution, and other consequences of anarchy.

Empire is a threat when some states have too much illegitimate power. Anarchy is a threat when some states have too little legitimate power.

By themselves or in combination, empire and anarchy have the potential to frighten Americans into abandoning our democratic republic for another kind of political system. Putting our hopes for security in a far less limited government, we can create a garrison state that pursues a policy of precautionary militarism. Or we can seek to save limited government by creating a tributary state that pursues a policy of precautionary appeasement. Or, losing our faith in the ability of the government to protect us, we can engage in an every-household-for-itself scramble of precautionary survivalism, the result being a castle society.

It is not enough, then, for America's strategists to protect the American people from direct threats to their physical security. American strategists must also protect the American way of life by preventing the domination of the international system by imperial and militarist states and the disruption of the international system by anarchy. Even if empire or anarchy elsewhere do not kill any Americans, they may have the potential to kill the American way of life by making democratic republicanism incompatible with the nation's physical security and incompatible with independence from foreign domination or foreign chaos.

The purpose of the American way of strategy is to defend the American way of life by means that do not endanger the American way of life.

Chapter 2

The American Way of Strategy

The world must be made safe for democracy.

—Woodrow Wilson, 1917[1]

FOR MORE THAN TWO CENTURIES, mainstream American foreign policy has sought to protect the two elements of American republican liberty—the freedom of the American state from other states and the freedom of Americans from their own state—by means of the American way of strategy. The American way of strategy is a synthesis of two traditions, liberal internationalism and realism.

Liberal internationalism and realism are often thought to be opposites. Liberal internationalists emphasize the norms of world order; realists, the realities of power politics. Properly understood, however, liberal internationalism and realism are complementary, not antithetical.[2] Liberal internationalism is a doctrine of legitimacy politics; realism, a doctrine of power politics.

In the realm of legitimacy politics, liberal internationalism holds that the two fundamental norms of the global system should be self-determination and nonintervention. Self-determination means that a state is legitimate only if it rests on the consent of the people—with the people usually, but not necessarily, defined as a nation by extra-political criteria of shared culture, language, and other aspects of common identity. Nonintervention means that no state can conquer or subvert another; with few exceptions, legitimate warfare is limited to self-defense.[3]

In the realm of power politics, realism holds that nations must be guided by considerations of power as well as morality. In a system of sovereign states, lasting peace can be established by several means, including the domination of one power, shifting alliances, or the collaboration of all major powers.

Liberal internationalists argue that the United States should promote its security by promoting a liberal international system. Realists argue that the United States should promote its security by pursuing prudent strategies in power politics. Both schools are right.

American statesmen at their best have always promoted liberal internationalism as the basis of world order. At the same time, the wisest American statesmen have been guided by realism in adopting a series of security strategies in response to different challenges in different eras.

Liberal Internationalism Is Not Inevitable

Since the eighteenth century, American statesmen have believed that American security costs would be lowest in a society of states rather than in a world of empires. According to the historian Hedley Bull, "A society of states (or international society) exists when a group of states, conscious of certain common interests and values, form a society in the sense that they conceive themselves to be bound by a common set of rules of their relations with one another, and share in the working of common institutions."[4] In the absence of overarching imperial structures, voluntary trade and alliances unite different societies, each with its sovereign state. Liberal internationalism is only one of a number of regional and global systems that have existed in history or that can be imagined. The present liberal international system was established by the adoption of the United Nations Charter in 1945. Germany's National Socialists and their allies sought a different world order, based on racial imperialism, while Marxist-Leninists sought to create an alternate world order based on "proletarian internationalism." Before World War II, a few European empires, which rejected the principle of national self-determination, dominated most of the world. And throughout most of recorded history, regional empires, like the Roman and Chinese, and civilizations that fused religious and secular authority, like Christendom and the world of Islam, were typical.

Liberal internationalism, then, as a way of organizing the world, is neither traditional nor inevitable. The United States promoted the reorganization of the world along liberal international lines in the mid-twentieth century because this relatively new and historically unprecedented system of global order serves both American interests and American ideals. Liberal internationalism serves American interests because a world divided into many sovereign nation-states is less threatening to the United States, a gigantic nation-state, than a world divided into a handful of powerful multinational empires or a world divided into many states too weak to preserve their sovereignty by suppressing anarchy in their own territories. And liberal internationalism serves American ideals because national self-determination is the precondition for democratic republicanism, a system of government incompatible with foreign rule over subject peoples.

A World Safe for Democracy, or a Democratic World?

Liberal internationalism is not to be confused with democratic revolutionism. In George W. Bush's second Inaugural Address in 2005, he claimed that it was "the policy of the United States to seek and support the growth of democratic movements and institutions in every nation and culture, with the ultimate goal of ending tyranny in our world."[5] This declaration of a global crusade for democracy on behalf of the United States, rhetorical or serious, represented a radical and unwise departure from the historic American way of strategy.

Americans have always believed that democracy, defined as democratic republican liberalism, is the best form of government in theory. But wise Americans have always recognized that democracy may not be the best form of government for a country in two cases.

First, external or internal threats may make an authoritarian system necessary in the interest of security and basic public order. The entire American way of strategy is an attempt to minimize the external dangers to democratic republics like the United States, both by creating a global society of sovereign states capable of thwarting empire and anarchy and by creating a system of power politics that favors peaceful civilian states. But while a peaceful and orderly world makes democracy more likely by reducing the incentive of countries to organize themselves as garrison states or castle societies, it does not make democracy inevitable everywhere. Even when external global and regional conditions are favorable, some societies may still be incapable of successful democratic republican government if they lack the separation of church and state, high literacy, and a broad and stable middle class.

For mainstream American statesmen and strategic thinkers, democratic republicanism of the American style is the best form of government only where the combination of external geopolitical conditions and internal social conditions permit democratic republicanism to be established and maintained.

Some Societies Are Not Prepared for Democracy

The Founders of the United States took it for granted that not all societies were capable of being organized as democratic republics of the American kind. Hamilton wrote to the Marquis de Lafayette in 1799 that "what may be good at Philadelphia may be bad at Paris and ridiculous at Petersburgh."[6] Adams declared that the project of establishing republican governments in the Latin America of his day was "as absurd as similar plans would be to establish democracies among the birds, beasts and fishes."[7] Later in 1821 Adams wrote: "Strait is the gate and narrow is the way that leads to liberty and few nations, if any, have found it."[8]

Jefferson, caught up in enthusiasm for the French Revolution, believed it would "produce republics everywhere."[9] During the Reign of Terror he wrote: "My own affections have been deeply wounded by some of the martyrs to the cause, but rather than it should have failed, I would have seen half the earth desolated. Were there but an Adam and Eve left in every country, and left free, it would be better than as it is now."[10] Soon disillusioned, Jefferson told Lafayette that the French revolutionaries had failed to recognize "the imprudence of giving up the certainty of such a degree of liberty, under a limited monarch, for the uncertainty of a little more under the form of a republic."[11] In a letter to John Adams on September 4, 1823, referring to struggles in Europe and Latin America, Jefferson predicted that in the long run "all will attain representative government, more or less perfect." In some cases, however, Jefferson thought that this would take the form of constitutional monarchy rather than democratic republicanism: "[Representative government] is now well understood to be a necessary check on kings, whom they will probably think it necessary to chain and tame, than to exterminate. To attain all this however rivers of blood must yet flow, and years of desolation pass over."[12] President Jefferson carried on a friendly correspondence with Tsar Alexander, whom he regarded as an enlightened autocrat capable of gradually preparing the backward Russian people for representative government in future generations.[13]

More than any other American president, Woodrow Wilson is identified with the promotion of democracy abroad. But Wilson, who was a leading American political scientist before he became president, expressed scholarly doubts about whether all societies were capable of democratic and constitutional government. In "Self-Government in France" (1879), an unpublished essay, Wilson argued that republicanism was likely to fail in France because the middle classes were "not of the stuff of which trustworthy citizens are made" and French peasants were "almost hopelessly ignorant." Wilson argued that liberal democracy suited France "as ill as independence of parental authority fits a child."[14] Like John Adams, who argued that Britain was a monarchical republic, Wilson was willing to consider constitutional monarchies like Britain and Imperial Germany as "democracies" like the United States. According to Wilson, "the Prussian constitution was an excellent instrument [for Japan] to copy."[15] Wilson, who admired Bismarck and suggested that Imperial Germany's weighted vote for the upper classes be adopted in American municipal elections, wrote: "Not universal suffrage constitutes democracy. Universal suffrage may confirm a coup d'etat which destroys liberty."[16]

Recognizing that not all societies are ready for democracy defined as liberal democratic republicanism, American statesmen, in addition to promoting peace as the external precondition for democracy, have usually preferred to promote two political preconditions for democracy, rather than democracy itself. The two political preconditions are national self-determination and human rights. The freedom of a community from rule by foreigners, and respect for human rights even on the part of a nondemocratic regime, are necessary, though not sufficient, conditions for the evolution of democratic republicanism in a country.

National Self-Determination as a Precondition for Democracy

No nation can be democratic if foreigners rule it against its will. However, popular sovereignty and democracy are not identical. A sovereign people may freely choose a form of government other than liberal democracy.

In 1795 George Washington wrote to the Marquis de Lafayette: "My politics are plain and simple. I think every nation has a right to establish that form of Government under which it conceives it shall live most happy; provided it infracts no right or is not dangerous to others. And that no governments ought to interfere with the internal concerns of another, except for the security of what is due to themselves."[17] Following the European revolutions of 1848, Abraham Lincoln, then a young politician, joined with political allies in Springfield, Illinois, in publishing a public letter that called for the independence of Ireland, Poland, Hungary, and other nations in Europe that were ruled by foreign nations or imperial dynasties. In a subsequent resolution on the subject, Lincoln and his colleagues wrote: "That is the right of any people, sufficiently numerous for national independence, to throw off, to revolutionize, their existing form of government, and to establish such other in its stead as they may choose." But Lincoln and his friends then declared that "it is the duty of our government neither to foment, nor assist, such revolutions in other governments."

In the twentieth century, Americans supported the self-determination of nations, whether the newly independent nations were democratic or not. Woodrow Wilson declared: "I am proposing, as it were, that the nations should with one accord adopt the doctrine of President Monroe as the doctrine of the world: that no nation should seek to extend its polity over any other nation or people, but that every people should be left free to determine its own polity, its own way of development, unhindered, unthreatened, unafraid, the little along with the great and powerful."[18] Walter Lippmann, who had served Wilson as an adviser, wrote of U.S. entry in World War I: "Nor did the United States go to war to make the world safe for all democracies: if it had seemed probable that Germany would be defeated by Czarist Russia, the United States would have remained neutral because its vital interests in the North Atlantic would have remained secure. The war was certainly not engaged to overthrow the Kaiser and to make Germany a democratic republic: if the Germans had not broken into the Atlantic and threatened the whole structure of our Atlantic defenses, private citizens would still have made faces at the Kaiser, but the nation would not have made war upon him."[19] In World War II, the alliance to which the United States belonged, the United Nations (which gave its name to the international organization founded in 1945), was made up chiefly of nondemocratic states, including the authoritarian states of Latin America. The United States was the only democracy among the "Big Four" that led the alliance—the British Empire, the Soviet Union, and Nationalist China. Outside of the British Isles and the white dominions, the British Empire was nondemocratic; Stalin's Soviet Union was a totalitarian tyranny that ruled a multinational empire; and Chiang Kai-shek's Nationalist China was an authoritarian dictatorship. The goal of the United Nations in World War II was liberating conquered nations from the Axis powers—Germany, Japan, and Italy—not imposing democratic government in every country on earth.

Similarly, it was to preserve the right of nations to choose their own forms of government, not to launch a democratic crusade, that President Harry Truman announced what became "the Truman Doctrine" in 1947: "I believe that it must be the policy of the United States to support free peoples who are resisting attempted subjugation by armed minorities or by outside pressures." In the context of the Cold War, by "free peoples" Truman meant not liberal democracies, but countries independent of Soviet control, intimidation, or subversion. The purpose of the Truman Doctrine was to ensure that independent states—including noncommunist dictatorships like those of South Korea and South Vietnam, which the United States went to war to preserve—would not be invaded by Soviet bloc countries or taken over by Soviet-sponsored communist movements. Truman's successor as president, Dwight Eisenhower, declared in 1953: "Every nation's right to a form of government and an economic system of its own choosing is inalienable . . . Any nation's attempt to dictate to other nations their form of government is indefensible."[20]

Human Rights as a
Precondition for Democracy

In traditional American thought, only some nations are capable of establishing and maintaining successful democratic republican governments. Other forms of government can be legitimate. But all legitimate governments, of whatever form, should be liberal in the sense of respecting basic human rights, which according to the traditional American understanding do not include the right to vote.

The Declaration of Independence reflects the idea that governments of different types may secure the same basic set of rights. "We hold these truths to be self-evident, that all men are created equal, that they are endowed by their Creator with certain unalienable Rights, that among these are Life, Liberty and the pursuit of Happiness.—That to secure these rights, Governments are instituted among Men, deriving their just powers from the consent of the governed,—That whenever any form of Government becomes destructive of these ends, it is the Right of the People to alter or to abolish it, and to institute new Government, laying its foundation on such principles and organizing its powers in such form, as to them shall seem most likely to effect their safety and Happiness." The drafters of the Declaration, foremost among them Thomas Jefferson, had an opportunity to state that only democratic governments could "secure these rights" including "Life, Liberty and the pursuit of happiness." Instead, the drafters spoke of "any form of Government" that "becomes destructive of these ends." The assumption is that forms of government other than democracy could secure rights and derive "their just powers from the consent of the governed." Two tests of the legitimacy of a government are suggested by the Declaration. First, the government, no matter what its form, must secure the basic rights of the governed. Second, it must rest on the consent of the governed, which may take the form of tacit consent. As long as a state protects the rights of a people and governs with their consent, it can take "any form."

In his identification of "the four freedoms" in his address to Congress of January 6, 1941, President Franklin D. Roosevelt did not make the promotion of democracy central to his message. At the time, there were hardly any democratic governments in the world outside of the United States and Britain and its dominions. The number of constitutionally elected governments declined from thirty-five in 1920 to seventeen in 1938 to twelve in 1944.[21] And as we have seen, the goal of defeating the Axis powers required the United States to ally itself with various nondemocratic regimes—the Soviet Union, Nationalist China, and dictatorial states in Latin America. The right to vote was not one of Roosevelt's "Four Freedoms."

But the freedoms that he did list provide the internal and external conditions for the secure establishment of democratic republicanism in a country. Roosevelt's Four Freedoms are "freedom of speech and expression," "freedom of every person to worship God in his own way," "freedom from want," and "freedom from fear." The first two of these—freedom of speech and freedom of religion—are individual rights secured by the internal constitution of a state. The second pair—freedom from want and freedom from fear—refer to the national security and prosperity of entire countries, not individuals. Roosevelt made the international nature of the second pair of freedoms clear in his speech: "The third is freedom from want, which, translated into world terms, means economic understandings which will secure to every nation a healthy peacetime life for its inhabitants—everywhere in the world. The fourth is freedom from fear, which, translated into world terms, means a world-wide reduction of armaments to such a point and in such a thorough fashion that no nation will be in a position to commit an act of physical aggression against any neighbor—anywhere in the world."[22]

Roosevelt's Four Freedoms, when they are remembered at all, tend to be dismissed as noble propaganda. In fact they are a good summary of the internal and external preconditions for the establishment and maintenance of a liberal society, whether it has a democratic political system or not. The internal conditions are freedom of speech and separation of church and state, which have existed to some extent in every liberal society, whether it had universal suffrage democracy or not. Freedom of religion includes freedom from state-imposed secular political religions, like fascist nationalism and Marxism-Leninism, as well as freedom from a state-sponsored supernatural creed like Christianity or Islam.

As a practical matter, liberalism, defined as the institutional protection of human rights, is much easier to achieve than democracy. An autocratic regime can improve its human rights policy very quickly; it need only stop torturing people, executing them without trial, confiscating their property, and censoring the media. It is much easier to ask an autocratic regime to stop violating human rights than it is to ask it to democratize itself. In the first case, it need only change a few of its policies; in the second case, it must abdicate.

The distinction between human rights and voting rights is not evidence of hypocrisy. It follows naturally from the American Creed of democratic republican liberalism. Americans are democratic republican liberals. They are liberals first and republicans second. All government should be liberal, even if only some governments can be democratic republics. Americans should support basic freedoms everywhere, but should support democratic republicanism only where external or internal conditions do not doom it to failure. The American republican liberal ideal has always been a world of liberal states, not all of them republican, rather than a world of republican states, not all of them liberal. The American tradition is one of support for global liberal reform, not global democratic revolution.

Promoting Democracy by Example,
Not Force

Rather than promote democracy directly, most American statesmen have been content to promote the external preconditions for democracy, the most important of which are sustained international peace in power politics and national self-determination in legitimacy politics. American statesmen have also encouraged the internal preconditions for democracy, including the granting of basic rights to all people by their governments. The most important way in which the United States has promoted democracy, however, has been to set an example that can inspire other nations.

In the first essay in *The Federalist*, Alexander Hamilton wrote: "It has been frequently remarked that it seems to have been reserved to the people of this country, by their conduct and example, to decide the important question, whether societies of men are really capable or not, of establishing good government from reflection and choice, or whether they are forever destined to depend, for their political constitutions, on accident and force. If there be any truth in the remark, the crisis, at which we are arrived, may with propriety be regarded as the era in which that decision is to be made, and a wrong election of the part we shall act, may, in this view, deserve to be considered as the general misfortune of mankind."

As the leader of the effort to save the American Union during the Civil War, President Lincoln repeatedly argued that the fate of democracy elsewhere in the world depended on its success in the United States. In the Gettysburg Address he defined the U.S. Civil War as a test of whether the United States "or any nation so conceived [in liberty] and so dedicated [to the proposition that all men are created equal] can long endure."[23] His point was that if the American experiment ended in civil war and disintegration, then the opponents of democracy around the world could argue that the democratic republic on the scale of the modern nation-state was an inherently unstable and unworkable form of government.

But Lincoln viewed those who advocated using the U.S. military to "export democracy" with derision. In his speech "Discoveries and Inventions" on February 11, 1859, Lincoln mocked "Young America," the symbol of Manifest Destiny, and suggested that talk about spreading democracy on the part of American expansionists was a disguise for other motives: "He is a great friend of humanity; and his desire for land is not selfish, but merely an impulse to extend the area of freedom. He is very anxious to fight for the liberation of enslaved nations and colonies, provided, always, they *have* land, and have *not* any liking for his interference. As to those who have no land, and would be glad of help from any quarter, he considers *they* can afford to wait a few hundred years longer"[24] (emphasis in original).

Lincoln's hostility to the idea of wars to promote democracy was shared by the Founders. During the wars of the French Revolution, French radicals declared war on all monarchical regimes and claimed that by invading neighboring countries France was bringing republicanism to them. On November 19, 1792, the French government declared that "it will accord fraternity and assistance to all peoples who shall wish to recover their liberty." Hamilton rejected this as "little short of a declaration of war against all nations, having princes and privileged classes," while Jefferson, despite his support for the French Revolution, observed that "the French have been guilty of great errors in their conduct toward other nations, not only in insulting uselessly all crowned heads, but endeavoring to force liberty on their neighbors in their own form."[25]

The classic statement of the argument that the United States should exemplify democracy rather than evangelize for it was made by John Quincy Adams in an address on the Fourth of July in 1821: "Wherever the standard of freedom and independence has been or shall be unfurled, there will her [America's] heart, her benedictions and her prayers be. But she goes not abroad in search of monsters to destroy. She is the well-wisher to the freedom and independence of all. She is the champion and vindicator only of her own."[26]

A World Safe for Democracy

The goal of U.S. foreign policy, to use Woodrow Wilson's phrase, has been to make the world safe for American democracy. More than any other system of world order, liberal internationalism minimizes the security costs of the American republic in two ways. First, the existence of many sovereign states makes it more difficult, though not impossible, for a hostile power to assemble an empire beyond America's borders with enormous human, natural, and industrial resources. Second, the assignment of all territories and populations in the world to a sovereign state with responsibility for policing them reduces the need for Americans to defend their interests against anarchy abroad. By minimizing the dangers of empire and anarchy, liberal internationalism reduces the incentive for Americans to seek their security by abandoning liberty in a garrison state, sovereignty in a tributary state, or both liberty and sovereignty in a castle society.

In promoting a favorable international order that would make an American garrison state, tributary state, or castle society unnecessary, the United States has been guided by enlightened self-interest, not altruism. By promoting liberal internationalism as the organizing system of world politics, while preventing the rise of a global hegemon based in Europe or Asia, Americans primarily have sought to preserve their own republican liberal way of life, not to bring liberty or democracy to other nations.

Even so, a world that is safe for American democracy is likely to be one that is safe for democracies in many other countries as well. At best, though, a world with low security costs is a necessary, not a sufficient, condition for liberal democratic governments. Recognizing that not all societies have been capable of successful democratic republican liberalism, American leaders have preferred to emphasize two of democracy's necessary conditions: the external condition of national self-determination, defined as the right of each people to choose its own form of government, and the internal condition of basic human rights. With some exceptions, Americans throughout their history have preferred to provide an example of democracy, rather than to try to impose democracy as a form of government on other nations by coercion.

A world safe for democracy need not be a democratic world. However, it will be a world in which more countries can become democratic republics like the United States without endangering their safety.

Power Politics and the American Way of Life

As we have seen, a liberal international system helps to preserve the American way of life by keeping American security costs lower than they might be otherwise. It does so by dividing humanity among many sovereign states based on national self-determination. Because most nation-states are small and relatively weak, the principle of national self-determination reduces the threat of empire by making it illegitimate for nations to augment their military power by conquering other nations, annexing their territories, and exploiting their populations. And the threat of international anarchy is reduced, as long as all states are fully sovereign in the sense that they can exercise effective control over their territories in order to reduce cross-border terrorism, crime, and unregulated immigration.

A liberal international system imposes fewer costs on America's republican liberal way of life than its predecessor, the European imperial system, and possible alternatives like the world orders sought by fascists, communists, and Muslim theocrats. By itself, however, the liberal international system is insufficient to preserve American security at low cost. Even in a world organized along liberal international lines, empire is still a threat, in the form of the intimidation by some countries of others by means short of outright conquest, and anarchy remains a threat if some countries are incapable or unwilling to police their territories to control terrorism, crime, or migration.

The Fallacies of Liberal Utopianism

Liberal internationalism does not entail liberal utopianism, which, however, has often been associated with it. From the eighteenth century to the present, liberal utopian theories have come in two kinds—"liberal peace theory," which attributes peace to the external relations among states, and "democratic peace theory," which attributes peace to the internal constitutions of states. Liberal peace theory, also known as interdependence theory, holds that as a result of increasing trade states will become so economically intertwined that war will be unthinkable.[27] Democratic peace theory holds that democracies are inherently nonaggressive and that democracies will never go to war with one another.[28]

Some American statesmen have endorsed one or both of these ideas. Woodrow Wilson declared: "A steadfast concert for peace can never be maintained except by a partnership of democratic nations."[29] Bill Clinton claimed that promoting democracy leads to peace because "democracies don't attack each other."[30] Harry Truman endorsed interdependence theory, claiming that "nations are interdependent and that recognition of our dependence upon one another is essential for life, liberty, and the pursuit of happiness of all mankind."[31]

Liberal utopians are correct that trade and cooperation among states tend to be correlated with international peace. They are also correct that the combination of liberalism and democracy within states tends to be correlated with international peace. But they get cause and effect backward.

Economic interdependence, international cooperation, liberalism, and democracy are not causes of international peace; they are its results.

Warring states do not trade with each other. And warring states also tend
to be illiberal and undemocratic. In times of international or domestic danger, individual liberties and democratic dissent tend to be curtailed in the
name of national security. An absence of war and high military tensions does
not guarantee that states will engage in trade and constructive diplomacy
with each other, nor does it guarantee that states will have liberal and democratic internal constitutions. But peace makes all of these things more likely.

In *The Federalist,* coauthored in 1787 by James Madison, John Jay, and
Alexander Hamilton to persuade citizens in New York and other states to
ratify the federal constitution, Hamilton made this argument: "Safety from
external danger is the most powerful director of national conduct. Even the
ardent love of liberty will, after a time, give way to its dictates . . . Frequent
war and constant apprehension, which require a state of constant preparation, will infallibly produce [standing armies]." Hamilton dismissed both
democratic peace theory and liberal peace theory, which were already familiar in the eighteenth century: "The genius of republics (say they) is pacific; the spirit of commerce has a tendency to soften the manners of men,
and to extinguish those flammable humors which have so often kindled
into wars . . . Are not popular assemblies frequently subject to the impulses
of rage, resentment, jealousy, avarice, and of other irregular and violent
propensities? . . . Has commerce hitherto done any thing more than change
the objects of war?"[32]

The American political scientist Mark E. Pietrzyk describes this venerable insight associated with Hamilton and like-minded thinkers as the thesis that "peace facilitates democracy": "In general, conditions of frequent
war and unstable peace contribute to the dominance of military organization in a government—either the army actually assumes control of the government, or a civilian government takes on a military character, with a
powerful executive ruling coercively. Long periods of stable peace, on the
other hand, permit the development of a government not based predomi-
nantly on military organization. Under peaceful conditions, a government
is more likely to assume a minimal role of maintaining law and order and
basic security, without becoming overbearing or escaping the control of
society."[33]

This is the fundamental insight of the American way of strategy: *peace makes republican liberalism possible*. Only in a peaceful world can liberal and democratic societies flourish. Peace is not the result of liberty and democracy but their cause.

The Realist Tool Kit

Peace itself must be created and maintained by power. A world state might establish and preserve global peace, but republican liberals reject that option because it would require the end of the independence of the United States and other self-governing communities. The question then becomes: how can peace be established among sovereign states with no common superior capable of enforcing the law? The answer is provided by realism.[34]

International peace in a society of sovereign states must be based on patterns of power that, unlike world federalism or world empire, are compatible with the continued existence of many independent states. These patterns of power include hegemony (the informal dominance of a single power, called the *hegemon* after the Greek word for "leader"), concert of power (the shared hegemony of two or more great powers), and balance of power (rival alliances of great powers). What is sometimes described as a fourth pattern, spheres of influence, really is a version of hegemony in which a number of powers accept the prerogative of others to act as hegemons in their own regions. The relations of great powers—that is, states that are major military powers, whether they are rich or poor in per capita terms—define all of these systems. Great powers are the main actors in world politics because, despite the juridical and political equality of sovereign states, military power has always been concentrated in a few states in every system of multiple states.

These three options—hegemony, concert of power, and balance of power—provide the basic tool kit of realist statecraft. Some realists have favored one instead of another. But in different eras, or in different regions, each of these strategies may be best for a particular state or the society of states as a whole. For example, American statesmen and strategic thinkers have usually agreed on the need for U.S. hegemony in North America but often have disagreed about the best policy to pursue in regions outside of North America: U.S. hegemony, a great power concert, or a role in a balance of power system.

Properly understood, realism consists merely of a set of methods used in power politics. The tools of realism can be used to promote a world based on freedom or one based on tyranny. Realism is like a knife, which can be used by a criminal to torture and kill or by a surgeon to save a life. Statesmen with radically different goals and visions of world order may be realists, in the sense that they follow the logic of realism for tactical or strategic reasons. Hitler was a realist when he temporarily teamed up with Stalin to launch World War II; on February 26, 1945, Hitler even mused that "in a spirit of implacable realism on both sides" he and Stalin might have established "a durable entente."[35] For his part Franklin Roosevelt was a realist when he teamed up with Stalin in order to defeat Hitler. In both cases Stalin was acting as a realist. But despite their common use of realist techniques, Hitler, Stalin, and Roosevelt sought radically different world orders—a fascist world order, a communist world order, and a liberal internationalist world order, respectively.

Liberal internationalists thus can be realists, just as fascists, communists, and Muslim theocrats can be realists. Realism is compatible with any number of historic and conceivable world orders. Properly defined, realism should not be confused with the nineteenth-century German school of *Machtpolitik* (power politics), which held that an untrammeled state should maximize its power at all costs. American realists are not power-maximizing statists; they are state-limiting liberals. In the interests of individual and communal liberty, they want the state to be limited to the minimal level of strength compatible with national safety. Even relatively "statist" American realists like Alexander Hamilton and the two Roosevelts look like libertarians by comparison with continental European practitioners of *Machtpolitik* or *Realpolitik*. American realism is a strategic doctrine that has as its purpose the preservation of the republican liberal way of life of the American people, not the maximization of the relative power of the United States.

American statesmen have included some who have neglected the realities of power politics, like Woodrow Wilson following World War I. But the mainstream American way of strategy has protected the American way of life by making the world less dangerous with a combination of liberal internationalism in the realm of norms and realism in the realm of power politics.

α

Fear and American Strategy

The Greek historian Thucydides, in his history of the Peloponnesian Wars, observed that states might be motivated to go to war by fear, glory, or pursuit of profit.[36] A fourth motivation for war unknown to the ancient Greeks, zeal, was added by the crusading supernatural religions of Christianity and Islam and crusading secular creeds like illiberal nationalism and Marxism-Leninism. As a commercial republic, the United States has preferred trade to war as the route to profit, and as a civilian republic the United States, unlike republican France, has lacked a tradition that equates national greatness with military glory. Protestant religious zeal, in the form of missionary fervor with respect to Asia and Christian Zionist support of Israel, has influenced U.S. strategy but has not determined its broad outlines. And the influence of secular ideological zeal for promoting liberalism or democracy on actual U.S. strategy is often exaggerated by defenders and critics of U.S. foreign policy alike.

This is as it should be. Glory, profit, and zeal are illegitimate as the basis of the grand strategy of a civilian, commercial, and secular republic. Reasonable fear, the rationale that remains, is a legitimate basis for strategy.

For more than two centuries the main motive for American security strategy has been the fear, sometimes unreasonable but usually justified, of other great powers, and in particular of six great powers: Britain, France, Germany, Japan, Russia, and China.

Fear of British and French influence and power in North America inspired the United States to incorporate vast territories contiguous to U.S. borders that had been ruled or at least claimed by the moribund Spanish Empire, from Florida to Texas and California. Fear of Germany and Japan inspired the United States to establish its hegemony in North America, to obtain a network of naval bases, and finally to take part in two wars against Germany, as a suspicious ally of Japan in the first and as an enemy of Japan in the second. Following World War II, fear that Russia would fill the power vacuums in Europe and Asia inspired the United States to adopt the strategy of containment, while anxiety about German and Japanese militarism or neutralism inspired the United States to treat those two conquered nations as protectorates rather than to rehabilitate them as independent military powers. Individuals and groups in the United States have often supported American strategies for reasons of their own: economic, ethnic, religious, ideological. But while American leaders have sometimes misled the American public about the details of U.S. foreign policy, the publicly stated purpose of successive American security strategies has always been their genuine purpose: enhancing American security.

Fear has guided American security strategy since the end of the Cold War. The United States feared the restoration of Japan and Germany as independent great powers, and feared as well the revival of Russian strength and the rise of Chinese power. The United States sought to make its temporary Cold War protectorates over Japan and Germany, now reunited, permanent. And the United States continued discreetly and sometimes crudely to contain China and post-Soviet Russia. The United States justified these policies in terms of a grand strategic bargain between it and the other great powers. The United States indefinitely would pay the costs of defending the interests of all of the other great powers, in their own regions and in the oil-producing Middle East, a region of concern to all. In return for accepting the unilateral U.S. security guarantee, the other great powers would remain relatively disarmed and would not challenge America's role as the dominant or hegemonic power in their own neighborhoods. The bargain was enforced by U.S. threats of arms races and containment policies directed at potential challengers. The premise was that the costs of U.S. hegemony, while significant, would be far lower than the costs that the United States would be forced to pay in a multipolar world of mutually suspicious and well-armed great powers or in a world in which a hostile power established hegemony over Asia, the Middle East, or Europe.

U.S. hegemony in North America succeeded in lowering U.S. security costs after it was established around 1900. But the attempt to establish U.S. global hegemony beginning in the 1990s is a different matter. The world is not the Caribbean. In the long run, America's regional hegemony in North America probably cannot be translated into U.S. hegemony in the world at an acceptable cost in American money and the lives of American soldiers. Nor can the policy of free security that the United States provides to other wealthy industrial nations be explained to the American public, which almost certainly would reject the strategy if it understood it.

In the early decades of the twenty-first century, it is clear that the attempt by the United States to establish its own global hegemony cannot be sustained. It is unclear, however, what American strategy will succeed it, and whether that strategy will be compatible with the American way of life.

PART II

A WORLD SAFE FOR
AMERICAN DEMOCRACY

Chapter 3

Independence, Unity, and the American Way of Life

> There is no one article of my political creed more clearly
> demonstrated to my mind than this, that we shall proceed
> with giant strides to honor and consideration, and national
> greatness, if the union is preserved; but that if it is once
> broken, we shall soon divide into a parcel of petty tribes at
> perpetual war with one another, swayed by rival European
> powers, whose policy will agree perfectly in the system of
> keeping us at variance with one another.
>
> —John Quincy Adams, 1796[1]

THE AMERICAN WAY OF LIFE IS MUCH OLDER THAN THE UNITED STATES. In fact, the United States was founded to preserve it.

The United States of America was established during the American War of Independence of 1775–83. The American Union subsequently was solidified by the adoption of the federal Constitution of 1787 and rescued by the defeat of the Southern attempt at secession in 1861–65.

Each of these events had different immediate causes. And Americans on all sides were driven by various motives in each of these periods. But whatever their other purposes were, the independence of the United States, the adoption of the federal Constitution of 1787, and the preservation of the Union during the Civil War helped to defend the American way of life.

The threat to the American way of life posed by the centralizing British government in the 1760s and 1770s was direct. Britain threatened to substitute direct rule for self-government in some if not all areas of American colonial life, converting what were effectively self-governing dominions in a loose federal empire into directly administered provinces in a centralized empire. A centralized British Empire in North America ruled from London might have been compatible with individual liberty, but not with republican liberty, defined as the right of American communities to a high degree of self-government.

In the cases of the adoption of the federal constitution and the U.S. Civil War, the dangers to American republican liberty were indirect. If the United States had disintegrated into two or more independent governments, as a result of the weakness of the Articles of Confederation or the success of the Confederate war of secession, then North America might have been "Balkanized" among a number of independent English-speaking countries. At best, the division of North America like Latin America among many small, mostly weak governments would have harmed prosperity, by preventing the formation of a continental market and requiring each state to have its own redundant currency and trade policies. At worst, conflicts among the petty sovereign states of North America might have been manipulated by European and Asian great powers, including Britain and France in the nineteenth century, and perhaps Germany, Russia, and Japan in the twentieth. In order to hold their own against each other, or against European or Asian great powers, these lesser North American republics might have had to turn themselves into regimented and militarized garrison states.

For this reason, the bloody war for American independence, the bloodless campaign for the adoption of the federal Constitution, and the bloody crusade for preservation of the Union were vital to the preservation of the liberty of Americans. Defending liberty in the United States required not only independence from British rule, but also unity, in order to prevent the freedom and prosperity of Americans from becoming a casualty of trade wars and actual wars among the shattered fragments of the former United States.

Something to Do with Taxes

Many people remember vaguely that the American Revolution had something to do with taxes. A few remember that the issue was whether the power to tax lay with London or the American colonies. But this was a surrogate for the real issue: preserving the American way of life.

In the first two-thirds of the eighteenth century, the British colonists in North America developed a distinctive way of life quite different from that of their British cousins. Something like Britain's aristocratic society endured in the South and parts of the Northeast. But in general, colonial society was characterized by a degree of middle-class prosperity and widespread property ownership unknown in any other society in the world. Not only were America's yeoman farmers, artisans, and merchants better off than most Britons and Europeans, but also the cost of government was much lower.

The trouble began in the aftermath of the French and Indian War (Seven Years' War) of 1754–63. The British imperial government insisted that the colonists pay more of the costs of their own defense. The colonists, however, feared that the London parliament was trying to destroy the system of colonial self-government that had grown up in the preceding generations. They remembered that the London parliament had destroyed the Scottish parliament in 1707 (it would eliminate the Irish parliament in 1801). They feared that the same thing was now happening to them. They would pay ever higher taxes, even as their colonial assemblies lost authority to the London parliament. As a result, British North America might come to resemble Ireland or Scotland, impoverished countries where absentee landlords held vast tracts of land and where major decisions were made by well-connected aristocrats and merchants in London with little or no accountability to the people whom they ruled.

In 1774–75, American colonial leaders sought equality within the British Empire, not independence from it. Reluctant to break with Britain, the American colonists proposed various kinds of imperial federalism, in which foreign affairs and defense would be left to imperial authorities in London, while the colonies, individually or with a common legislature, would control their own domestic policy. The Declaration of Rights and Grievances adopted by the First Continental Congress in 1774 stated: "We have not raised armies with ambitious designs of separating from Great Britain." The Continental Congress declared that it was willing to "cheerfully consent to the operation of such acts of the British Parliament, as are bona fide restrained to the regulation of our external commerce . . . "[2]

In his *Summary View of the Rights of British America* (1774), Thomas Jefferson asserted that the original colonists, having left Britain, continued "their union with her by submitting themselves to the same common Sovereign, who was thereby made the central link connecting the several parts of the Empire thus newly multiplied."[3] According to this theory, the British Empire was a federal empire, with a number of independent legislatures, sharing the same monarch. This American theory of imperial federalism explains why the Declaration of Independence denounces the king, who was acknowledged to have authority over the colonies, rather than the

London parliament, which, according to the colonists, had never possessed any jurisdiction in North America. In a sentence in Jefferson's draft of the Declaration of Independence that Congress deleted, Jefferson summarized the theory: "We have reminded [our British brethren] . . . that in constituting indeed our several forms of government, we had adopted one common kind; thereby laying a foundation for perpetual league and amity with them; but that submission to their parliament was no part of our constitution."[4] This claim was plausible. While the London parliament had sometimes regulated trade and imperial military affairs, all of the colonial governors were appointed by the king alone, without the approval of the London parliament, and the elected assemblies in the colonies had sole control over money bills.

The British Rejection of Imperial Federalism

What the American colonists were proposing, then, was something like the relationship between Britain and its white dominions from the late nineteenth century onward, in which the United Kingdom, Canada, Australia, and New Zealand were all self-governing countries, each with its own legislature, sharing a common head of state, the British monarch. If the British had agreed to such an arrangement in the late eighteenth century, the rupture between Britain and what became the United States might never have occurred.

However, ordinary Englishmen had reason to reject the doctrine of imperial federalism that the Americans proposed. For one thing, the growth of the American colonies in population and power threatened to make North America the center of gravity of the British Empire by the mid-nineteenth century. The British Isles might have become minor provinces of a superpower centered on the Great Lakes and the Mississippi. (Some might assert that this has occurred anyway.)

Nor could eighteenth-century Britons contemplate the possibility of a king ruling many separate realms without alarm. English history contained many examples of monarchs who repressed the English population with the help of foreign subjects or mercenaries—Scots, Irish, Danes. If George III, who was the ruler of tiny Hanover in Germany as well as of Britain, could employ Hessian soldiers from his German domain in an attempt to repress his rebellious American subjects, what would prevent the monarch

of a federal British Empire from using Virginian and Pennsylvanian soldiers to crush dissent in England itself?

By the time Britain's white dominions established their autonomy within
the British Empire in the late nineteenth century, such a threat was no longer
plausible. In the course of the nineteenth century, the British monarch became a largely ceremonial figurehead. No British citizen today would fear
that the British monarch would send Canadian or Australian troops to
arrest the British prime minister or shut down parliament. But in the eighteenth century the subordination of the British monarchy to parliament
was still far from established. A powerful monarch in a federal British Empire
might have been able to play one self-governing domain against another in
a game of divide and rule.

Given the reasonable American insistence on imperial federalism, and
the equally reasonable British fear of its consequences, a divorce may have
been inevitable. When the London parliament, with the support of George
III, insisted on its unlimited power over the colonies, the Americans reluctantly adopted their second choice: independence.

This history may be familiar but the point is not. For Americans, the
independence of the United States from Britain and its organization as a
democratic republic was a means to an end, not an end in itself. The end
was the safeguarding of the communal right to self-government and the individual liberties that the British settlers in America had already enjoyed for
generations under British rule. Americans adopted one strategy for defending the American way of life against imperial centralization—independence
as a democratic republic—only because their first choice, self-government
within a federal monarchical empire, was rejected. Democratic republicanism and national independence were only two of several possible methods
for preserving what by 1776 was the traditional American way of life, characterized by personal liberty, widespread property ownership, low taxes,
and an inexpensive military.

This explains what otherwise might seem puzzling in a letter President
Washington wrote to the French minister on January 1, 1796: "Born, Sir, in
a land of liberty; having early learned its value; having engaged in a peril-
ous conflict to defend it; having, in a word, devoted the best years of my
life to secure its permanent establishment in my own country, my anxious
recollections, my sympathetic feelings, and my best wishes are irresistibly
excited, whensoever, in any country, I see an oppressed nation unfurl the

banners of Freedom."[5] When Washington said that he had been born "in a land of liberty," he was not referring to the United States, which did not exist in his youth; he was referring to his native Virginia and the other colonies of British North America. The purpose of the American Revolution was not to make the British colonies free, in the sense of respecting the liberties of their inhabitants. They were already free, in that sense. It was to secure that freedom against British imperial encroachment—"to secure its permanent establishment," in Washington's words—that the colonies became free in the sense of independence.

Preventing a North American Balance of Power: National Unity

Following independence, the first priority of most of the leaders of the United States was maintaining the union of the states, to prevent Britain or other European great powers from engaging in a divide-and-rule policy in North America. In his circular letter to the state governments of June 8, 1783, George Washington wrote that "this is the favorable moment to give such a tone to our Federal Government, as will enable it to answer the ends of its institution, or this may be the ill-fated moment for relaxing the powers of the Union, annihilating the Cement of the Confederation, and exposing us to become the sport of European politics, which may lay one State against another to prevent their growing importance, and to serve their own interested purposes."[6]

Whether or not they were encouraged by foreign powers, wars and strategic rivalries among the former British colonies might have led to the decline of republican liberty in them as a result of the defensive militarization of their societies. This argument was first made during the debates over the ratification of the federal Constitution.

The Anti-Federalists, opponents of the new and strong federal Constitution drafted at the Philadelphia Constitutional Convention in the summer of 1787, argued that strengthening the Union would create a government as dangerous to the American way of life as the British Empire had been. An overly powerful central government, imposing high taxes and maintaining a standing army, would threaten the liberties and prosperity of ordinary Americans. The Federalists, supporters of the new constitution, turned this argument against the Anti-Federalists. In the Federalist Papers, a series of newspaper essays published in 1787–88 to encourage New York and other states to ratify the new federal constitution, Alexander Hamilton, James Madison, and John Jay argued that government and military costs would be higher in a fragmented America than in an integrated federal state. It would cost less to support a single federal military than many state militaries. In Federalist 8, Hamilton warned that "if we should be disunited, and the integral parts should either remain separated, or, which is most probable, should be thrown together into two or three confederacies, we should be, in a short course of time, in the predicament of the continental powers of Europe—our liberties would be a prey to the means of defending ourselves against the ambition and jealousy of each other."[7] Each of the states or several confederacies would need its own expensive military establishment, at a great cost in personal liberty and economic freedom.

Hamilton warned: "Frequent war and constant apprehension, which require a state of constant preparation, will infallibly produce [standing armies]. The weaker states, or confederacies, would first have recourse to them to put themselves upon an equality with their more potent neighbors. They would endeavor to supply the inferiority of population and resources by a more regular and effective system of defense, by disciplined troops, and by fortifications. They would, at the same time, be necessitated to strengthen the executive arm of government, in doing which their constitutions would acquire a progressive direction towards monarchy. . . . Thus we should, in a little time, see established in every part of this country the same engines of despotism which have been the scourge of the old world."[8]

In his Farewell Address, drafted by Hamilton, George Washington made a different but related argument. "While, then, every part of our country thus feels an immediate and particular interest in union, all the parts combined cannot fail to find in the united mass of means and efforts greater strength, greater resource, proportionably greater security from external danger, a less frequent interruption of their peace by foreign nations; and, what is of inestimable value, they must derive from union an exemption from those broils and wars between themselves, which so frequently affect neighboring countries not tied together by the same governments, which their own rival ships alone would be sufficient to produce, but which opposite foreign alliances, attachments, and intrigues would stimulate and embitter. *Hence, likewise, they will avoid the necessity of those overgrown military establishments which, under any form of government, are inauspicious to liberty, and which are to be regarded as particularly hostile to republican liberty.* In this sense it is that your union ought to be considered as a main prop of your liberty, and that the love of the one ought to endear to you the preservation of the other"[9] (emphasis added). The United States as a federal nation-state could obtain security at a lower cost in taxes and liberty than any independent state or league of several states by taking advantage of economies of scale in spending on defense.

The ratification of the federal Constitution averted the immediate danger that the newly formed United States might break up. The greatest test of the Union was yet to come.

The Civil War and the American Way of Life

On December 20, 1860, South Carolina announced its secession from the United States. In the months that followed ten other Southern slaveholding states, alarmed by the election to the presidency of Abraham Lincoln, the leader of the antislavery Republican Party, followed South Carolina and formed the Confederate States of America. The Civil War began on April 12, 1861, when Confederate forces fired on federal troops at Fort Sumter in Charleston, South Carolina, and ended when Robert E. Lee surrendered the Army of Northern Virginia at Appomattox Courthouse on April 9, 1865. More than half a million soldiers on both sides had died, and Southern society was crippled and warped for generations.

The domestic effects of the Civil War, including the end of slavery in the United States and the strengthening of the federal government, were revolutionary. But the geopolitical effects were just as significant. If the Confederacy had secured its independence, it is unlikely that the disintegration of the United States would have ended. Texas and other parts of the Confederacy might have broken away to become independent republics. The remnant of the United States might have crumbled into Northeastern, Midwestern, and Western federations.

In 1798 Thomas Jefferson had rejected those who argued that the South should secede in response to the temporary control of the federal government by New Englanders: "If on a temporary superiority of the one party, the other is to resort to a scission of the Union, no federal government can ever exist. If we rid ourselves of the present rule of Massachusetts and Connecticut, we break the Union, will the evil stop there? Suppose the New

England states alone cut off, will our nature be changed? . . . Immediately, we shall see a Pennsylvania and a Virginia party arise in the residuary confederacy, and the public mind will be distracted with the same party spirit. . . . If we reduce our Union to Virginia and North Carolina, immediately the conflict will be established between the representatives of these two states, and they will end by breaking into their simple units."[10] The conversion of the map of the United States into a crazy quilt of petty sovereignties would have brought about the nightmare of generations of American statesmen— the "Balkanization" of North America.

The costs of disunity provided a powerful argument to the Unionists during the Civil War. In his second annual address to Congress on December 1, 1862, which was an address to the rebel South as well, President Lincoln argued that the division of the United States would be an economic disaster. Speaking of the interior of the country, Lincoln wrote: "And yet this region has no sea-coast, touches no ocean anywhere. As part of one nation, its people now find, and may forever find, their way to Europe by New York, to South America and Africa by New Orleans, and to Asia by San Francisco. But separate our common country into two nations, as designed by the present rebellion, and every man of this great interior region is thereby cut off from some one or more these outlets, not perhaps, by a physical barrier, but by embarrassing and onerous trade regulations."[11]

Because he was trying to persuade the South to return to the Union, Lincoln did not dwell on the possibilities of conflict between the successor states of a disintegrated United States. Other American statesmen, however, had long warned that the break-up of the Union might lead to war among rival republics, in alliance, perhaps, with different foreign great powers.

In Federalist 4, John Jay warned of the disasters that would follow if the United States "split into three or four independent and probably discordant republics or confederacies, one inclining to Britain, another to France, and a third to Spain, and perhaps played off against each other by the three . . . "[12] And in Federalist 7, Alexander Hamilton wrote of "the probability of incompatible alliances between the different States, or confederacies, and different foreign nations" and warned that "America, if not connected at all, or only by the feeble tie of a simple league, offensive and defensive, would, by the operation of such jarring alliances, be gradually entangled in all the pernicious labyrinths of European politics and wars; and by the destructive contentions of the parts into which she was divided, would be likely to become a prey to the artifices and machinations of powers equally the enemies of them all. *Divide et impera* [divide and rule] must be the motto of every nation that either hates or fears us . . . "[13] John Quincy Adams wrote in 1796: "There is no one article of my political creed more clearly demonstrated to my mind than this, that we shall proceed with giant strides to honor and consideration, and national greatness, if the union is preserved; but that if it is once broken, we shall soon divide into a parcel of petty tribes at perpetual war with one another, swayed by rival European powers, whose policy will agree perfectly in the system of keeping us at variance with one another."[14]

That this was not an idle fear is proven by the hope of the Confederates that war between Britain and the United States would secure the independence of the South, in the same way that France's war against Britain had secured the independence of the United States. Most of the British elite was sympathetic to the South, and the United States and Britain came close to war over incidents arising from the struggle between North and South. In the early 1800s the government of Spain had secretly conspired with Americans, including the governor of the Louisiana Territory, General James Wilkinson, who, unknown to the U.S. government, was a spy for Spain.[15] In the 1840s Britain and France maneuvered to discourage Texas from joining the United States and hoped to encourage a balance of power system in North America.

Even in the absence of hostilities among new countries carved out of the ruins of the United States, the costs of maintaining separate military establishments would have been substantial. And in the absence of a common internal U.S. market, the costs of different currencies, tariffs, tolls, and other devices would have retarded the growth of North American agriculture and industry. The costs of militarization and economic inefficiency would have fallen hardest on ordinary Americans in a disunited America.

Germany and Italy, each a cultural nation divided among many mostly weak governments, were cited by some Americans as examples of the evils of disunion. In his own speech at Gettysburg on November 19, 1863, eclipsed by Lincoln's more famous Address, the American orator and statesman Edward Everett told the audience: "In Germany, the wars of the Reformation and Charles V, in the sixteenth century, the Thirty Years' war in the seventeenth century, the Seven Years' war in the eighteenth century, not to speak of other less celebrated contests, entailed upon that country [Germany] all the miseries of internecine strife for more than three centuries. . . . In Italy, on the breaking up of the Roman Empire, society might be said to be resolved into its original elements—into hostile atoms, whose only movement was of mutual repulsion."[16] Before the Civil War, an American visitor wrote about the consequences of the division of Italy among many independent governments: "They are all of them what our South Carolina is, alone fortunately, in its character—all for self—ready to throw the world into universal confusion and war, rather than not be able to have her own way—like a petted baby. A few Carolinas would reduce our country to the miserable condition of the Italian republics. The want of a spirit of union and amity has destroyed them."[17]

Lincoln was accused by critics in his time and later generations of being a tyrant who waged an unjust war. But while his administration sometimes abused its emergency powers, President Lincoln insisted on a fair election in the midst of the crisis, and before his assassination ruled out the idea of severe mass punishment of the defeated rebels. Like other American statesmen, he was haunted by the question he framed in his address to the special session of Congress he called on July 4, 1861, at the beginning of the bloodiest conflict in American history: "Must a government, of necessity, be too strong for the liberties of its own people, or too weak to maintain its own existence?"[18]

The victory of the federal government in the Civil War helped the United States to avoid facing this tragic dilemma. The triumph of the Union averted the danger that the territory of the United States would be occupied by two or more rival countries, with enmities manipulated by foreign great powers and with republican constitutions of government and society warped to the point of breaking by the demands of defense.

A Union of Potential Nations

"The United States is imperial in area," the American historian Frederick Jackson Turner wrote in 1932. "If we lay a map of Europe upon a map of the United States constructed to the same scale, the western coast of Spain would coincide with the coast of Southern California, Constantinople would rest near Charleston, South Carolina; Sicily, near New Orleans; and the southern coast of the Baltic would fall in line with the southern coast of

Lake Superior." Turner described the United States as "a union of potential nations."[19]

American statesmen from Washington to Lincoln were determined that these "potential nations" should never be born, out of fear of a Balkanized North America. But the breakup of the United States into smaller countries was not the only way that North America might have been Balkanized. New countries on the borders of the United States, some or all of them allies or colonies of hostile extra-hemispheric great powers, might have been formed by Anglo-American settlers, British colonists, Mexican rebels, European immigrants, and others in the former French, Spanish, and Mexican territories from the Gulf Coast to the Mississippi Valley to Texas and California. That threatening possibility was averted by the geographic expansion of the United States.

Chapter 4

Averting a Balance of Power in North America: Power Politics and American Expansion

> We dismiss one other monarch from the continent. One by one they have retired—first France, then Spain, then France again, and now Russia—all giving way to the absorbing Unity declared in the national motto, E pluribus unum.
>
> —Charles Sumner[1]

Forget the covered wagon, when you think of the expansion of the United States in the nineteenth century. Think instead of ships. Sailing ships.

The present-day United States was assembled from bits and pieces of coastline that contained strategically important seaports like New Orleans, San Francisco, and San Diego. To be sure, these strips of coastline came with huge continental territories attached. With the purchase of New Orleans from France, the United States got the Mississippi River Valley as a bonus. By wresting control of San Francisco and San Diego from Mexico during the Mexican War, the United States got control of California's Inland Empire, the Rocky Mountains, and the Desert Southwest. But American strategists were chiefly after harbors, not the immense acreage that was included in the bargains and glamorized by the folklore of pioneer America.

In thinking about genuine schooners and forgetting "prairie schooners" or covered wagons, it is best to forget about the prairie, too. Today there are fewer people in the Great Plains than in the Los Angeles metropolitan area. Most people in the United States have always lived within a few hundred miles of a coastline, including the coastlines of the Great Lakes, which form a kind of inland sea. Most of the rest have lived near major rivers. While producing some decentralization, the train, car, and plane have hardly altered this pattern. The United States is a continental country with a coastal population. Instead of the bald eagle, the symbol of the American republic should have been the seagull.

The oceans are highways, not barriers. Forget the claim that the United States had no serious enemies in the nineteenth century because it was protected by the oceans. During the War of Independence, the British found it easy to land forces at points of their choosing along the thin, inhabited coastal strip of colonial America. It was much harder for Americans to go overland from one place to another. Independence was won for the United States largely by the French fleet, which first diverted British forces by threatening the British West Indies and finally bottled up British warships in the Chesapeake Bay, enabling George Washington to force the surrender of General Cornwallis at Yorktown, Virginia.

But the vulnerability of coastal America to foreign naval power was illustrated in 1814, during the War of 1812, when the British Navy burned Washington and then sailed up the Chesapeake, only to be prevented from burning Baltimore, Maryland, as well by the U.S. garrison at Fort McHenry, whose victory is commemorated in the U.S. National Anthem by Francis Scott Key: "the rockets' red glare, the bombs bursting in air, / Gave proof through the night that our flag was still there . . . " American coastal forts protected far more Americans than were ever protected from Native Americans on the Western frontier by U.S. Army stockades.

Hollywood prefers Indian wars to naval battles and General Custer to Captain John Paul Jones. Nevertheless, understanding American strategy in the nineteenth century begins with a conscious effort to forget covered wagons, prairie farms, and U.S. Cavalry stockades, and to focus on schooners, port cities, and coastal fortifications. Driving U.S. territorial expansion was the determination of American leaders to deny Britain and France control or influence over two coasts that were as important for American security as for American commerce: the Gulf Coast and the Pacific Coast.

America's First Grand Strategy: Isolation

Before the twentieth century, the United States lacked the military and economic might to contemplate a strategy of American global hegemony, as distinct from regional North American hegemony. Nevertheless, the United States could have participated in the balance of power wars of Europe, as an ally of one or more European powers, from the Napoleonic era onward. American leaders consciously rejected American participation in the European balance of power system, because they feared it was incompatible with America's republican constitution and middle-class society.

At the same time, U.S. statesmen recognized that the balance of power system in Europe produced beneficial results for the United States. The division of Europe among competing great powers prevented any single power from dominating the resources and population of Europe, the richest and most powerful part of the world, and then turning its attention to the Western Hemisphere. During the Napoleonic Wars, which in effect constituted a world war, Thomas Jefferson, both as president and private citizen, showed a shrewd awareness of the importance of a balance of power in Europe for U.S. security in North America. Referring to Napoleon, Jefferson wrote to a correspondent in 1814, while both the United States and France were engaged in separate wars with Britain: "It is cruel that we should have been forced to wish any success to such a destroyer of the human race."[2] Around the same time, he wrote to another correspondent: "Surely none of us wish to see Bonaparte conquer Russia, and lay thus at his feet, the whole continent of Europe. . . . It cannot be to our interest that all Europe should be reduced to a single monarchy. The true line of interest for us, is, that Bonaparte should be able to effect the complete exclusion of England from the whole continent of Europe, in order, by this peaceable engine of constraint, to make her renounce her views of dominion over the ocean. . . . And this would be effected by Bonaparte succeeding so far as to close the Baltic against [Britain]. This success I wished him the last year, this I wish him this year; but were he again advanced to Moscow, I should again wish him such disasters as would prevent his reaching St. Petersburg. And were the consequences even to be the longer continuance of our war [against Britain], I would rather meet them than see the whole force of Europe wielded by a single hand."[3] Jefferson believed that the United States would be more secure if Napoleon's France and Britain each were strong enough to check the other.

Before World War I, the United States chose to play the role of a "free rider"—opportunistically benefiting from the internecine power struggles of Europe, without contributing to them. The classic statement of America's grand strategy of isolation or non-entanglement is found in President Washington's Farewell Address of 1796, drafted by Alexander Hamilton.

Washington told his fellow citizens: "Europe has a set of primary interests which to us have none, or a very remote relation. Hence she must be engaged in frequent controversies, the causes of which are essentially foreign to our concerns. Hence, therefore, it must be unwise in us to implicate ourselves by artificial ties in the ordinary vicissitudes of her politics, or the ordinary combinations and collisions of her friendships or enmities." Washington continued: "Our detached and distant situation invites and enables us to pursue a different course . . . Why forego the advantages of so peculiar a situation? Why quit our own to stand upon foreign ground? Why, by interweaving our destiny with that of any part of Europe, entangle our peace and prosperity in the toils of European ambition, rival ship, interest, humor or caprice?" He concluded: "It is our true policy to steer clear of permanent alliances with any part of the foreign world . . . Taking care always to keep ourselves by suitable establishments on a respectable defensive posture, we may safely trust to temporary alliances for extraordinary emergencies."[4]

America's first grand strategy of isolation combined a refusal to engage in alliances with any European great power with the gradual expulsion of extra-hemispheric powers from America's neighborhood by means first of territorial growth and later of regional hegemony. The fact that the European powers tied each other down in wars and arms races permitted the United States to increase its security at low cost by means of territorial expansion and the establishment of its own sphere of influence in North America. When, toward the end of the nineteenth century, a united Germany proved to be too powerful to be restrained by its European neighbors without American help, America's first grand strategy of isolation became obsolete.

Averting a North American Balance of Power by Means of Expansion

The expansion of the United States in North America in the nineteenth century is often portrayed as the result of a messianic conception of America's "Manifest Destiny." But Manifest Destiny is something of a myth. The continental expansion of the United States was motivated largely by the determination of Americans to ensure that the great powers of Europe did not use North America as a battleground in the future, as Britain and France had done during the seventeenth and eighteenth centuries, when their North American colonists and allied Indian nations waged proxy wars against each other on behalf of London or Paris.

Most of the territory into which the United States expanded had been ruled at one time by the Spanish Empire. Jefferson described the United States as "the nest from which all America, North and South is to be peopled." Spain, "too feeble" to hold onto its North American territory, would maintain it only "till our population be sufficiently advanced to gain it from them piece by piece . . . "[5] The long decay of Spanish imperial control in North America created power vacuums on the borders of the United States. American leaders feared that Britain or France, the dominant European maritime powers until the mid-nineteenth century, would fill those power vacuums and threaten the United States with military encirclement or economic strangulation—either of which would threaten the American way of life.

The Louisiana Purchase

In 1801, when he learned that Spain was about to transfer the Louisiana Territory back to France by treaty, President Jefferson wrote in alarm: "There is on the globe one single spot, the possessor of which is our natural and habitual enemy. It is New Orleans, through which the produce of three-eighths of our territory must pass to market. . . . The day that France takes possession of New Orleans . . . seals the union of two nations, who, in conjunction, can maintain exclusive possession of the ocean. From that moment, we must marry ourselves to the British fleet and nation."[6] The danger of foreign control of the mouth of the Mississippi was illustrated in 1802, when the Spanish government ended the U.S. right of deposit (passage of goods without customs duties) at New Orleans.

When France offered to sell the United States all of the Louisiana Territory in April 1803, Jefferson moved quickly, announcing the treaty on the Fourth of July, the twenty-seventh anniversary of the Declaration of Independence. Jefferson himself was unsure about the constitutionality of the transaction, but in his second Inaugural Address in 1805 he argued "is it not better that the opposite bank of the Mississippi should be settled by our own brethren and children, than by strangers of another family? With which shall we be most likely to live in harmony and friendly intercourse?"[7]

Jefferson also hoped that the Louisiana Purchase would strengthen the agrarian basis of American society, by providing enormous tracts of land that could be carved into small farms, at the expense, needless to say, of the Indian inhabitants.

The Floridas

After France sold New Orleans and the Louisiana Territory, Spain continued to control the Southern coastline east of New Orleans or "West Florida" as well as "East Florida" or the peninsula. The lack of unimpeded river access from the South to the Gulf of Mexico threatened U.S. security and commercial interests. After having tried unsuccessfully to purchase the Floridas from Spain in 1802, President Jefferson wrote in 1807 to his ally James Madison that apparently imminent war with Britain would provide the United States with an excuse to seize them. In the summer of 1808, Jefferson ordered the Secretary of War to be prepared to move: "Mobile, Pensacola, and St. Augustine, are those we should be preparing for. The enforcing the embargo would furnish a pretext . . . "[8] The declaration of a short-lived "Republic of West Florida" established by American settlers in 1810 was followed by U.S. seizure of much of West Florida.

In 1811, Jefferson's successor as president, James Madison, fearful of British designs on the Floridas, asked Congress for power to prevent "the occupancy thereof by any other foreign Power." Congress passed a secret resolution authorizing the president to seize Florida east of the Perdido "in the event of an attempt to occupy the said territory, or any part thereof, by any foreign government," by which Congress meant the British, as Secretary of State James Monroe told the French ambassador to Washington.[9]

Although the United States used the issue of British violations of America's right as a neutral maritime nation as a pretext, the underlying strategic reason for the War of 1812 was the desire of American "War Hawks" to end Britain's encirclement of the young republic by taking Canada along with Florida, then controlled by Spain, an ally of Britain. The prospect of seizing the long-sought Spanish Floridas explains much of the fervent support for the war in the Southern states.

Southern War Hawks viewed the conquest of Canada as a bribe given to Northern Republicans voting with them in favor of a war whose main purpose was acquisition of the Gulf Coast and Florida peninsula. One War

Hawk offered a toast: "Florida and Canada;—A fee simple in the one, a mortgage upon the other." In the words of one Southern hawk, Representative Felix Grundy of Tennessee: "I therefore feel anxious not only to add the Floridas to the South, but the Canadas to the North of this empire."[10] Many Westerners who battled Indians armed by the British shared the view of Grundy, three of whose brothers had been killed by Indians: "We shall drive the British from our Continent—they will no longer have an opportunity of intriguing with our Indian neighbors . . . "[11] The United States tried but failed to conquer Canada in the War of 1812. But the hope of many Americans that Canada would join the Union, as a result of invitation rather than conquest, persisted for generations.

After the United States declared war on Britain in 1812, Jefferson was optimistic: "The acquisition of Canada this year, as far as the neighborhood of Quebec, will be a mere matter of marching, and will give us experience for the attack of Halifax the next, and the final expulsion of England from the American continent."[12] But the "second war for independence" was a debacle. Both the British and the Americans invaded Spanish Florida and briefly occupied Pensacola. The British not only repulsed the Americans who tried to conquer Canada but also captured and burned down Washington, D.C. Only the victory of General Andrew Jackson at the Battle of New Orleans on January 8, 1815, which occurred before news of peace between Britain and the United States reached that city, permitted Americans to treat the War of 1812 as anything other than a debacle.

The United States did not immediately achieve the goal of the incorporation of the Floridas. In December 1813, Jefferson referred to the threat of British control of the Floridas as a justification for their conquest by the United States, in a letter to a friend in Spain: "We are in a state of semi-warfare with your adjoining colonies, the Floridas . . . The commanding officers in the Floridas have excited and armed the neighbouring savages to war against us . . . This conduct of the Spanish officers will probably oblige us to the possession of the Floridas, and the rather as we believe the English will otherwise seize them, and use them as stations to distract and annoy us."[13]

In 1812 American filibusters declared a republic in East Florida. But the incident embarrassed the United States, and on April 19, 1814, Monroe formally declared, "The United States to at peace with Spain, no countenance can be given to the proceedings of the revolutionary party in East Florida, if it is composed of Spanish subjects,—and still less can it be given

to them, if it consists of American citizens, who . . . will be liable to cen-
sure."[14] The attempt of the Gutierrez-Magee expedition of 1812–13 to detach Texas from the Spanish Empire was a failure as well.

Having invaded Florida in 1812 during the war, General Andrew Jackson invaded a second time in 1818, burning villages of Indians and runaway slaves from the United States and executing two British traders along
with Indian leaders. Spain finally ceded its remaining territorial claims to
the United States in the Adams-Onis Treaty of 1819, which reaffirmed the
Spanish claim to Texas, to the outrage of many in the United States.

No Substitute for Statecraft

The conduct of U.S. foreign policy during the Napoleonic Wars between
the 1790s and 1815 demonstrates that there is no substitute for sound
statecraft. The first two presidents, George Washington and John Adams,
along with Alexander Hamilton, all associated with the Federalist Party,
agreed that the United States should act as a de facto ally of Britain in the
global struggle of the Wars of the French Revolution from 1793 to 1815.
The military hegemony of France in Europe would threaten the United
States far more than the naval mastery of Britain, with its small army, ever
could. Behind the shield of British power the United States could seize strategic territories claimed by France and Spain along the U.S. borders.

The strategy of the "Virginia dynasty" of Southern Republican presidents that began with Jefferson's election in 1800 was misguided by comparison. Jefferson hoped that a unilateral embargo on U.S. cotton and
agricultural exports to Europe would bring Britain and France to their knees;
instead, the "O-Grab-Me," as the embargo was called, wrecked the U.S.
economy and inspired some Northern merchants to favor the secession of
New England, without affecting the trans-Atlantic power struggle at all.
Jefferson's friend and successor as president, James Madison, was even more
incompetent as a strategist. In 1812 President Madison wrote Jefferson to
ask what the former president thought of the idea of the United States
waging war simultaneously against Britain and its enemy France; to his
credit, Jefferson replied in alarm that this was "a solecism worthy of Don
Quixote."[15] In September 1814 President Madison ingloriously fled as
Washington, D.C., was set afire by British occupiers, his capital as well as
his strategy in ruins.

The Origin of the Monroe Doctrine

Following the end of the Napoleonic Wars in 1815, all of Spain's Latin American colonies except for Cuba and a few other West Indian islands won their independence from Spain. Brazil gained its independence from Portugal in 1825. The secession of the Latin American countries from Spain and Portugal was encouraged and welcomed by Britain, which hoped to dominate their trade. The United States had owed its own success in its struggle for independence from 1776 to 1782 in part to the intervention of France, which had helped to strip Britain of its major North American colonies. Similar reasoning led Britain to support the independence of mainland Latin American colonies of Spain, which had frequently been a French ally.

In public British Foreign Minister Canning explained on December 12, 1826: "I have already said, that when the French army entered Spain, we might, if we chose, have resisted or resented that measure by war. But were there no other means than war for resorting the balance of Power? . . . I resolved that if France had Spain, it should not be Spain 'with the Indies.' I called the New World into existence, to redress the balance of the Old."[16] Two years earlier in December 1824, in a secret memo to the British Cabinet, Canning argued that Britain should recognize the independence of Mexico from Spain not only to profit from Mexican commerce but also to check the United States: "The other and perhaps still more powerful motive is my apprehension of the ambition and ascendancy of the U[nited] S[tates] of Am[erica] . . . I need not say how inconvenient such an ascendancy may be in time of peace, and how formidable in case of war." Canning continued: "I believe we now have the opportunity (but it may not last long) of opposing a powerful barrier to the influence of the U[nited] S[tates] by an amicable connection to Mexico, which from its position must be either subservient to or jealous of the U[nited] S[tates]."[17]

As early as 1799 Alexander Hamilton had argued that the United States should promote the independence of Spain's Latin American colonies in order to weaken France, then Spain's ally, writing that "if universal empire is still to be the pursuit of France, what can tend to defeat the purpose better than to detach South America from Spain, which is the only Channel, through which the riches of Mexico and Peru are conveyed to France? The Executive ought to be put in a situation to embrace favorable conjunctures for effecting the separation." This was Hamilton's euphemistic way of suggesting that the United States in a war with France should consider intervening in Latin America to promote its independence from France's ally Spain, in addition to seizing New Orleans and the Louisiana Territory from Spain, which then controlled them.[18]

In 1821, when Russia suggested that the European powers help Spain regain control of Latin America, Canning proposed that Britain and the United States issue a joint declaration opposing any further European imperialism in the Americas while renouncing territorial ambitions of their own. President Monroe's Cabinet, unaware of Canning's privately expressed desire to block U.S. influence in Latin America, debated the U.S. response. Arguing for a unilateral effort by the United States to discourage further European colonization of the Americas, Secretary of State John Adams told President Monroe and his fellow Cabinet members: "We have no intention of seizing Texas or Cuba. But the inhabitants of either or both may exercise their primitive [i.e. natural] rights, and solicit a union with us. . . . Without entering now into the enquiry of the expediency of our annexing Texas or Cuba to our Union, we should at least keep ourselves free to act as emergencies may arise, and not tie ourselves down to any principle which might immediately afterwards be brought to bear against ourselves."[19] In 1823, in his annual address to Congress, President James Monroe enunciated what became known as "the Monroe Doctrine," warning outside powers: "We should consider any attempt on their part to extend their system to any portion of this hemisphere as dangerous to our peace and security. With any existing colonies or dependencies of any European power we have not interfered and shall not interfere."[20]

Britain, France, and the Texas Question

America's westward expansion is often attributed to the ideology of "Manifest Destiny." But strategy, not idealism, drove American annexations. And strategy in turn was driven by fear. In the mid-1840s, fear of Britain led the United States to annex Texas, partition Oregon, and seize California from Mexico.

In 1844 a British author, David Urquhart, published a novel entitled *Annexation of Texas, a Case of War Between England and the United States.*[21] The Anglo-American crisis of the 1840s was triggered by the movement to annex Texas. Like the short-lived Republic of Florida created by

U.S. filibusters in Spanish territory in 1810, the Republic of Texas was detached from Mexico in 1835–36 by a coalition of immigrants from the United States and Europe and their native allies, after several previous attempts by Americans to "revolutionize" Texas had failed. To prevent Texas from joining the Union as a slave state and upsetting the balance of power between slave and free states in the U.S. Senate, the Northern states successfully opposed the admission of Texas for a decade. During that time Texas was recognized as an independent country by Britain and France, while Mexico regarded it as a renegade province.

In 1825, when President Adams offered to buy Texas from Mexico, British Foreign Secretary Canning viewed Mexico as a check upon the United States.[22] In 1830 Lord Aberdeen, then Foreign Secretary, told the Mexican ambassador of British opposition to U.S. acquisition of Texas. In 1843, in response to President Tyler's support for Texas annexation, Britain and France agreed to work together to prevent it.[23] In the same year in a public letter, Andrew Jackson advocated incorporating Texas to check Britain.[24] The following year Britain and France were alarmed when President James K. Polk made the annexation of Texas an issue in his successful 1844 presidential campaign.

Both Britain and France preferred a balance of power in North America to U.S. hegemony. Britain also saw the Republic of Texas as a potential source of cotton for its mills and a potential market independent of the United States, which levied tariffs on British imports. As Ashbel Smith, a former diplomat of the Texas republic in London and Paris, recalled, "Great Britain desired to find in Texas a market for her merchandize 'without having to climb over the United States tariff.' These are Lord Aberdeen's words to me . . . Their statesmen made no secret of their willingness to see an independent state established on the southwest border of the American union which should arrest its further extension in that direction and prevent encroachment on the territories of Mexico," the foreign commerce of which "had long been done mostly with or through British merchants."[25] In 1844 Aberdeen proposed that Britain and France would guarantee the independence of Texas on condition that Mexico recognize the sovereignty of the Texas republic. The U.S. representative to Paris protested to Prime Minister Guizot "that Texas must be absorbed [by the United States] in order to guard against the danger of England's controlling her . . . "[26] The proposed Franco-British guarantee never came about because Mexico refused to recognize the independence of Texas.

Anglo-American Rivalry Over Oregon

The Texas issue was joined by the questions of Oregon and California. In the Adams-Onis Treaty of 1819, Spain had ceded to the United States all Spanish territorial claims above the forty-second parallel north of the Rocky Mountains. In 1818 Britain agreed with the United States to exercise joint occupancy in the Oregon Territory. In renewed negotiations in 1826–27, both powers agreed to continue the condominium, because each feared that it would lose out from a partition of the territory that would deprive it of access to the valuable Juan de Fuca Strait. This was the motive of John Quincy Adams, the U.S. negotiator, as well as of British Foreign Secretary Canning, who said he would not approve a treaty "by which England would have foregone the advantage of our immense direct intercourse between China and what may be, if we resolve not to yield them up, her boundless establishments on the N.W. Coast of America."[27]

In the mid-1840s, agitation for the U.S. annexation of Oregon, to deny it to Britain, was a by-product of agitation for the annexation of Texas. In 1844 the Democrats ran on the slogan "Fifty-four forty or fight." Inasmuch as fifty-four forty latitude was the border of Russian-controlled Alaska, the slogan was a demand that Britain withdraw completely from the Pacific Northwest or risk war with the United States. In 1845–46 Britain showed its strength by sending three warships to Oregon waters.[28] The Polk administration ordered Commodore John D. Sloat to move his squadron closer to Oregon and California in order to watch the British. Sloat was also ordered to send "rifles or other small arms" to the American settlers in the Willamette Valley of Oregon, "taking all possible care that they fall into the hands of no one who is unfriendly to the United States. These orders you will keep secret."[29]

Polk wanted to avoid war with Britain, as long as a partition of the Oregon territory at the forty-ninth parallel gave the United States control of the Juan de Fuca Strait. In the end, Britain and the United States compromised so that each would control one side of the strait.

The Danger of a British California

According to one historian, "In the opinion of contemporary British diplomats the situation in California was intimately connected with events in

Mexico and Texas, and British agents, prophesying the destruction of the Mexican state, frequently advocated the acquisition of California as some compensation for American expansion in other directions."[30]

In 1841 Sir Richard Pakenham, the British ambassador to Washington, sent a memo to British Foreign Secretary Palmerston urging British colonization of California, a policy rejected by Lord Aberdeen when he replaced Palmerston.[31] In 1844, an Irish priest named Eugene McNamara proposed colonizing California with immigrants from Ireland, shortly before the Irish Potato Famine. In the same year, the British vice-consul in Monterey, California, was contacted by members of the California elite who requested "the protection of Great Britain, in a similar manner to that of the Ionian isles, but to remain for the present under the direct Govt. of one of its natives . . . "[32] Passing this request on to London, the vice-consul wrote: "I feel myself in duty bound to use all my influence to prevent this fine country from falling into the hands of any other foreign power than that of England."[33] Aberdeen rejected British support for a revolt by Californians against Mexico but wrote: "It is, however, of importance to Great Britain, while declining to interfere herself, that California, if it should throw off the Mexican yoke, should not assume any other which might prove inimical to British interests. . . . Great Britain would view with much dissatisfaction the establishment of a protectoral power over California by any other foreign state."[34]

The journalist John O'Sullivan coined the phrase "Manifest Destiny" in his essay "Annexation," which appeared in July 1845. The phrase made its first appearance in the context of O'Sullivan's discussion of the Franco-British opposition to the U.S. annexation of Texas: "England, our old rival and enemy; and . . . France, strangely coupled against us" had united "for the avowed object of thwarting our policy and hampering our power, limiting our greatness and checking the fulfillment of our manifest destiny to overspread the continent allotted by Providence for the free development of our yearly multiplying millions."[35] American newspapers noted French Prime Minister Guizot's declaration in July 1845, the same month in which O'Sullivan's essay appeared: "It behooves France to preserve the balance of power in the Western Hemisphere."[36] Indirectly responding to this and similar statements, James K. Polk, in his first annual message to Congress in December 1845, declared: "The rapid extension of our settlements over our territories heretofore unoccupied, the addition of new States to our

Confederacy, the expansion of free principles, and our rising greatness as a nation are attracting the attention of the powers of Europe, and lately the doctrine has been broached in some of them of a 'balance of power' on this continent to check our advancement . . . Jealousy among the different sovereigns of Europe, lest any of one of them might become too powerful for the rest, has caused them anxiously to desire the establishment of what they term the 'balance of power.' It can not be permitted to have any application on the North American continent, and especially to the United States."[37]

In October 1845, Thomas O. Larkin, the U.S. consul in California, was given secret additional duties as a "confidential agent" and told by his superiors that the policy of the United States "is to let events take their course, unless an attempt should be made to transfer [the inhabitants of California] without their consent either to Great Britain or France."[38] In his secret instructions of November 10, 1845, to John Slidell, his envoy to Mexico, President Polk warned that "both Great Britain and France have designs upon California . . . The possession of the Bay and harbour of San Francisco, is all important to the United States . . . The advantages to us of its acquisition are so striking that it would be a waste of time to enumerate them here. If all these should be turned against our country by the cession of California to Great Britain, our principal commercial rival, the consequences would be most disastrous."[39]

Polk's concern was not unreasonable. Around this time the *London Times* wrote: "England must think of her own interests, and secure the Bay of Francisco and Monterey . . . to prevent those noble ports from becoming ports of exportation for Brother Jonathan [a derogatory name for the United States] for the Chinese market."[40] Americans were alarmed by rumors that Mexico had agreed to sell its claim to California and Texas to Britain. The rumors were partly based on fact; in 1839, the Mexican Congress had agreed to give British bondholders one hundred million acres in Texas (still claimed in its entirety by Mexico), Chihuahua, Sonora, New Mexico, and California, in return for British assumption of Mexico's national debt. The deal, however, was never completed.[41] After the U.S.-Mexican war broke out, the Mexican government in May 1846 offered to give California to Britain as security for a loan, but British leaders rejected the idea, because by then California was under U.S. control.[42]

Texas, California, and the Mexican War

In March 1845 Congress passed a resolution of annexation of Texas. On July 4, 1845, the Texas legislature unanimously approved annexation, and President Polk signed the act on December 29 of that year. A Mexican general, Antonio Paredes, used the issue of Texas, which many Mexicans still regarded as a renegade province, to seize power, and Mexican troops attacked and killed U.S. troops stationed on the north side of the disputed Rio Grande boundary. In response, Congress declared war on Mexico on May 23, 1846.

Polk, like presidents Jackson and Tyler before him, had offered to purchase California from Mexico. While there is no evidence that Polk deliberately provoked war with Mexico, he foresaw that the U.S. annexation of Texas, still claimed by Mexico, might lead to war and an opportunity for the United States to seize California by force.

Earlier in June 1845 the Polk administration had given Commodore John D. Sloat secret instructions to seize San Francisco and blockade other California ports to deny them to the British and French, if the United States declared war on Mexico. In spring 1846 one U.S. naval commander was ordered by Washington to "ascertain as exactly as you can the nature of the designs of the English and French" with respect to California and to "distribute the accompanying constitutions of the State of Texas printed into Spanish," evidently to encourage the Californians, like the Texans, to declare their independence from Mexico and then apply for admission to the United States.[43]

When war broke out between the United States and Mexico in March 1846, the U.S. Navy carried out its standing instructions to seize the ports of California. The brief declaration by Americans in California of a "Bear Flag Republic" was rendered irrelevant by U.S. military occupation. Earlier in 1842, to the embarrassment of the government in Washington, U.S. Naval officers, under the mistaken impression that Mexico and the United States were at war over Texas, seized Monterey and claimed California for the United States, only to withdraw when the error was discovered. This time the seizure was permanent.

The Mexican War ended on February 2, 1848, when the two countries signed the Treaty of Guadalupe Hidalgo, which ceded California and much of today's American Southwest and Mountain West to the United States, in return for more than eighteen million dollars. In 1853 the Gadsden Purchase added a strip of former Mexican land that the United States hoped to use for a Western railroad. Polk unsuccessfully sought to buy Cuba from Spain as well.

On September 23, 1845, Aberdeen lamented: "We might have established our *Protectorate* [over California] long ago, if we had thought proper."[44] British prime minister Peel overruled Aberdeen's suggestion of an Anglo-French alliance "to unite in resisting American aggression," as this would commit Britain and France to war with the United States, concluding that "we have no alternative but to leave the field open to the U. States."[45]

"It will be worth a war of twenty years to prevent England acquiring it," Waddy Thompson, the U.S. ambassador to Mexico in the 1840s, said of California.[46] "Fear of England more than any other factor carried manifest destiny to the Pacific in 1845," according to historian Norman A. Graebner.[47] Graebner explains: "National expansion in the 1840s was in essence not westward at all. It was a northward and southward movement along a coastline, and it is to be understood primarily in terms of specific objectives on that coastline . . . The goal of American foreign policy was to control the great harbors of San Francisco, San Diego and Juan de Fuca Strait. With their acquisition expansion on the coastline ceased."[48] Another historian, D. W. Meinig, agrees: "The Americans saw Britain as an aggressive jealous power that was ready to exploit any opportunity to curb, annoy, or belittle the United States . . . American intervention or involvement in the Floridas, Cuba, Texas, Mexico, Yucatan, California, and Hawaii was in some degree motivated by fear of the British."[49] In the words of Frederick Merk: "The chief defense problem was the British, whose ambition seemed to be to hem the nation. On the periphery of the United States, they were the dangerous potential aggressors. The best way to hold them off was to acquire the periphery."[50]

Power Politics and the Map of North America

During the U.S. Civil War, the French emperor Louis Napoleon took advantage of the distraction of the United States in order to invade Mexico and set up a puppet government under the Austrian Prince Maximilian von Hapsburg. In the draft of a public letter justifying his actions, Napoleon wrote that "we shall have erected an insuperable barrier against the encroachments of the United States," a sentence that was absent from the published version.[51] Following the Union victory in 1865, the U.S. government stationed troops along the Mexican border. Unwilling to risk war with the United States, Napoleon pulled out the troops and abandoned Maximilian to be executed. A French journalist bitterly observed: "We went in the name of Europe to weaken America [but] the Yankees have made Europe retreat."[52] The Monroe Doctrine had been vindicated. Never again did any European great power attempt to conquer an independent country in the Western Hemisphere.

While Britain refused to intervene in the U.S. Civil War, most of the British elite hoped for a Confederate victory that would result in the division of the United States into two or more weaker countries, a result that would strengthen British influence in North America, particularly in the Anglophile, free-trade South. During the Civil War, Russia tilted toward the North in order to deter Britain from entering the conflict on behalf of the Confederacy. This inspired Oliver Wendell Holmes to write a poem, "America to Russia": "Though watery deserts hold apart / The worlds of East and West, / Still beats the selfsame human heart / In each proud Nation's breast."

Although American republicanism and Tsarist despotism were polar opposites in terms of political values, the two continental powers on the periphery of the European system had long enjoyed good relations based on shared geopolitical interests. In 1812 Russia took the initiative in offering to broker an end to the war between the United States and Britain, in the hope that Britain could then concentrate its power against their common enemy Napoleon.

In the 1840s and 1850s, Britain, with France as its sometime ally, was trying to thwart the expansion of the United States in North America by strategies that included an Anglo-French guarantee of the independence of the Republic of Texas. At the same time Britain, with France at its side again, was concerned about the expansion of Russian power and influence in the Balkans, Central Asia, and East Asia, where Britain and France had obtained trade concessions from China at gunpoint during the "Opium Wars" of the 1840s. When Britain and France sought to block Russian expansion toward the Mediterranean in the Crimean War in 1854, three hundred Kentucky riflemen volunteered to fight for Russia against the despised British.[53]

The Russian government, seeking to rid itself of Alaska in order to consolidate its lines of defense, tried to persuade the United States to buy Alaska, in order to prevent "Russian America" from becoming part of British North America. U.S. Secretary of State William Seward pushed the treaty that obtained "Seward's Folly" through the United States Senate.

March 31, 1867, was an important date in the history of North America. Only hours before Seward signed the Alaska treaty with Russia in Washington, D.C., in London Queen Victoria signed the British North America Act that created the self-governing Dominion of Canada as of July 1, 1867. The two signing ceremonies were not unrelated.

Alarmed by the military power displayed by the U.S. federal government in the Civil War, and concerned that the United States might turn covetous eyes northward, the British government hastily had cobbled together its North American provinces into a federation. Although Canadians themselves wanted their country, which shared a monarch with Britain, to be known as "the Kingdom of Canada," Lord Monck, the British governor-general, suggested the innocuous title "Dominion" in order not to "open a monarchical blister on the side of the Americans."[54]

By subjugating the South, expelling France from Mexico, and inadvertently inspiring the consolidation of Canada, the United States gave the map of mainland North America the shape that it has retained since 1867. Senator Charles Sumner's response to the rounding out of the territory of the continental United States by the purchase of Alaska was this: "We dismiss one other monarch from the continent. One by one they have retired—first France, then Spain, then France again, and now Russia—all giving way to the absorbing Unity declared in the national motto, E pluribus unum."[55]

Democratic Republicanism and the Methods of U.S. Expansion

In his inaugural address of March 4, 1853, President Franklin Pierce declared: "It is not to be disguised that our attitude as a nation and our position on the globe render the acquisition of certain possessions not within our jurisdiction eminently important for our protection."[56] While territorial expansion did not violate America's democratic republican principles, wars of imperial conquest did. For this reason, purchase was the preferred method for obtaining foreign territory that was most in keeping with the principles of a civilian, commercial republic. With more idealism than accuracy, President James Buchanan in his 1858 address to Congress claimed that the American preference for purchasing foreign territories was "due to our national character. All of the territory which we have acquired since the origin of the Government has been by fair purchase from France, Spain, and Mexico or by the free and voluntary act of the independent Republic of Texas in blending her destinies with our own."[57]

The term "filibuster" comes from the Spanish word *filibustero*, derived from the Dutch word *vrijbuiter* for "free-booter" or "pirate" by way of the French *filibustier*. The method of "filibustering"—the infiltration of foreign territories by American settlers, who would then try to secede and join the territory to the United States—looked like American imperialism to the governments whose territory was coveted, when it was tried successfully in West Florida, Texas, and Hawaii and unsuccessfully in East Florida, Nicaragua, and Cuba. Whatever their personal motives, the filibusters, by enacting the ritual sanctified by the American Revolution of declaring independence against autocratic tyranny, appealed to the American principle of self-determination.

From Territories to States

Republican principles required that all new territories be converted into states with rights identical to those of the original states. The alternative of making the new domains national territories forever was never considered. That would have required the American settlers in the new lands to be ruled indefinitely by military governors appointed by Washington. Such a system of internal colonialism would have been incompatible with American democratic republicanism. Indeed, the process of turning territories into states was sometimes hasty, because of discontent with federal rule by the settlers and the discomfort of America's leaders with the quasi-imperial nature of temporary territorial government.

As Henry Cabot Lodge observed, the United States had a "record of conquest, colonization and expansion unequalled by any power in the nineteenth century."[58] American expansion was imperialism, but it was the imperialism of a republican settler state whose ideology discouraged the rule of one nationality over another. Critics of American "imperialism" often fail to note that "empire" in the eighteenth and early nineteenth centuries was a synonym for "state or "domain" or "realm"; only later did it become identified with what was earlier known as colonialism or the colonial policy. David Ramsay was not talking about an American equivalent of British imperialism when he wrote in 1778 during the War of Independence: "We have laid the foundations of a new empire, which promises to enlarge itself to vast dimensions, and to give happiness to a great continent."[59] He meant only that the United States would expand. President Jefferson wrote to the residents of the Indiana Territory in 1805: "By enlarging the empire of liberty, we multiply its auxiliaries, and provide new sources of renovation, should its principles, at any time, degenerate, in those portions of our country which gave them birth."[60] By "empire of liberty" Jefferson meant only "zone" or "area of liberty." His point was that yeoman farmers in the American West might keep the spirit of democratic republicanism alive even if the decadent, class-stratified states of the East Coast became bastions of oligarchy.

America's republican ideology was responsible not only for the rationale of expansion and its methods but also for the limits to territorial extension. Part of the American democratic republican tradition was the belief that a republic required a sense of common identity among its citizens and therefore had to correspond to a relatively homogeneous community. White-only immigration laws were sometimes justified in terms of this republican ideal, as well as by racist theories of nonwhite inferiority. Most Americans in the nineteenth century were also opposed to annexing territories densely populated by allegedly "unassimilable" nonwhite populations. For example, following the Mexican War the "all-Mexico movement" was defeated by opponents who limited U.S. territorial annexations to areas with only small populations of Mexican mestizos and Indians. Similar arguments were made at the time of the Spanish-American War against admitting the U.S. protectorates of Cuba, Puerto Rico, and Hawaii, with their nonwhite majorities, as states. As late as 1941, President Franklin Roosevelt told Secretary of State Cordell Hull that Puerto Rico and other U.S. territories should not be annexed, on the grounds that granting citizenship to their inhabitants "would stir up question[s] of racial stocks by virtue of their new status as American citizens."[61]

Historians have sometimes explained American expansionism as the result of American racism, without acknowledging the degree to which the former was checked by the latter. If Americans had been less racist, the territory of the United States would probably be much more extensive today.[62]

Manifest Destiny or a
Slave Power Conspiracy?

Many historians have explained the continental expansion of the United States primarily or exclusively in terms of purely economic factors, such as the desire of American farmers for new land or a "slave power conspiracy" on the part of Southern slave owners to expand and secure the zone of plantation slavery inside U.S. borders. These factors contributed to political support for U.S. annexation of the Floridas, the Louisiana Territory, Oregon, Texas, California, and the Southwest. Nonetheless, the main purpose of those annexations was the elimination of British and French power or influence from areas contiguous to the United States.

In defending the Louisiana Purchase, President Jefferson argued that the agrarian basis of American democratic republicanism could be preserved for generations if the Louisiana Territory were divided into small farms for American settlers. But new land for settlement was a side effect of a policy intended to deny New Orleans and the mouth of the Mississippi to Britain or France. In the same way, the Manifest Destiny agitation of the 1840s was manipulated, if not fabricated, by politicians in order to mobilize public support for the strategic goal of denying Britain influx or control over the key ports of San Diego and San Francisco and the Strait of Juan de Fuca on the West Coast.

It is true that much of the Southern elite viewed the annexation of both the Floridas and Texas as a way to extend plantation slavery, deny havens to runaway slaves, and increase the representation of the South in the U.S. Senate. Some Southerners argued that if Texas was not annexed, the Texas republic might abolish slavery in its borders as the price of an alliance with Britain, which had led the global antislavery campaign since it had abolished slavery in its own empire in the 1830s. Even so, enthusiasm for Western expansion was limited in the South and strongest in the North.[63]

Southern expansionists looked southward, not westward. They dreamed of new slave states in Cuba and other Caribbean islands and in Central

America. In this sense there was a genuine "slave power conspiracy," but its goals, apart from the annexation of Texas, were thwarted in the 1850s and forgotten after the South's defeat in the Civil War. Half a century later, when the U.S. finally established a Caribbean sphere of influence during and after the Spanish-American War, its purpose was to deny naval bases to Imperial Germany and other great powers, not to provide the upper class of the Deep South with new plantations and additional U.S. Senators. The most prominent advocate of an expansive U.S. Naval policy was Theodore Roosevelt, a progressive Northeastern champion of U.S. Naval power who was deeply unpopular among Southern voters. Naval expansion, like westward expansion, had far greater political support in the North than in the South.[64]

Averting a Balkanized North America

Each wave of American expansion coincided with a period of intense geopolitical tension with a particular great power with ambitions in North America. Britain and France, the leading powers in Europe and the world until the late nineteenth century, preferred a weak United States and a North American balance of power to a strong United States that was the hegemon of North America. Attempts to explain U.S. territorial expansion chiefly in terms of American culture ("Manifest Destiny") or a search for markets or resources are simply wrong. From the acquisition of the Louisiana Territory and the Floridas to the annexation of Texas, partition of Oregon, and conquest of California, the United States was motivated to expand by a determination to deny strategic territories on its borders to rival great powers.

None of this excuses the suffering inflicted on Mexicans and Indians by the United States in the course of its territorial expansion. But the alternatives must be realistically assessed. The Mexican government, bankrupt and weakened by ceaseless coups, revolutions, and civil wars, was incapable of holding on to all of the territory it had inherited from the Spanish Empire. In the 1820s the Central American states broke away from Mexico and in the 1830s Mexico lost Texas and Yucatan, which was later conquered and reabsorbed. If California and the American Southwest had not been seized by the United States in the Mexican War, they still would have been lost to Mexico, in all likelihood. If the region had not become a British protectorate, it probably would have been carved up among several weak and unstable filibuster republics populated by emigrants from the United States, like the Republic of Texas.

The American Indian nations were too few, poor, and divided to form a modern state or states of their own. They were doomed to be the wards of the modern countries that divided up North America among them. As it turned out, if the short-lived Republic of Texas is not counted, there have been only three such modern states, the United States, Mexico, and Canada. But even if there had been more post-colonial states in North America, including a Republic of California and a Confederate States of America, the original inhabitants of the continent still would have been forced to negotiate the best terms of surrender they could obtain from the governments of the new countries in whose internationally recognized borders they found themselves.

A Balkanized North America was a dangerous possibility. "There could have arisen a polyglot Florida Republic, a Francophone Mississippian America, a Hispanic New Biscay, a Republic of the Great Lakes, a Columbia—comprising the present Oregon, Washington, and British Columbia," the historian Eric Wolf has speculated.[65] Another historian, D. W. Meinig, has imagined "a continuing independent Republic of Texas; an infiltrated but continuing Mexican state of New Mexico; a de facto independent [Mormon] Commonwealth of Deseret beyond the canyonlands of the Colorado . . . and, out of the swirl of the Gold Rush, a new Republic of California."[66] The thought of these never-created countries may be entertaining. But the division of North America among a much smaller United States and a number of weak and unstable countries on its borders would have had the same harmful consequences as the division of North America among a number of English-speaking republics as the result of the disintegration of the United States in civil war.

Critics of nineteenth-century American expansion must acknowledge the costs of the alternative. In 1943 Walter Lippmann pointed out that Britain was the only great power with a common border with the United States, the Canadian border. "If the boundaries of 1783 had remained the boundaries of the United States, the young Republic would have had to live with France as her neighbor on the Mississippi and with Spain on the frontier of Georgia. This would have left the United States with small means within its narrow limits, and committed to the defence of a long land frontier against the shifting combinations of three great European powers."[67] A smaller

United States with a greater number of potential enemies on its borders probably would have been forced to have a far more militarized society.

The Success and Obsolescence of American Isolationism

"Today the United States is practically sovereign on this continent and its fiat is law upon the subjects to which it confines its interposition," U.S. Secretary of State Richard Olney declared in 1895. Olney added that "its infinite resources combined with its isolated position render it master of the situation and practically invulnerable as against any or all other powers."[68]

The occasion of Olney's statement was a dispute between Venezuela and Britain's South American colony of Guiana. Olney insisted that the United States had the right to mediate disputes between countries in the Western Hemisphere and extra-hemispheric powers like Britain. After President Grover Cleveland hinted at the use of American armed force in his annual address to Congress in December 1895, Britain gave in to U.S. pressure and consented to arbitration.

Only 112 years after winning its independence from the British Empire, the United States was indeed "practically sovereign" in North America. It had expanded from the Atlantic seaboard to the Gulf Coast and the Pacific Ocean. And the victory of the Union in the Civil War of 1861–65 had ensured that the United States would not disintegrate into two or more squabbling successor states. Geographic expansion and political unity had done more than make the United States the dominant nation in the Americas and potentially the most powerful country in the world. By averting the formation of a balance of power system in North America that might have been manipulated by Britain and other outside powers and thereby keeping U.S. defense costs low, territorial expansion and national unity had helped to preserve the civilian and individualist American way of life that the United States had been founded to defend.

But the isolationist strategy presupposed a balance of power in Europe. As the twentieth century dawned, it became clear to perceptive American thinkers and statesmen that the old European balance of power system was in danger of failing. When it collapsed, America's policy of isolation could no longer be maintained. Long before World War I, the United States was in need of a new strategy.

Chapter 5

Why the United States Fought in World War I

> ... [I]f Germany won it would change the course of our civilization and make the United States a military nation ...
>
> —Woodrow Wilson[1]

ON APRIL 9, 1865, GENERAL ROBERT E. LEE, commander of the Army of the Confederate States of America, surrendered to General Ulysses S. Grant of the United States Army at the courthouse in Appomattox, Virginia. The U.S. Civil War, which had cost more than six hundred thousand lives, was over. The defeat of the South's attempt to secede had left the United States intact as a continental nation-state with enormous industrial and military potential.

North America was not the only region in which a civil war led to the emergence of a new great power in the 1860s. On November 9, 1867, the fifteenth Tokugawa shogun, Tokugawa Yoshinobu, ceded his powers to the Japanese emperor under pressure from an alliance of the military leaders of two Japanese provinces, Satsuma and Choshu. In May 1869, Yoshinobu's armies finally were defeated in battle in Hokkaido. The "Meiji Restoration" of 1866–69 was disguised as the restoration of the powers of the Japanese emperor, reduced for generations to a figurehead by the ruling Tokugawa shoguns. In reality it was a civil war won by military oligarchs who were determined to launch Japan on a program of modernization from above.

Even more significant was the civil war in the 1860s in Germany, a cultural nation long divided into many states, of which Prussia and Austria were the most powerful. Using a dispute over Schleswig-Holstein as a pretext, Prussia launched a war against Austria on June 15, 1866. Seven weeks later on August 23 Austria signed the Treaty of Prague, which excluded the Habsburg monarchy from influence in Germany. The Prussians consolidated the states of Germany outside of Austria into the North German Confederation, which was converted into the German Empire following Prussia's defeat of France in the Franco-Prussian War of 1870. Amid the splendor of the Hall of Mirrors in the French palace of Versailles, Prussia's King Wilhelm I was crowned as emperor or Kaiser (Caesar). Like Japan under the Meiji oligarchs, the new German Empire was a regime dominated by aristocrats and military officers committed to modernizing their society without liberalizing or democratizing it.

Seventy-four years after the coronation of Wilhelm I as German emperor at Versailles, in the French city of Rheims the representatives of another German regime surrendered to the U.S. General Dwight Eisenhower, supreme commander of Allied forces in Europe. On May 7, 1945, acting on behalf of Admiral Karl Doenitz, whom Adolf Hitler had designated as his successor before committing suicide in his bunker on April 30, German General Alfred Jodl signed the instrument of unconditional surrender. Four months later, on board the USS *Missouri*, anchored in Tokyo Bay, General Yoshijuro Umezu, chief of the Japanese Army General Staff, signed another instrument of surrender on behalf of the government of Japan, in the presence of General of the Army Douglas MacArthur and Admiral Chester W. Nimitz of the United States. Of the three great powers that had been consolidated in civil wars in the 1860s, two were defeated and in ruins and one was the most powerful nation on the earth.

The Obsolescence of American Isolationism

America's first grand strategy of isolation served the American people well. The balance of power system in Europe ensured that no single great power would be able to dominate Europe and threaten North America. While the European powers kept each other down, American leaders strove to avert a North American balance of power system that would force the militarization of American society. They did so by preserving America's national unity, expanding America's borders, and making North America a regional sphere of influence, at the expense of Britain, France, and Spain. With the exception of the Civil War, which also averted the Balkanization of North America, these measures cost very little, yet they ensured that America's defense costs remained low. In 1900 in per capita terms the United States had by far the lowest expenditure on the military of any great power in the world.

But the grand strategy of non-entanglement assumed two conditions: the safety afforded the United States by its geographic distance from other great powers and a balance of power in Europe.

From antiquity until the early modern era, the small number of liberal republics or constitutional monarchies that, unlike republican Athens and republican Rome, endured over time usually enjoyed low security costs because they had natural geographic defenses. They were located on islands (Venice, Britain), peninsulas (the Netherlands), or mountains (Switzerland, San Marino). These geographic barriers freed these republics from the need to raise huge armies, which threatened political liberty, and from the need for high levels of taxation for military spending, which discouraged the formation of a prosperous middle class of the kind necessary in a republic. Alexander Hamilton pointed this out in Federalist 8: "There is a wide difference also, between military establishments in a country, seldom exposed by its situation to internal invasions, and in one which is often subject to them, and always apprehensive of them . . . The kingdom of Great Britain falls within the first description. An insular situation, and a powerful marine, guarding it in great measure against the possibility of foreign invasion, supercede the necessity of a numerous army within the kingdom . . . If, on the contrary, Britain had been situated on the continent, and had been compelled, as she would have been, by that situation, to make her military establishments at home co-extensive with those of the other great powers of Europe, she, like them, would in all probability, be at this day a victim to the absolute power of one man."[2] As Hamilton observed, a state surrounded on easily crossed land borders by powerful and potentially hostile neighbors often had no choice but to become an armed camp under executive rule in order to survive.

By the twentieth century, however, the industrialization of sea power and the development of airpower and motorized armies meant that the American republic could no longer count on geographic barriers to allow it to achieve security at low cost to a civilian, liberal way of life. "The safeguard of isolation no longer exists," a U.S. War College report concluded in 1915. "The oceans, once barriers, are now easy avenues of approach by reason of the number, speed, and carrying capacity of ocean-going vessels. The increasing radii of action of the submarine, the aeroplane, and wireless telegraphy all supplement ocean transport in placing both our Atlantic and Pacific coasts within the sphere of hostile activities of overseas nations."

The authors complained: "The great mass of the public does not yet realize the effect of these changed conditions upon our schemes of defence."[3]

Even as the industrialization of warfare was diminishing the value of the geographic defenses of the United States, the balance of power in Europe, the other condition for America's historic isolationist policy, was endangered. The unification of Germany in 1870 and its subsequent military and industrial growth had created a state too powerful to be restrained by European rivals alone. From 1871 to 1890, German Chancellor Otto von Bismarck, obsessed by the "nightmare of coalitions," was careful to avoid antagonizing Germany's powerful neighbors. But German caution in foreign policy came to an end in 1890, when the young Kaiser Wilhelm II dismissed Bismarck and launched Germany's new *Weltpolitik* (global policy). Not content for Germany to be the greatest European power, the Kaiser and his officials wanted Germany to become a power of global reach and importance.

German-American Naval Rivalry

Between the end of the Napoleonic Wars in 1815 and the unification of Germany in 1870, Britain had managed to dominate the seas while preserving a balance of power among the five great powers of the European "pentarchy"— Britain, France, Russia, Prussia, and Austria. On the continent Germany's unification threatened the European balance, while ambitious German *Weltpolitik* threatened not only Britain but also the United States at sea.

As early as the 1880s, the United States was engaged in naval rivalry with the newly created Imperial Germany.[4] In 1888–89, the United States and Germany almost came to blows over control of the Samoan Islands and the two countries also clashed over the question of control of Hawaii. The first five topics of German war-planning exercises in 1897–98 involved war between Germany and the United States.[5] In August 1897 Theodore Roosevelt wrote, "Germany is the Power with which we may very possibly have ultimately to come into hostile contact."[6]

Even before the outbreak of the Spanish-American War in 1898, some German leaders wanted Imperial Germany to support Spain against the United States.[7] During the Spanish-American War, Imperial Germany dispatched a fleet to Manila Bay, in order to strengthen German claims on the Philippines if the United States abandoned the islands. Tensions rose to the point at which Admiral Dewey informed the German commander, Vice-

Admiral Otto von Diederichs, who later became Germany's admiralty chief, that "if Germany wants war, all right, we are ready."[8] The prospect that the Philippines would be seized by Germany or other great powers led the McKinley administration to decide to turn the entire archipelago into a U.S. protectorate, at the cost of a bloody and inhumane war in which the United States killed more than two hundred thousand Filipinos. In 1898 the same strategic rationale led the United States to annex Guam and Hawaii, which it had long contested with Germany.

On July 27, 1898, John Hay, the U.S. ambassador to Britain, warned his friend, Massachusetts Senator Henry Cabot Lodge: "The jealousy and animosity felt towards us in Germany . . . can hardly be exaggerated. . . . They want the Philippines, the Carolines, and Samoa . . . "[9] Germany purchased the Marshall and Caroline Islands from Spain in 1899, having acquired leases in China's Shangtung Province in 1898.

In the words of one historian, "Behind the advocacy of the annexation of Cuba and Hawaii lay not so much a growing American imperialism as a concern for the safety of the isthmian canal and the American continent."[10] The Teller Amendment of 1898 prevented the United States from annexing the former Spanish colony of Cuba. But the Platt Amendment to the army appropriations bill of 1901, along with provisions the United States forced the Cubans to include in their constitution, made Cuba a U.S. protectorate, chiefly to forestall possible German influence. In 1934 Elihu Root explained: "You cannot understand the Platt Amendment unless you know something about the character of Kaiser Wilhelm the Second."[11] Earlier in 1930 Root had written: "We went into Santo Domingo [in 1904] for the sole purpose of keeping Germany from taking it."[12]

In December 1903 Major General Arthur MacArthur, the father of General Douglas MacArthur, predicted "a war in the immediate future between the United States and Germany" in which the Philippines and Hawaii would be central.[13] U.S. defenses in the Philippines were strengthened in 1903–4 more out of fear of Germany than of Japan.[14] For its part, Japan seized Taiwan in 1894 and Korea in 1910.

American concerns about Imperial Germany were not without foundation. "Operationsplan III," devised by the German Navy between 1898 and 1906, provided for German naval attacks against East Coast cities like New York and Boston in the event of a German-American war, while Germany's Pacific Fleet, based in Asia and Latin America, attacked American and British shipping. The German Admiralty's Chief of Staff Buchsel explained to the Kaiser in 1903 that "direct pressure on the American east coast" should take the form of "a merciless offensive designed to confront the American people with an unbearable situation by the spread of terror and by damaging enemy trade and property."[15]

While Germany's plans for war against the United States were offensive, U.S. plans were purely defensive. The United States devised War Plan Black to defeat a possible German naval invasion of the Caribbean, attacks on the East Coast, or German seizure of key Caribbean islands. Only in 1917 did the U.S. military begin planning for an American expeditionary force to Europe.[16]

The Anglo-American Rapprochement

Henry Cabot Lodge, the Massachusetts Senator who long served as chairman of the Senate Foreign Relations Committee, complained in 1895 that "from 1776 England's policy has been one of almost studied unfriendliness" toward the United States.[17] But in *America's Economic Supremacy* (1900), Brooks Adams, a member of the influential circle that included Theodore Roosevelt and Lodge, wrote that "the risk of isolation promises to be more serious than the risk of an alliance." He called on "Englishmen and Americans to combine for their own safety" against the threats of Germany and Russia in Europe, and to prevent either Japan or Russia from turning China into a colony: "the United States could hardly contemplate with equanimity the successful organization of a hostile, industrial system on the shore of the Pacific, based on Chinese labour . . . "[18]

In order to focus on the increasing threat to the British Isles from Germany, Britain conciliated Russia, Japan, and the United States at the end of the nineteenth century and the beginning of the twentieth. In 1895 Britain backed down when President Grover Cleveland intervened in a dispute between Britain and Venezuela and insisted on arbitration to prevent Britain from using force in America's sphere of influence. In 1898 Britain yielded again in another dispute with the United States over the Canadian border with Alaska. In 1902 in the Hay-Pounceforte Treaty, Britain acknowledged U.S. hegemony in the Caribbean and Central America. This was followed in 1903 by the U.S.-sponsored coup that severed Panama from Colombia, making possible the construction of the U.S.-controlled Panama Canal, which permitted America's Atlantic and Pacific Fleets to reinforce each other in the event of war with Germany or another great power. To reconcile U.S. recognition of legitimate European financial claims against Latin American countries with the need to deny Germany and other great powers an excuse for intervening in North America, Theodore Roosevelt announced the "Roosevelt Corollary" to the Monroe Doctrine in 1904, declaring that henceforth the United States would police delinquent Latin American creditor states on behalf of European powers.

Germany and the United States clashed again, when Germany, along with Britain and Italy, blockaded and bombarded Venezuela to punish its government for refusing to negotiate over investment claims made by their nationals. In 1906 the United States took part in the Algeciras Conference, convened to settle the rival claims of Germany and France in Morocco. The United States contributed to the anti-German majority vote at the conference, and President Theodore Roosevelt wrote privately that "I set [the Kaiser] on his head with great decision . . . "[19] In 1908 Roosevelt sent America's "Great White Fleet" around the world, signaling American naval strength and determination to other great powers, particularly Germany and Japan. Ominously, however, by the time that the Panama Canal opened in 1914, Germany had surpassed the United States as the world's second greatest naval power after Britain.[20]

The United States and the Rise of Japan

In the late nineteenth and early twentieth centuries, the United States and Britain shared a common concern about Japan as well as Germany. Ironically, half a century earlier the "opening" of Japan by the United States had been motivated largely by concern about Britain. Commodore Matthew C. Perry, whom President Millard Fillmore charged in 1853 to undertake a diplomatic mission to Japan to obtain trading rights for the United States and coaling stations for the U.S. Navy, had been wary of British naval power and influence in East Asia.[21] Naval rivalry with Britain in the mid-nineteenth century was also a factor in the U.S. annexation of Midway Island in 1867 and proposals by a series of presidents, rejected by the U.S. Congress, to buy or annex various Caribbean and Pacific islands.[22]

The "opening" of Japan to the West at American instigation, formalized in the Convention of Kanagawa in 1854, led to the Meiji Restoration of

1868, a revolution from above by Japanese military elites. They modernized Japan and turned it into a formidable power that fought wars with China in 1894–95 and Russia in 1904–5. Britain, worried about the growing threat of Imperial Germany, mended its fences with Japan as well as the United States and Russia. By means of the Anglo-Japanese alliance of 1902, a declining Britain hoped to prevent Japan from becoming a rival in Asia. In a different way, the United States also embraced Japan in the hope of restraining it. President Theodore Roosevelt, who volunteered to broker the peace that ended the Russo-Japanese War in part to prevent Japan from completely destroying Russian power in East Asia, appeased Japan by recognizing Korea as a Japanese colony.

American Imperialism Versus American Republicanism

Advocates of U.S. naval expansion in the late nineteenth and early twentieth centuries wanted a maritime empire of naval bases in the Caribbean and the Pacific to strengthen the United States in preparation for possible conflict with other great powers, particularly Germany and Japan. American navalists like Theodore Roosevelt and Alfred Thayer Mahan, whose book *The Influence of Sea Power Upon History, 1660–1783* (1890) influenced policymakers in Germany, Britain, and other countries in addition to the United States, believed that the United States should control strategic territories, if that was necessary to secure the sea lanes between the United States and other regions including Latin America, Asia, and Europe.

But naval bases came with countries and populations attached. Anti-imperialists in the United States argued that the acquisition of overseas colonies that, unlike the territories of the American West, could never become states and join the Union violated American republican traditions. Grover Cleveland, who as president had resisted pressure to propose the annexation of Hawaii, complained in 1898 of the "perversion of our national mission. The mission of our nation is to build up and make a greater country out of what we have instead of annexing islands."[23] Opponents of U.S. naval imperialism often had motives other than republican idealism. Many anti-imperialists in the South, for example, feared agricultural competition with U.S. colonies and U.S. rule over new nonwhite populations, and some feared that a stronger federal government would use its enhanced powers in the South.

In what became known as the Insular Cases in 1901, the U.S. Supreme Court rejected the argument against imperialism from the principles of American republicanism and held that the United States had the power perpetually to rule "unincorporated" territories whose inhabitants legitimately could be denied all rights except those derived from natural law. According to one justice, "A false step at this time . . . might be fatal to the development of what Chief Justice Marshall called the American Empire."[24] This was a grotesque misreading of American tradition. Marshall, like Washington, Jefferson, and other Founders, had used "empire" as a synonym for "country" or "nation" in eighteenth-century fashion, not in the later sense of coercive colonial rule of one population over another; indeed, Marshall had defended the rights of the Cherokee against the government of Georgia and the administration of Andrew Jackson. The Insular Cases had a sinister legacy. Invoking them as precedent, the administration of George W. Bush transferred prisoners from the wars in Afghanistan and Iraq to the U.S. naval base at Guantanamo Bay, Cuba, on the theory that they had no legal rights in this "unincorporated territory" and could be tortured in interrogations.

Notwithstanding the Supreme Court's endorsement of imperialism, the policy was short-lived. Appalled by the cost of the U.S. war to subjugate the Philippines from 1898 to 1902, the elite and public turned against further imperial adventures. Even Theodore Roosevelt in 1907 confided to William Howard Taft, who had been governor-general of the Philippines: "The Philippines form our heel of Achilles."[25] The United States granted the Philippines its independence in 1945, after recapturing the island chain from Japan during World War II. Otherwise the formal U.S. empire was limited to Puerto Rico and a handful of islands in the Caribbean and the Pacific.

Subsequently the United States continued to intervene militarily in its sphere of influence in the Caribbean and Central America, but even its prolonged occupations of Haiti (1915–1934) and Nicaragua (1912–1933) were meant to be temporary. While this may not have comforted the inhabitants of North American countries in which the United States intervened, unlike formal imperialism this kind of informal hegemony was compatible with America's own traditions as a democratic republic.

If the United States, instead of limiting its formal empire to a few strategic islands, had sought permanently to rule large populations against their will and without granting them rights, the United States might have been forced to maintain large military forces to repress unwilling subjects, with ominous consequences for the republic. As the political scientist Mark E. Pietrzyk observes, "when military campaigns result in the conquest of new lands and peoples, subsequent political conditions in the conquering state are likely to be characterized by a permanent increase in centralization and a decrease in liberty. This is because conquest tends to bring new sources of power and wealth to the conqueror, while the conquering state acquires more people of different cultures, decreasing social cohesion. The victims of conquest are not likely to consent to their new government, so unrelenting coercion is required."[26]

This point was made by William Graham Sumner in 1899, in his protest against American imperialism in the Caribbean and the Philippines entitled "The Conquest of the United States by Spain." Sumner warned that the acquisition of a colonial empire would force changes in the American system of government: "We see that the peculiarities of our system of government set limitations on us. We cannot do things which a great centralized monarchy could do. The very blessings and special advantages which we enjoy, as compared with others, bring disabilities with them . . . [W]e cannot govern dependencies consistently with our political system, and . . . if we try it, the State which our fathers founded will suffer a reaction that will transform it into another empire just after the fashion of all the old ones. That is what imperialism means. That is what it will be; and the democratic republic, which has been, will stand in history, like the colonial organization of earlier days, as a mere transition form."[27]

World War I: Germany's First Bid for Superpower Status

For half a century after 1914, most historians agreed that the great powers of Europe tragically had stumbled into an avoidable war. However, research in Imperial German archives in the 1960s revealed the truth: the *Kaiserreich* had deliberately launched a preventive war against Russia and its ally France, out of fear that growing Russian military power would soon make German dreams of European domination impossible to realize.

On December 8, 1912, in a secret meeting from which civilian policymakers were excluded, the Kaiser and his top military officers decided to plan a war against Russia and its allies. In order to prepare the German Navy for war with the British fleet, Admiral Tirpitz asked for "postponement of the great fight for one and a half years." Almost exactly one and a half years later, the "great fight" began.[28]

Following the assassination of Austrian Archduke Franz-Ferdinand in Bosnia by a Serb terrorist on June 28, 1914, the authorities in Berlin manipulated the conflict between Austria and Russia's ally Serbia to provide an excuse for the war to destroy Russian power that Germany had been planning for several years.

Imperial Germany was committed to a radical program of conquest and territorial expansion in Europe that differed little from that of Hitler's National Socialist regime a generation later. According to Chancellor Bethman Hollweg in his secret "September Program" of 1914: "France must be so weakened as to make her revival as a great power impossible for all time. Russia must be thrust back as far as possible from Germany's eastern frontier and her domination over the non-Russian vassal peoples broken."[29] The German chancellor was fond of the word "vassal": "At any rate, Belgium, even if allowed to continue to exist as a state, must be reduced to a vassal state, must allow us to occupy any militarily important posts, must place her coast at our disposal in military respects, must become economically a German province."[30] From Belgium, Germany would be able to blackmail Britain permanently by threatening an invasion or blockade.

The September program and other contemporary expansionist programs discussed by German officials repeated a few themes, with different details. Germany would annex portions of France with mineral resources important for military-industrial power. In the east, Germany would annex a "Polish Strip" that in some plans foreshadowed Hitler's *Lebensraum* scheme and would be ethnically cleansed of Poles and Jews and colonized by ethnic Germans. The Russian Empire would be broken up and Poland, Ukraine, and other Eastern European nations would be subordinated to the Reich. In the Middle East, Germany and its Turkish ally would try to control the Persian Gulf oil fields. Some members of the German elite also wanted a belt of German colonies through central Africa from the South Atlantic to the Indian Ocean, while others dreamed of a German economic sphere of influence in South America. With France crushed, Russia shattered, Britain intimidated, and the United States isolated and tied down by conflicts with Mexico and perhaps Japan, Imperial Germany would be in a position to dominate the world by dominating the world's richest and most powerful region, Europe.

German-American Rivalry in Mexico During World War I

In 1915 Secretary of State Robert Lansing wrote in his diary: "It comes down to this: Our possible relations with Germany must be our first consideration; and all our intercourse with Mexico must be regulated accordingly."[31]

Mexico had long played an important role in Germany's anti-American strategy. When, in 1907, Mexico agreed to let Germany establish coaling stations on its coasts, William Buchsel, chief of staff of the German Admiralty, declared that this would be "a thrust . . . into the very basis of the Monroe Doctrine."[32] The Kaiser speculated about turning Baja California into a German colony.[33]

The Mexican Revolution that began in 1910 became a proxy war, in which the United States supported the Mexican leader Venustiano Carranza against his rivals General Victoriana Huerta and Pancho Villa who received aid from Imperial Germany. By World War I, the navies of the great powers had completed their conversion from coal to oil. This made Mexico, which provided one quarter of the world's oil supply, as important as Saudi Arabia later would be.[34]

On April 21, 1914, the U.S. Marines seized control of the Mexican port of Veracruz. The message to the U.S. naval commander was as follows: "SEIZE THE CUSTOMS HOUSE. DO NOT PERMIT WAR SUPPLIES TO BE DELIVERED TO HUERTA GOVERNMENT OR ANY OTHER PARTY." The public reason given by the Wilson administration was the refusal of the Mexican government to make an adequate public apology for the mistaken arrest of several U.S. sailors weeks earlier in the port of Tampico. In secret President Wilson told congressional leaders that the goal was to intercept the *Ypiranga*, one of three German ships sailing to Veracruz with munitions intended for Huerta. The U.S. intervention not only angered Mexicans, including Carranza, but also failed in its purpose, because the German arms were delivered to Huerta through another port.[35] Following his defeat, a German military cruiser took General Huerta into European exile.[36] Later Huerta, financed by Germany, was arrested in New Mexico and charged with violating U.S. neutrality laws; he died while awaiting trial in El Paso, Texas, on January 13, 1916.[37]

Wilson explained to one of his political allies that "[Germany] wishes an uninterrupted opportunity to carry on her submarine warfare and believes that war with Mexico will keep our hands off her and thus give her liberty of action to do as she pleases on the high seas. It begins to look as if war with Germany is inevitable. If it should come—I pray God it may not—I do not wish America's energies and forces divided, for we will need every ounce of reserve we have to lick Germany."[38]

German-American Rivalry in the Caribbean

After the outbreak of World War I in 1914, the United States, although nominally neutral until 1917, helped Britain and France keep their war efforts going. The United States treated Britain's blockade of Germany as legitimate, but insisted that unrestricted German submarine warfare violated the rights of neutral nations like the United States and the laws of war. Between 1915 and 1917, when it resumed unrestricted submarine warfare, Germany, seeking to avoid direct conflict with the United States, agreed to restrictions on submarine warfare against ships traveling to Britain and France from North America. This made it easier for supplies from the United States to bolster the British and French war efforts.

On July 11, 1915, Wilson's Secretary of State Robert Lansing called for "the prevention by all means in our power of German influence becoming dominant in any nation bordering the Caribbean or near the Panama Canal."[39] To this end, the Wilson administration moved quickly to deny German access to three strategic harbors in the Caribbean: Mole-Saint-Nicolas in Haiti, Samana Bay in the Dominican Republic, and the Danish West Indies. On July 28, 1915, several hundred U.S. Marines landed at Port-au-Prince, Haiti. The U.S. military also occupied the Dominican Republic in 1915, and in 1916 the United States, by threatening to seize the West Indies to deny their use by Germany, pressured Denmark to sell the islands to the United States.[40] Franklin Roosevelt, then assistant secretary of the navy, declared in 1915: "Our national defense must extend all over the western hemisphere, must go out a thousand miles into the sea."[41]

Haiti had been a key Caribbean country that Imperial Germany sought to bring under its influence. By 1914 the U.S. State Department estimated that German merchants controlled 80 percent of Haitian commerce.[42] The U.S. government became alarmed by the role of German merchants in financing revolutions in Haiti. In order to "Germanize the descendants of Germans established in Haiti" and foster reverence for the Kaiser, the imperial foreign office funded a German school in Port-au-Prince in 1912.[43]

After the United States entered the war against Germany formally in April 1917, Washington pressured its client government in Haiti to intern Germans, to confiscate their property, and to declare war against Germany.[44] As in the Philippines, atrocities committed by U.S. soldiers were the subject of newspaper exposes and congressional investigations in the United States. Franklin Roosevelt, who had served Wilson as assistant secretary of the navy, was criticized when, during his campaign for the vice presidency as part of the Democratic ticket in 1920, he joked, "You know I have had something to do with the running of a couple of little republics. The facts are that I wrote Haiti's constitution myself, and, if I do say it, I think it a pretty good Constitution."[45]

The United States Enters World War I

On January 31, 1917, Germany resumed unrestricted submarine warfare, a policy that it had abandoned after the sinking on May 7, 1915, of the ocean liner *Lusitania*, with many Americans on board, had created outrage in the United States. On February 3, the Wilson administration responded to the new German policy of unrestricted submarine warfare by severing diplomatic relations between the United States and Germany.

On February 17, 1917, the German foreign minister sent a telegram to the German ambassador in Mexico, which the British obtained and revealed to the American people. The "Zimmerman Telegram" read: "We intend to begin unrestricted submarine warfare. We shall endeavor to keep the United States neutral. In the event of this not succeeding, we make Mexico a proposal of alliance on the following basis: make war together, make peace together, generous financial support, and an understanding on our part that Mexico is to recover lost territory in Texas, New Mexico and Arizona."[46] In 1916 the *Tägliche Rundschau* of Berlin declared: "We consider it not worth denying that Germany is egging Mexico into war in order to prevent the export of arms to the Allies."[47]

The outrage of the American public at the promise of Imperial Germany to help Mexico dismember the United States, together with the resumption of unrestricted submarine warfare, led Congress to respond positively to Wilson's request, on April 6, 1917, for a declaration of war against Germany. Wilson's idealistic vision—"The world must be made safe for democracy"—coexisted with geopolitical realism. If German submarine warfare cut off Britain and France from American support, then Imperial Germany, which had displayed its intention to encircle the United States in North America, would succeed in becoming the dominant military power in Europe. In addition, the Wilson administration recognized that if British and French power in Asia collapsed, the power vacuum might be filled by Japan. The United States might find itself in a tripolar world, between a German Empire in Europe and an Asia dominated by Imperial Japan. Indeed, Imperial Germany hoped that Japan as well as Mexico would go to war against the United States.[48]

Why America Fought

Even before World War I, the historian Henry Adams had spoken for many Americans who understood the new requirements of American defense: "We have got to support France against Germany and fortify the Atlantic System beyond attack; for if Germany breaks down England and France, she becomes the center of a military world, and we are lost."[49]

Had a general war broken out earlier in Europe, the United States might have intervened earlier. In 1910 Theodore Roosevelt confided to a friend in the German diplomatic service that the United States would have intervened in 1906 if, at the time of the First Moroccan crisis, Germany had invaded France. "I certainly would have found myself compelled to interfere. As long as England succeeds in keeping 'the balance of power' in Europe, not only in principle, but in reality, well and good; should she however for some reason or other fail in doing so, the United States would be obliged to step in at least temporarily, in order to restore the balance of power in Europe, never mind against which country or group of countries our efforts may have to be directed."[50]

In "A War of Self-Defense," a government pamphlet published in August 1917, Secretary of State Lansing wrote: "Imagine Germany victor in Europe because the United States remained neutral . . . Let me then ask you, would it be easier or wiser for this country single-handed to resist a German Empire, flushed with victory and with great armies and navies at its command, than to unite with the brave opponents of that Empire in ending now and for all time this menace to our future?"[51] On February 3, 1917, the *New York Times* declared in an editorial that the victory of Imperial Germany would mean "either that we buy freedom from molestation by perpetual poltroonery, or that within a few years we shall be engaged in a new war for independence against an incomparably more formidable foe. And for that war, unless we adopted a permanent policy of non-resistance, we should be compelled to begin instant preparations."[52]

Walter Lippmann, who served the Wilson administration as an advisor, explained "the undeclared . . . foreign policy which determined the participation of the United States in the first German World War." Lippmann wrote that "many Americans saw in 1917 that if Germany won, the United States would have to face a new and aggressively expanding German empire which had made Britain, France, and Russia its vassals, and Japan its ally. They saw that in such a position the defense of the Western Hemisphere would require immense armaments over and above those needed in the Pacific, and that America would have to live in a perpetual state of high and alert military preparedness. It was in this very concrete and practical sense . . . that a German victory in 1917 would have made the world unsafe for the American democracies from Canada to the Argentine."[53] The political scientist and historian Robert J. Art agrees: "The threat of a German victory in World War I provoked Woodrow Wilson's fear that America's democratic system would be subverted by the huge military buildup that the United States would require to protect itself from the German hegemon."[54] In Wilson's own words to his adviser Colonel Edward M. House, "if Germany won it would change the course of our civilization and make the United States a military nation . . . "[55]

In April 1917 the United States entered World War I in order to save the American way of life, not from a German conquest of the United States, but from the need to sacrifice American liberty in order to preserve American independence in a world dominated by Imperial Germany by constructing a regimented Fortress America. A generation later, for the same reason, the United States went to war with Germany again.

Chapter 6

World War II and the American Way of Life

> No realistic American can expect from a dictator's peace international generosity, or return of true independence, or world disarmament, or freedom of expression, or freedom of religion—or even good business. Such a peace would bring no security for us or for our neighbors. Those who would give up essential liberty to purchase a little temporary safety deserve neither liberty nor safety.
>
> —Franklin Roosevelt, 1941[1]

THE WORLD WAR ONLY RECEIVED THE ROMAN NUMERAL "I" after the second global conflict of the twentieth century began. Apart from a few pessimistic thinkers, no one at the time realized that "the world war" or "the great war" was merely the first in a series that would include not only World War II but also the Cold War, which some have viewed as three episodes in a Seventy-Five Years' War of the twentieth century.[2]

In hindsight, the interwar decades of the 1920s and 1930s were an armistice between two rounds of conflict between Germany and an anti-German coalition of Britain, France, Russia, and the United States. Fifteen million died as a result of the first round, and as many as fifty million as a result of the second. In the second war against Germany, as in the first, the United States took part in order to avoid the need to choose between the equally grim alternatives of a defiant, regimented Fortress America or a submissive American tributary state in a world dominated by a German Empire.

Woodrow Wilson and the League of Nations

In his address to Congress of January 22, 1917, President Wilson declared: "In every discussion of peace that must end this war, it is taken for granted that the peace must be followed by some definite concert of power which will make it virtually impossible that any such catastrophe should ever overwhelm us again."[3]

The idea of a league of nations to enforce peace was popular at the time, particularly among British and American liberals. Liberal utopians dreamed of "the parliament of man, the federation of the world," to use Tennyson's phrase.[4] Realists preferred the idea of a concert or cartel limited to a small number of great powers. This was the conception of Theodore Roosevelt, who said in his 1905 annual address to Congress: "Our aim should be from time to time to take such steps as may be possible toward creating something like an organization of the civilized nations, because as the world becomes more highly organized the need for navies and armies will diminish."[5]

Wilson's trusted adviser Colonel Edward M. House and his Secretary of State Robert Lansing both favored the idea of an exclusive great power concert, a global version of the nineteenth-century Concert of Europe. In the spring of 1914 House, traveling to Europe as Wilson's informal ambassador, had won assent from the British for his proposal of an American-British-German concert, but failed to persuade the Kaiser to agree to cut back the German Navy in order to reassure Britain. After the United States entered the war, Wilson asked House to draft a plan for the postwar League of Nations. In his diary on July 5, 1918, House asked rhetorically "why permit [smaller powers] to exercise a directing hand upon the nations having to furnish not only the financial but the physical force necessary to maintain order and peace? I am sorry to come to this conclusion, because it does not seem toward the trend of liberalism. However, the idealist who is not practical oftentimes does a cause more harm than those frankly reactionary."[6] On July 14, 1918, House recommended to Wilson "that the League might be confined to the Great Powers."[7]

Like House, Secretary of State Lansing had a traditional great power alliance in mind. Lansing reluctantly lobbied the Senate to ratify the League of Nations Covenant, but his candor in testimony before the Senate enraged Wilson and he soon resigned as secretary of state. In a posthumously published memoir Lansing complained that "the international agency, which the President described to me in July, 1917, which was simple, practical and without any sort of executive power, and to the support of which most conservatives could subscribe, was a very different type of agency from the completed machinery of the League with its Council and Assembly and

Secretariat, which the President in 1919 wrote into the Covenant that was laid before the Peace Conference." Lansing observed that Wilson's vision was "possibly too ideal for a practical and selfish world and too coldly impartial for human nature."[8]

Wilson was convinced that his grandiose version of the League of Nations would be necessary to save the world from war in the future. On the way to the Peace Conference Wilson said of the League: "If it won't work, it must be made to work."[9] Wilson prevailed on other heads of government at the Versailles Conference to include the League of Nations Covenant in the Versailles Treaty (actually five treaties) that spelled out the postwar treatment of Germany and its allies. He dismissed traditional statecraft as obsolete, in the new age of universal harmony based on international public opinion: "National purposes have fallen more and more into the background; and the common purpose of enlightened mankind has taken their place. The counsels of plain men have become on all hands more simple and straightforward and more unified than the counsels of sophisticated men of affairs, who still retain the impression that they are playing a game of power and are playing for high stakes."[10]

Wilson was deeply committed to the idea of collective security, a system in which all nations in the world, powerful and weak, automatically would unite to punish any aggression by any country anywhere. Article 10 of the League of Nations Covenant required every member to come to the defense of any that was attacked. Henry Cabot Lodge of Massachusetts, the influential Republican chairman of the Senate Foreign Relations Committee, was a realist like Roosevelt, House, and Lansing. He was unwilling to favor the ratification of the treaty, unless a reservation was added that preserved the right of the U.S. Congress, which has the power to declare war under the U.S. Constitution, to choose whether to go to war or not on a case-by-case basis. Wilson believed that this would doom the whole project and refused to compromise.

On November 19, 1919, the Senate failed to ratify the Versailles Treaty. During a desperate cross-country train trip undertaken to rally popular support for the treaty, Wilson collapsed from a stroke and remained an invalid for the rest of his term as president. Although there were enough votes to ratify the treaty on the second attempt on March 19, 1920, Wilson ordered loyal Democrats to vote with opponents rather than accept the reservations and the treaty failed a second and final time. The United States refused to join the League of Nations, and Wilson left office a broken and bitter man. The United States joined the United Nations after World War II only because the UN Charter safeguards the "constitutional processes" of member states and because the UN Security Council only has the power to recommend, not command, military action by member states.[11]

The Anglo-American Treaty of Guarantee to France

In a memo of March 18, 1919, one of British Prime Minister Lloyd George's colleagues, Arthur James Balfour, dismissed what he called the "lurid picture" of a future Germany drawn by the French: "They assume that the German people will always far outnumber the French; that as soon as the first shock of defeat has passed away, Germany will organize herself for revenge; that all our attempts to limit armaments will be unsuccessful; that the League of Nations will be impotent; and, consequently, that the invasion of France, which was fully accomplished in 1870, and partially accomplished in the recent War, will be renewed with every prospect of success."[12]

To prevent a revival of German power, the French wanted to detach the Rhineland and turn it into a buffer state between France and Germany. Lloyd George opposed this on the grounds that it would create an "Alsace-Lorraine in reverse" and the proposal violated the American ideal of national self-determination. Lloyd George proposed, and Wilson accepted, the idea of an Anglo-American guarantee to France if France would acquiesce in Germany's territorial integrity. As House noted in his diary of March 20, 1919, "It is practically promising only what we promise to do in the League of Nations, but since Clemenceau does not believe in the League of Nations it may be necessary to give him a treaty on the outside."[13] American realists like Lodge approved of the idea of an Anglo-American alliance with France against German revanchism.

Unfortunately Wilson, obsessed with the League, refused to allow the proposed Anglo-American treaty of guarantee to exist "on the outside" of the League system, to use House's term. House's proposed draft, accepted by Clemenceau and Lloyd George, read: "we solemnly pledge to one another our immediate military, financial, economic and moral support of and to one another in the event Germany should at any time make a like unprovoked and unwarranted attack against either one or more of the sub-scribing Powers."[14] The revised draft that Wilson gave to the French government on March 28, 1919, however, read: "In a separate treaty by the United States, a pledge by the United States, *subject to the approval of the Executive Council of the League of Nations*, to come immediately to the assistance of France as soon as any unprovoked movement of aggression against her is made by Germany"[15] (emphasis added).

Wilson doomed the Anglo-American security treaty with France by including clauses that subordinated the treaty to the cumbersome machinery of the League. According to Article III of the treaty of guarantee: "The present Treaty must be submitted to the Council of the League of Nations, and must be recognized by the Council, acting if need be by a majority, as an engagement which is consistent with the Covenant of the League. It will continue in force until on the application of one of the Parties to it the Council, acting if need be by a majority, agrees that the League itself afford sufficient protection."[16] Instead of a traditional U.S. alliance with Britain and France, which Lodge and other realists would have supported, Wilson insisted that the treaty be in effect only temporarily until the League of Nations could assume responsibility for the protection of France and every other country in the world.

The Anglo-American treaty of guarantee to France was signed on the same day, June 28, 1919, that the Versailles Treaty with Germany was signed. The treaty of guarantee's own language stated that it would be submitted to the U.S. Senate at the same time as the Treaty of Versailles. But Wilson, perhaps afraid that the Senate would pass the American-French security pact and reject the Treaty of Versailles in the absence of reservations, sent the Senate the Treaty of Versailles by itself and sent the guarantee treaty only nineteen days later.

Lodge had promised the French ambassador to the United States that the security treaty would be ratified.[17] However, after the second rejection of the Treaty of Versailles on March 19, 1920, Lodge allowed the treaty of guarantee to France to die in the Senate Foreign Relations Committee without ever being brought before the Senate for a vote. He explained later: " There was no desire on the part of Senators of either party at that stage to bind the United States irrevocably with agreements to go to war again under certain prescribed conditions."[18] Nor would it have made any sense for the Senate to vote on the American-French guarantee treaty, which was subject to approval and termination by the League Council, after it was clear that the United States was not going to be a member of the League Council. By seeking to ensure that a Franco-American alliance could not exist outside of his beloved League system, Wilson had merely ensured that both would fail. Because the American security pact with France was never ratified, the British guarantee to France, dependent upon the American guarantee, was allowed to lapse by the British government, which did not want unilaterally to guarantee the safety of France from Germany without the backing of the United States.

The Interwar Years

Wilson's defenders have often argued that World War II could have been averted, if the United States had joined the League of Nations. But even if the United States had joined it would have been no more likely than Britain or France, which belonged to the League, to go to war to prevent German remilitarization or Japanese imperialism until a remote peril became an imminent one. Moreover, the League Council suffered from the unanimity rule that later paralyzed the Security Council. The paradox of formal collective security organizations like the Council of the League of Nations or the Security Council of the United Nations is this: if the great powers agree, they do not need a formal organization, and if they do not agree, then the formal organization will be paralyzed.

Another myth, influenced by John Maynard Keynes's book *The Economic Consequences of the Peace* (1919), holds that the harsh treatment of Germany by the victors under the Treaty of Versailles caused the rise of Hitler and World War II. In fact the victors of World War I were far more lenient toward Germany than Germany had been to defeated Russia in the 1918 Treaty of Brest-Litovsk and than the victors of World War II were to defeated Nazi Germany and Japan in 1945. German nationalists like Hitler were angry chiefly because Germany had been defeated in its first bid for European and global hegemony. In a second book entitled *A Revision of the Treaty* (1922), Keynes declared: "That [France] has anything to fear from Germany in the future which we can foresee, except what she may herself provoke, is a delusion."[19]

The real mistake made by the United States and the other victors involved their misunderstanding of actual power realities following the war.

The postwar expansion of the British and French Empires in the former Ottoman Middle East masked their actual weakness. France had been defeated in 1870 and barely rescued in World War I. The long-term erosion of British military, industrial, and financial power would become evident quickly in World War II.

The United States and Britain should have guaranteed France's security. But a U.S.-British-French alliance alone would have been insufficient, without Russian participation. With little help from its Austrian and Turkish allies, Germany had been so powerful in World War I that only a coalition of the three major powers, Britain, the United States, and Russia, had been able to stop it. It was foolish to believe that anything short of a continuation of that wartime alliance could have deterred Germany. Indeed, Germany was potentially even stronger in the 1920s, because the breakup of the Austrian Empire and the liberation of Russia's Eastern European empire had surrounded Germany with weak, small states.

But the Soviet Union was an unstable, revolutionary pariah state, engaged in savage internal repression and bloodletting. Stalin's Russia sometimes opposed and sometimes opportunistically collaborated with Germany both under the Weimar Republic and Hitler, while the United States returned to an anachronistic isolationism and refused to grant diplomatic recognition to the Soviet Union until 1933. With Britain repeatedly rejecting France's harsh but realistic view of the German threat and trying to act as umpire between Germany and France, it was no surprise that Hitler, on coming to power, could spend a decade rebuilding German military strength in preparation for the second war for German hegemony.

Some in Britain resented the way that the United States initially stayed out of both world wars, allowing Britain to bear most of the costs at first. But this was in part the unintended consequence of the illusion of British power. In 1914 and again in 1939 many Americans were convinced that Britain was a superpower capable of defeating Germany without U.S. help. Had Britain's actual debility been recognized, the debate in the United States about intervention in both world wars would have been different. Americans can hardly be faulted for believing that Britain was the world's leading military power when this was widely believed in Britain itself.

A final reason for the failure of the United States and Britain to balance Germany after 1919 was the American way of life and the closely related British way of life. The two nations shared a common heritage of civilian government, low taxation, and low military spending. To defeat the Indians and police America's sphere of influence in North America, the United States had needed only a small regular army and the U.S. Marines. The expansion of Britain, like that of the United States, had come chiefly at the expense of poor and primitive peoples, and Britain controlled India with Indian troops and Indian taxes. Both of the English-speaking great powers looked to naval power for their safety, and the public in each was hostile to peacetime conscription and large standing armies. In both the United States and Britain, the public demanded the demobilization of the armed forces when World War I ended. In both countries, many conservatives thought that armies were too expensive, while many liberals hoped that the League of Nations and international treaties made armies obsolete. Had any American or British politician proposed maintaining forces adequate to protect France and deter Germany in the 1920s or 1930s, the proposal would have been rejected by public opinion. If only in the short run, dictatorship enjoyed a genuine advantage when it came to mobilizing a nation for war. The United States and Britain armed themselves only at a very late stage, when Germany and its allies had become so powerful and dangerous that considerations of security overrode the liberal suspicion of the military that was deeply rooted in the cultures of both English-speaking nations. The United States and Britain learned to their cost that it sometimes is necessary to curtail the liberal way of life, if only temporarily, in order to save it.

Hitler's War Aims

Hitler's territorial goals were similar to those of the Kaiser and the officials of Imperial Germany: the reduction of France and other continental European states to vassal states, the annihilation of Russian power, and ethnic German colonization of Eastern European *Lebensraum*. But Hitler was far more radical and murderous. Once war broke out, Hitler's Social Darwinist view of world history in terms of race war and racial purity inspired him to order the mass killing of Europe's Jews, gypsies, homosexuals, and the handicapped and the reduction of the Slavic nations of Eastern Europe to the status of serfs who would labor for the German master race.

Hitler thought that Imperial Germany's emphasis on naval power and overseas colonies unwisely had alienated the British, a kindred "Teutonic" nation that had provided a model for a German Empire in Eastern Europe by conquering and ruling the nonwhite populations of India and Africa. In his second, never-published book of 1928, Hitler looked to Britain and Italy as allies in "a new association of nations, consisting of individual states with a high national [racial] value, which would then stand up to the threatening overwhelming of the world by the American Union. For it seems to be that the existence of English world rule inflicts less hardship on present-day nations than the emergence of an American world rule."[20] Envisioning a future "German-British army" in 1942, Hitler mused: "I don't see much future for the Americans. In my view, it's a decayed country . . . Everything about the behavior of American society reveals that it's half Judaised, and the other half negrified . . . " Hitler concluded that "in spite of everything, I like an Englishman a thousand times better than an American."[21] He predicted: "I shall no longer be there to see it, but I rejoice on behalf of the German people at the idea that one day we will see England and Germany marching together against America."[22] According to Hitler, "There's nobody stupider than the Americans."[23]

Hitler may have envisioned conflict with the United States sooner rather than later. In 1939, he approved ambitious plans for the German Navy, authorizing 4 aircraft carriers, 6 battleships, 8 heavy cruisers, and 233 submarines.[24] According to notes taken in 1941 by the commander of the German Navy, "After the Eastern campaign, he reserves the right to take severe action against the United States."[25] In November and May 1941 Hitler discussed using the Azores as a base for deploying long-range bombers against American cities.[26] In 1937 Messerschmitt began designing an aircraft referred to alternately as "the America Bomber" and "the New York Bomber" that would be capable of bombing New York City and other American cities; the German government granted the contract in 1940.[27] German government scientists and engineers also worked on an intercontinental missile dubbed the "America Rocket" and on submarine-launched rockets that could be used against the United States.[28] Engineer Eugen Albert Sänger worked on a space plane that would be able to fly into the upper atmosphere and bomb targets in the United States before gliding down to safety in a region of Asia controlled by Germany's ally Japan.[29]

The German historian Andreas Hillgruber has summarized Hitler's ambitions: "Germany, in alliance with Japan and if possible also Britain, would in the first place isolate the USA and confine it to the Western hemisphere. Then, in the next generation, there would be a 'battle of the continents' in which the 'Germanic empire of the German nation' would fight America for world supremacy."[30]

America Besieged?

In the years leading up to the U.S. entry in World War II, American interventionists made the same argument that proponents of U.S. intervention in World War I had made: a German victory would threaten the American way of life by forcing the United States to militarize its society and regiment its economy.

Douglas Miller, who had observed Hitler's government as a U.S. diplomat in Berlin for six years, argued that the United States would have to abandon its individualistic, commercial way of life in a world divided by one or a few totalitarian empires. In *You Can't Do Business with Hitler* (1941), he stressed the dangers the United States would face if "left alone in a friendless totalitarian world, forced to adjust its democratic economy under pressure from across both oceans . . . "[31] A Fortress America would be necessary: "Our enemies would have under their flags 80 to 90 percent of the human race. They would command the oceans outside the zone of our effective naval and air patrol near our shores . . . We should have to be a whole nation of 'Minutemen,' ready to rush to arms at the first sign of invasion. Our children would not, of course, expect to enjoy 'a better world' under such conditions."[32] Miller described the National Socialist system of trade, based on exchange controls, clearing agreements, subsidies, bilateral treaties, and other instruments of imperial autarky: "Totalitarian trade methods are political and military in purpose. Mere economic considerations carry no weight."[33] Miller predicted: "A totalitarian Europe would operate its economy through highly organized, central control. We should not be able to negotiate agreements with individual firms over there. Everything would be routed through a government agency."[34] The U.S. government would have no choice but to take control of American trade: "Just how can we maintain our system of free enterprise if our government is thus forced directly into all the deals which concern trade with the outside world? . . . We should be on a fair way to planned economy and a system of State Socialism."[35] Roosevelt's former budget director, Lewis L. Douglas, used another analogy: "To retreat to the cyclone cellar here means, ultimately, to establish a totalitarian state at home."[36]

President Roosevelt echoed these themes. In January 1939 Roosevelt summoned the members of the Military Affairs Committee of the Senate to a secret meeting. Warning the senators of the aggressive plans of the Axis powers, Roosevelt argued that the security of the United States depended on keeping U.S. island bases in the Pacific secure from Japanese attack and preserving the "continued independence of a very large group of nations" in Europe. If Hitler defeated Britain and France, their colonies in Africa and elsewhere would fall under German control. The president told the senators:

"The next perfectly obvious step, which Brother Hitler suggested in the speech yesterday, would be Central and South America. Hitler would dominate Europe and would say to [those] in the Argentine, 'Awfully sorry, but we won't buy your wheat, meat, or corn unless you sign this paper.' And the paper that the Argentine is asked to sign says, 'Number one, we will take your corn and pay for it in our goods and we will pay for your cattle in our goods and we will pay for your wheat in our goods and we will select the goods. Then, next, you have got to turn over all your military defense and training to our officers. Oh, yes, you can keep the flag.'. . . And then next would come Brazil. . . . Central America? Properly equipped and with the knowledge of how to get the right people to do it for us, we could stage a revolution in any Central American government for between a million and four million dollars. In other words, it is a matter of price."

Roosevelt concluded that "we cannot afford to sit here and say it is a pipe dream . . . It is the gradual encirclement of the United States by the removal of first lines of defense. That [are] in Europe and the Mediterranean area."[37] In a speech he delivered at the University of Virginia on June 10, 1940, FDR justified U.S. aid to Britain and France by arguing that in a world dominated by the Axis empires the isolated American people would be "lodged in prison, handcuffed, hungry, and fed through the bars from day to day by the contemptuous, unpitying masters of other continents."[38]

Roosevelt made the case before the entire nation in his address to Congress of January 6, 1941, which began: "I address you, the members of this new Congress, at a moment unprecedented in the history of the union. I use the word 'unprecedented' because at no previous time has American security been as seriously threatened from without as it is today . . . " The president continued: "Armed defense of democratic existence is now being gallantly waged in four continents. If that defense fails, all the population and all the resources of Europe and Asia, Africa and Australia will be dominated by conquerors. And let us remember that the total of those populations in those four continents, the total of those populations and their resources greatly exceeds the sum total of the population and resources of the whole of the Western Hemisphere—yes, many times over." Roosevelt dismissed the idea of peaceful co-existence with the fascist empires: "No realistic American can expect from a dictator's peace international generosity, or return of true independence, or world disarmament, or freedom of expression, or freedom of religion—or even good business. Such a peace would bring no security for us or for our neighbors. Those who would give up essential liberty to purchase a little temporary safety deserve neither liberty nor safety."[39]

Garrison State or Tributary State?

The Kaiser had few admirers in the United States, even in the German-American community, and Hitler almost none. Most Americans who opposed U.S. intervention in World War II, like most anti-interventionists in World War I, were patriots who feared that participation in those conflicts would destroy the American way of life by militarizing American society and creating a dictatorial presidency.

Many isolationists argued that the balance of power in Europe itself would protect the United States, if Germany, the Soviet Union, and the British Empire thwarted one another. By 1940, however, German victories had made this argument implausible. Some isolationists responded by advocating policies that would have turned the United States in effect into a garrison state or a tributary state.

The famous aviator Charles Lindbergh, an isolationist who had attributed U.S. interventionist sentiment to the machinations of Jews and the British government, in a radio address of June 15, 1940, declared: "The men of this country must be willing to give a year of their lives to military training—more if necessary."[40] At the same time Lindbergh called for the United States to build military bases throughout North America "wherever they are needed for our safety, regardless of who owns the territory involved."[41] David Worth Clark, an isolationist senator from Idaho, proposed unilateral U.S. occupation of Canada and other neighboring countries, telling journalists: "We could make some kind of arrangement to set up puppet governments which we could trust to put American interests ahead of those of Germany or any other nation in the world."[42]

Other isolationists favored a tributary state strategy, arguing that the United States should appease the Axis powers and consent to abide by the rules of their new global order. After Hitler's Foreign Secretary Joachim von Ribbentrop declared on July 1, 1940, that Germany would respect the Monroe Doctrine as long as the United States did not "interfere" in Europe, Hamilton Fish, a leading isolationist, responded: "We want America for Americans and Europe for Europeans, and that is a good American doctrine."[43]

In *America and a New World Order* (1940), Graeme Howard, vice president of overseas operations for General Motors, proposed that the United States adapt to the world that Hitler and his allies were creating by conquest. Denouncing both "blind internationalism" and "naïve isolationism" in favor of "cooperative regionalism," Howard wrote: "The world of tomorrow may contain various major regions: Continental Europe, a British Empire, a Union of Soviet Republics, a Latin-Mediterranean Federation, an American Federation, and a New Order of Asia." In order to take its place in the new world order imposed by force by the Axis powers, the United States should form a largely autarkic North American bloc of its own that could engage in government-managed trade with the other imperial blocs. The GM vice president dismissed freedom of trade as an antiquated notion: "If we concede the emergence of regionalism on tomorrow's horizon, then the most-favored-nation clause is as impractical an aspiration as universal free trade."[44]

The United States, Germany, and Japan

The debate in the United States over intervention ended when Japan attacked Pearl Harbor on December 7, 1941. Eight days later Germany declared war on the United States.

Hitler's declaration of war against America sometimes has been regarded as a strategic blunder. But from Hitler's perspective, Germany already was at war with the United States in the North Atlantic. In May 1942 he explained that "the Japanese alliance has been of exceptional value to us, if only because of the date chosen by Japan for her entry into the war. It was, in effect, at the moment when the surprises of the Russian winter were pressing most heavily on the morale of our people, and when everybody in Germany was oppressed by the certainty that, sooner or later, the United States would come into the conflict. Japanese intervention was, therefore, from our point of view, most opportune."[45] Hitler's hope that Japan would tie down the United States was vindicated. More than half of the divisions of the U.S. Army were in the Pacific by late 1942; as late as the end of 1943 more members of the U.S. Armed Forces were deployed against Japan than against Germany.[46]

As early as the beginning of the twentieth century, an alliance of Germany and Japan against the United States was the source of speculation in both Imperial Germany and the United States. But Japan preferred the alliance it made with Britain in 1902 and used its participation on the British and American side in World War I to seize Germany's colonies in China. After the war, the British and Americans dispatched troops to Siberia during the Russian Civil War as much to deter their nominal Japanese allies from controlling Siberia as to defeat the Bolsheviks.

In the early 1920s, worried that in the event of a war with Japan Britain would be bound by treaty to fight on Japan's side, the United States pressured Britain into declining to renew the Anglo-Japanese alliance and sought to construct a new Asian order at the Washington Conference of 1921–22. Preserving the territorial integrity of China, the old Open Door policy shared by Britain and the United States, was the purpose of the nine-power treaty, signed by the United States, Britain, Japan, China, the Netherlands, Belgium, France, Portugal, and Italy. Naval disarmament was the subject of the five-power treaty (the United States, Britain, Japan, France, Italy) that allowed Japan to have three-fifths as many capital ships in its fleet as the United States and Britain each were allowed to have. Finally, the four-power treaty (the United States, Britain, Japan, and France) stipulated that the United States could not fortify Guam and the Philippines, while Britain was not allowed to create new fortified bases north of Singapore, as compensation for Japan's acquiescence in the limitation of its fleet by the five-power treaty. As the historian Corelli Barnett has observed, "This was tantamount to turning the waters off the Chinese coast into a Japanese lake; it deprived British and American concern for China's integrity of all substance; one treaty signed at Washington made nonsense of another."[47]

The Washington Treaty did not restrain Japan for long. In 1931 Japan invaded Manchuria and two years later withdrew from the League of Nations. In 1936 Japan signed a pact with Hitler and then the next year invaded China. Following the outbreak of World War II, the United States imposed an oil embargo on Japan. Emboldened by Hitler's successes, and hoping to buy time to seize Southeast Asia's oil, Japan crippled much of the U.S. Pacific Fleet at Pearl Harbor in a surprise attack on the morning of December 7, 1941. With a similar surprise attack that destroyed much of the Russian fleet at Port Arthur in Manchuria in 1904, Japan had begun the Russo-Japanese War of 1904–5.

Japan, however, was a great power of the second rank, whose success depended on a German victory. Notwithstanding a series of Japanese victories in Asia, President Roosevelt and British Prime Minister Winston Churchill agreed on a strategy of first defeating the greater threat of German domination of Europe. In the final days of the Pacific War the United States amended its policy of unconditional surrender to allow the Japanese monarchy to survive. But the United States never wavered from the policy of unconditional surrender in the case of Germany, which was to be not only defeated but also occupied and demilitarized. The United States and its allies were determined to ensure that Germany's second bid for world domination would be its last.

Chapter 7

The Cold War

As the Soviet Union mobilized the military resources of
Eurasia, increased its relative military capabilities, and
heightened its threat to our security, some would be tempted
to accept "peace" on its terms, while many would seek to
defend the United States by creating a regimented system
which would permit the assignment of a tremendous part
of our resources to defense. Under such a state of affairs
our national morale would be corrupted and the integrity
and vitality of our system subverted.

—NSC-68 (1950)[1]

ON JANUARY 11, 1944, SOVIET DEPUTY FOREIGN MINISTER IVAN MAISKY sent a
memorandum to Soviet dictator Josef Stalin. The memo by Maisky, who
had served as Soviet ambassador to Britain from 1932 to 1943, argued that
prospects were favorable for Soviet world domination following the end of
World War II. Maisky suggested that the Soviet government manipulate
popular fronts to bring communist satellite regimes to power throughout
continental Europe after the war. In a communist Europe dominated by
Moscow "no power or combination of powers . . . could even think of
aggression" against the Soviet Union, Maisky wrote, with the United States
and Britain in mind. In addition, Maisky advised, the Soviet Union should
also try to maximize its influence in China "by every means" while allowing the United States to exhaust itself in the conquest of Japan. By these
methods, the Soviet Union, following the conclusion of World War II, might
put itself in a position to dominate Europe and Asia from the English Channel
to the Sea of Japan, without ever firing a shot. Having launched World War
II in 1939 as Hitler's partner in the partition of Poland, Stalin was poised
to inherit the world.[2]

The Maisky memorandum, discovered following the end of the Cold
War, is not evidence of a coherent master plan by the Soviet leadership,

which improvised its policy under the pressure of events. But along with other evidence, it destroys the myth that the Cold War was a tragic accident as thoroughly as evidence from the Imperial German archives destroyed the myth that the great powers had drifted by mistake into World War I. Just as World War I resulted from a calculated bid by Imperial Germany to conquer Europe and dominate the world, so the Cold War resulted from Soviet aspirations to dominate Europe and Asia, aspirations discussed in Moscow even as World War II was still raging.

Unlike Imperial Germany and National Socialist Germany, the Soviet Union under Stalin and his successors hoped to achieve Eurasian and global hegemony by methods short of direct war with the United States and other major powers. Intimidation and subversion, rather than conquest, were the preferred weapons in the Soviet arsenal. The Cold War was the third world war. But it was a world war in slow motion, fought over four decades rather than a few years.

Debating Cold War Strategy

The same concerns that led the United States to intervene in the two world wars inspired America's determination to prevent the Soviet Union from dominating Eurasia by conquest, subversion, or military intimidation. NSC-68, the Truman administration policy paper that set forth arguments for the strategy of containment, discussed the danger to American society of a policy of isolation that would allow the Soviet Union to dominate Europe and Asia by intimidation or conquest: "As the Soviet Union mobilized the military resources of Eurasia, increased its relative military capabilities, and heightened its threat to our security, some [Americans] would be tempted to accept 'peace' on its terms, while many would seek to defend the United States by creating a regimented system which would permit the assignment of a tremendous part of our resources to defense. Under such a state of affairs our national morale would be corrupted and the integrity and vitality of our system subverted." Soviet hegemony in Europe and Asia, established by cold war rather than hot war, no less than German victory in either world war, would have presented the United States with a choice between sacrificing its diplomatic independence to preserve its republican liberal way of life or sacrificing its republican liberal way of life to preserve its diplomatic independence.

President Truman argued that if the Soviet Union was allowed to dominate Europe and Asia, an American garrison state would become necessary: "If communism is allowed to absorb free nations, then we would be isolated from our sources of supply and detached from our friends. Then we would have to take defense measures which might really bankrupt our economy, and change our way of life so that we couldn't recognize it as American any longer. . . . It would require a stringent and comprehensive system of allocation and rationing in order to husband our smaller resources. It would require us to become a garrison state, and to impose upon ourselves a system of centralized regimentation unlike anything we have ever known."[3]

The challenge confronting the United States during the Cold War was as difficult as it was straightforward. America's options were limited by the determination of American leaders to avoid militarizing American society. The United States had to prevent Soviet hegemony in Europe and Asia, in order to preserve the American way of life. U.S. victory in the Cold War would be a Pyrrhic victory if the United States resisted Soviet totalitarianism at the price of creating a garrison state at home.[4]

The determination to avoid creating an American garrison state was shared by Americans who advocated different strategies for dealing with Soviet aggression in Europe and elsewhere in the world. At one extreme were advocates of "strongpoint defense." This was a modified form of isolationism, which would commit the United States to defending only North America and islands off the shore of Eurasia including Britain and Japan.[5] At the other extreme was the strategy of "rollback." Theorists of rollback called on the United States to sponsor anti-Soviet rebellions in its new Eastern European Empire. Some even advocated a preventive nuclear war against the Soviet Union.[6]

Between the extremes of strongpoint defense and rollback was the strategy of containment. The strategy was given its name by the State Department's George Kennan, who advocated it in a "Long Telegram" from Moscow that he published in *Foreign Affairs* under the pseudonym "Mr. X." The United States would seek to prevent the Soviet bloc from expanding, by force or the sponsorship of communist revolutionary movements. But the United States would not attack the Soviet regime or directly intervene in the Soviet Empire in Eastern Europe. Instead, the United States would wait for military and economic pressure to bring about changes in Soviet policy and perhaps the Soviet government itself.[7]

When Kim Il Sung, the communist leader of North Korea, invaded non-communist South Korea in 1950, with the support of Stalin and Mao, who had seized power in China in 1949, the debate over U.S. Cold War strategy effectively ended. From 1950 until the end of the Cold War in 1989 the United States, despite serious setbacks including the defeat in Vietnam, pursued the strategy of containment. The repudiation of the more aggressive rollback strategy was confirmed when the United States refused to intervene as the Soviet Union crushed rebellions in East Germany in 1953, Hungary in 1956, and Czechoslovakia in 1968.

Dual Containment: Keeping the Soviets Out and the Germans and Japanese Down

In the form in which it finally coalesced, the U.S. containment strategy was one of dual containment. The United States sought to contain not only its communist enemies, the Soviet Union and China, but also to contain its new allies, the defeated Axis powers Germany and Japan.

The Cold War took the form that it did because of the decision of the United States, Britain, and the Soviet Union to pursue a policy of unconditional surrender against Germany and Japan. The two nations would not only be defeated, but also occupied and demilitarized. Even in defeat, however, Germany and Japan remained centers of industrial power that could contribute greatly to the military capacity of other powers. As hostility deepened between the Soviet Union and the West, temporary lines of occupation hardened into the frontier of a communist bloc in which communist rule was imposed or sponsored by Moscow. In the late 1940s and early 1950s Germany, China and Korea were divided between communist and non-communist governments; in 1954, following the first Indochina War, Vietnam was partitioned as well.

In the competition to control the populations and resources of the former Axis powers, the United States had the advantage. The Soviets played no part in the occupation of Japan and Italy. The United States, along with Britain and France, controlled the most populous and richest part of Germany, which became the Federal Republic of Germany and was known as West Germany until Germany was reunited in 1990.

What was to be done with Germany and Japan? If a reunited Germany and Japan were neutralized, a Soviet invasion was unlikely. However, the

Soviets might use the military weakness of a neutral Germany or a neutral Japan to extort economic deals that might strengthen the Soviet military-industrial base. Restoring West Germany and Japan as independent great military powers was unthinkable. The least dangerous option was the conversion of West Germany and Japan into military protectorates of the United States. Their new status as "civilian powers" disguised their actual status as semi-sovereign states, with sizeable restored militaries, under U.S. military direction. In this way, the resources of West Germany and Japan could be denied to the Soviet bloc without risking the re-emergence of German and Japanese militarism. According to the containment doctrine, "[I]ndustry was the key ingredient of power, and the United States controlled most of the centers of industry. There were five such centers in the world: the United States, Britain, West Germany, Japan, and the Soviet Union. The United States and its future allies constituted four of the centers, the Soviet Union just one. Containment meant confining the Soviet Union to that one."[8]

As the British statesman Lord Ismay remarked, the purpose of the North Atlantic Treaty Organization (NATO), established in 1949, was to "keep the Russians out, the Americans in and the Germans down." During the later stages of the Cold War, some Americans complained that the Japanese and Western Europeans were not spending enough on defense, compared to the United States. But these critics misunderstood the dual containment strategy. The Japanese and West Germans were not supposed to defend themselves on their own. They were supposed to concentrate on civilian industry while permitting the United States to defend them, thereby making a strong and potentially threatening Japanese or West German military unnecessary. Likewise, complaints about the size of the U.S. defense budget during the Cold War often missed the point. The U.S. defense budget was also the Japanese defense budget and the Western European defense budget and the defense budget of U.S. client states in Asia, the Middle East, and Latin America. It was the defense budget needed to defend all of America's protectorates, not the United States alone.

The assumption underlying the dual containment system was simple. Although providing security to Japan and West Germany was expensive, the United States might have had to spend far more money to hedge against possible conflict with those two powers if they had been independent military actors or even traditional, well-armed allies whose menace was merely potential. The makers of American Cold War strategy believed that it was better for the U.S. Navy to volunteer to be the Japanese Navy, and for the U.S. Army to volunteer to be the German Army, than for the United States to run the risks of the revival of German or Japanese militarism.

America as Hegemon: Capability and Credibility

America's Cold War strategy of dual containment required the United States to act as a hegemon, the leader of an informal empire with protectorates over client states, rather than as the leader of a traditional alliance of equals or near equals, like the alliances to which the United States belonged in World Wars I and II. America's hegemonic alliance was based on the unilateral extension of a U.S. security guarantee to clients, of which the most important were West Germany and Japan. The U.S. guarantee had to be credible. To prevent the Soviet Union from using its military buildup to intimidate America's client states into appeasement, the United States repeatedly had to prove both its military capability and its political resolve.

To prove its military capability, the United States had to match the Soviet Union in the arms race as well as be able to deter and repel a conventional Soviet assault on Western Europe or Japan. Matching the Soviet Union in the arms race was relatively easy for the United States, given its superior scientific and industrial base. But the American people were never willing to pay for the enormous standing military forces that would have been necessary to offset the Red Army's numerical advantage in Europe. As a result, from the Eisenhower years onward the United States was committed in practice if not theory to the first use of nuclear weapons to prevent Western Europe from being overrun by the Red Army and its auxiliaries. This strategy created political tensions between the United States and its European clients, particularly the West Germans. Europeans feared that if U.S. conventional forces in Europe were too small, in the event of a superpower conflict, the United States might resort to nuclear weapons too soon, turning Central Europe into an atomic wasteland. On the other hand, if U.S. conventional forces were too powerful, then the Americans and Soviets might wage an equally destructive conventional war on German territory while agreeing not to attack each other's extra-European homelands. It is hardly surprising that U.S.-European relations were strained by repeated crises of confidence and war scares that the Soviets did their best to exploit.

In addition to proving its military capability to protect its client states from Soviet intimidation or invasion, the United States had to prove that it had the requisite political resolve. In order to demonstrate its credibility as the hegemon of a global protectorate system, the United States waged a long series of proxy wars with the Soviet Union and its sometime ally, communist China. The bloodiest were in Korea and Vietnam. Of the four nations divided in the early Cold War between communist and noncommunist regimes—Germany, China, Korea, and Vietnam—only Germany was of intrinsic military value because of its industrial power. But American leaders believed that a U.S. failure to defend South Korea, South Vietnam, or Taiwan from forcible absorption by communist regimes might signal a lack of American resolve to more important clients like West Germany and Japan, as well as to nonaligned countries in other regions of the world, which might then drift into neutrality or pro-Soviet alignment to the benefit of the Soviet Union.

The Domino Effect and the Bandwagon Effect

America's Cold War policymakers were sometimes accused by their critics of basing their policy on an exaggerated fear that communist success in one country would lead to a wave of communist revolutions in a "domino effect." To a limited extent the geographic domino effect was genuine in Asia. Common borders permitted Stalin to help Mao gain power in 1949, allowed Russia and China to help Kim Il Sung win and keep power in North Korea, and helped North Vietnam survive and eventually conquer South Vietnam, Laos, and Cambodia. But the neighbors fell out as neighbors often do: China split with the Soviet Union in the 1960s and fought border skirmishes with it, and in 1979 China fought a brief war with Vietnam, by then a Soviet satellite.

Despite public rhetoric about falling dominoes, American policymakers were always more concerned about the "bandwagon effect." As George Kennan explained in the early Cold War: "One of the vital facts to be borne in mind about the international communist movement in the parts of Europe which are not yet under Soviet military and police control is the pronounced 'bandwagon' effect which that movement bears. By that I mean the fact that a given proportion of the adherents to the movement are drawn to it by no ideological enthusiasm . . . but primarily by the belief that it is the coming thing, the movement of the future . . . and that those who hope to survive—let alone thrive—in the coming days will be those who had the foresight to climb on the bandwagon when it was still the movement of the future."[9] American leaders feared that if the United States suffered a series of reverses in mostly symbolic contests with the Soviets, Soviet power would seem unstoppable, and weak nonaligned nations as well as American clients, while remaining noncommunist or anticommunist internally, might jump on the bandwagon with the Soviet Union for fear of being on the losing side in geopolitics.

The history of the twentieth century shows that this concern was well founded. In the 1930s, as German power and aggression grew, many weak states in Europe appeased Germany or allied themselves with it out of fear or opportunism. Toward the end of World War II, and again toward the end of the Cold War, many nonaligned countries in Latin America and other regions hastened to ally themselves with or befriend the United States, joining the team that was clearly about to win.

Both the Korean and Vietnam Wars were waged to reinforce America's reputation as the leader of a hegemonic alliance.[10] President Johnson explained in 1965: "Around the globe, from Berlin to Thailand, are people whose well-being rests, in part, on the belief that they can count on us if they are attacked. To leave Vietnam to its fate would shake the confidence of all these people in the value of America's commitment, the value of America's word."[11] In an internal memo in 1965, one of Johnson's advisers, John McNaughton, assigned weight to the various motives behind American policy in Indochina: "70%—To avoid a humiliating defeat (to our reputation as a guarantor); 20%—To keep South Vietnam (and the adjacent territory) from Chinese hands; 10%—To permit the people of South Vietnam to enjoy a better, freer way of life."[12] The same need to defend America's "reputation as a guarantor" underlay the American wars in Korea and Indochina, repeated U.S. confrontations with the Soviet Union over Berlin, and the U.S. defense of noncommunist Taiwan.

Limited War

While the containment strategy committed the United States to fight symbolic "credibility wars" on behalf of protectorates like South Korea, South

Vietnam, and, implicitly, Japan and West Germany, the need to avoid direct Soviet-American or Sino-American confrontation required that these wars remain limited. U.S. strategy in World War II had exploited America's strengths as an industrial, commercial, civilian power. Converted to wartime production, America's factories had turned out the weapons and machines needed to destroy the ability of Germany and Japan to wage war by smashing their armed forces and striking directly at their factories and cities far behind the lines.

The Cold War, by contrast, forced the United States to forfeit its strengths. Even before the Soviet Union developed an adequate nuclear deterrent in the mid-1950s, the United States sought to avoid the costs of a conventional world war with the Soviet Union or communist China. When General Douglas MacArthur sought to end the Korean War by attacking China, President Truman fired him. During the Vietnam War, the United States bombed North Vietnam, but never attacked North Vietnam's military supply lines in China and the Soviet Union. For its part, the Soviet Union operated under similar self-imposed restraints. Following the Soviet invasion of Afghanistan, Soviet forces were savaged by Afghan rebels supplied with arms by the United States and China, by that time an enemy of Moscow. But the Soviets never attacked Pakistan, which provided a sanctuary and source of supplies for the Afghan resistance.

The Cold War strategy of limited wars to prove U.S. credibility to U.S. protectorates including West Germany and Japan proved to be profoundly divisive and unpopular with the American people. During the Korean War, the anticommunist right rejected the doctrine of limited war, calling for all-out war on the Soviet Union and communist China. During the Vietnam War, the antiwar left questioned the doctrine of wars to prove U.S. credibility in areas of little or no intrinsic value to the United States.

The tactics as well as the strategy of the United States in the Cold War fit poorly with American traditions and ideals. What the historian Russell F. Weigley called "the American way of war," based on high technology and massive firepower, was effective in the Korean War, in which the United States was able to bring its overwhelming industrial superiority to bear in a conventional war of attrition, at the cost, however, of horrific damage to the people and landscape of Korea. In the later years of the Vietnam War as well, when that conflict evolved from a Hanoi-sponsored insurgency in the South into a conventional invasion of South Vietnam by North Vietnam, superior American firepower was effective. But in the period from 1964 to 1968, the U.S. attempt to combat a Hanoi-sponsored insurgency in South Vietnam by means of a firepower-based strategy of attrition cost so many American lives and created so much devastation in Vietnam that public opinion in the United States as well as in the world turned against the war. Rather than continue to pay a high price for what was only a limited interest, the United States abandoned South Vietnam to conquest by North Vietnamese regulars equipped and subsidized by the Soviet Union and China.

Containment and the American Way of Life

Just as divisive as the Cold War practice of limited war was the debate in the United States over containment strategy as a whole. From the 1940s until the 1980s, supporters of the Cold War were divided into two schools, which might be called the schools of "symmetrical containment" and "asymmetrical containment."

The symmetrical containment school, sometimes called "flexible response," held that the United States should be prepared to deter or defeat the Soviet Union or its proxies at every level of violence—counterinsurgency, all-out nuclear war, and every kind of conflict in between. The asymmetrical containment school preferred to concentrate on America's strength, particularly its advantages in airpower and nuclear power, early in the Cold War.

The two strategies differed in their costs. A consistent strategy of symmetrical containment would have required a high level of militarization of American society for the duration of the Cold War. In order to maintain a standing army capable of defeating Soviet forces in Europe in a purely conventional war, a peacetime draft far more comprehensive than the selective service system of 1949–73 would have been necessary, along with massive investments in civil defense and a high degree of mobilization of American industry. Because of its reliance on airpower and nuclear weapons, the asymmetric containment strategy, by contrast, imposed far fewer costs on the U.S. economy and the liberties of American citizens.

The strategy of symmetrical containment was associated with Democrats like Presidents Truman, Kennedy, and Johnson, while the strategy of asymmetrical containment was associated with the Republicans Eisenhower and Nixon. Democrats were far less troubled by a powerful and expensive federal government than were Republicans. Democrats also tended to view military conscription as a progressive tool of national socialization, while Republican conservatives and libertarians viewed the draft with horror. Eisenhower in particular was concerned about preventing an excessive military establishment from harming the civilian business economy. In his farewell remarks to the American people the former general warned of the dangers of an overly large "military-industrial complex."

The philosophical differences were reflected in different policies. Democrats sent U.S. troops in great numbers at enormous cost to fight Soviet-sponsored proxies directly in Korea and Vietnam. Eisenhower, a fiscal conservative, sought to keep defense spending limited by relying on a strategy that combined covert CIA campaigns in Iran, Guatemala, and elsewhere with the threat of "massive retaliation" in his New Look strategy, which promised "more bang for the buck" than the manpower-squandering Truman strategy. Inheriting the Vietnam War from Kennedy and Johnson, Nixon showed the traditional Republican preference for asymmetric containment by seeking to replace American soldiers with South Vietnamese troops backed by U.S. airpower in a strategy of "Vietnamization" and hoping that regional proxies like the Shah's Iran would protect American interests. While Harry Truman had favored a system of universal military training far more comprehensive and expensive than the selective service system, Richard Nixon abolished the draft. The fact that the major Democratic constituency was the labor movement while the major Republican constituency was the business community was reflected perhaps in the fact that Cold War Democrats favored a labor-intensive strategy while Cold War Republicans preferred a capital-intensive strategy.

The Crisis of Containment

In the 1970s the costs of the Vietnam War eroded American public support for the strategy of containment that had led to it. In 1972 only 32 percent of Americans polled thought the United States should go to war to defend West Berlin, and only 47 percent agreed that it was "worth going to war" if the Soviet Union invaded Western Europe.[13]

Meanwhile, far from America's Indochinese and Korean protectorates, the cost of America's informal containment of Japan and West Germany were also becoming evident. The postwar economic recovery of Western

Europe and Japan reduced America's share of global income without reducing America's share of military commitments. In 1953, the U.S. share of global manufacturing was 44.7 percent, almost twice that of war-shattered Europe's share of 26 percent.[14] By 1970, however, the European Economic Community's share of global gross domestic product (GDP), having grown to 24.7 percent, had surpassed that of the U.S. share, which had shrunken to 23 percent.[14] For its part, Japan was growing more rapidly than either the United States or Western Europe.

While the military realm remained bipolar, the world had become multipolar in the economic realm. In July 1971 President Nixon noted that there were now five centers of economic power in the world, the United States, the Soviet Union, Western Europe, Japan, and China: "These are the five that will determine the economic future and, because economic power will be the key to other kinds of power, the future of the world in other ways in the last third of this century."[16] Nixon's response was to seek to share America's military burdens with other countries, in accordance with what became known as the Nixon Doctrine. In an "Address to the Nation on the War in Vietnam" on November 3, 1969, Nixon declared, "we shall look to the nation directly threatened to assume the primary responsibility of providing the manpower necessary for its defense."[17]

Nixon and Henry Kissinger, his national security adviser and later secretary of state, tried to substitute a classical balance of power approach for containment by pitting the Soviet Union against China. As a way to rescue the embattled South Vietnamese regime, this was a failure; notwithstanding their rivalry, the Soviet Union and China shared the goal of a North Vietnamese victory and the expulsion of the United States from Indochina. Nixon's policy of assigning responsibility for security in the Persian Gulf to the Shah of Iran also backfired, when the Iranian Revolution of 1979 brought the Ayatollah Khomeini's anti-American regime to power.

Like Nixon, Jimmy Carter experimented with less costly alternatives to containment. He sought to distinguish himself from his predecessors by warning against an "inordinate fear of communism" and stressing human rights, rather than anticommunism, as the basis of U.S. strategy. However, following the Soviet invasion of Afghanistan, the Carter administration returned to the containment strategy.

Ronald Reagan, elected president in 1980, brought the containment strategy to a successful conclusion. Reagan's foreign policy was a synthesis of the two rival schools of containment, reflecting Reagan's foreign policy advisers who included former Democrats, the so-called neoconservatives, and lifelong Republicans. Reagan's massive conventional military buildup had its roots in the traditional Democratic strategy of symmetrical containment/flexible response advocated by the Truman and Kennedy administrations. Unlike Eisenhower, Reagan spent lavish sums on the military-industrial complex, on the gamble, which turned out to be correct, that by ramping up the arms race the United States could force the Soviet Union into an economic crisis. Reagan talked like the Democrats Kennedy and Carter about universal freedom and human rights, but in his aversion to reliance on large-scale U.S. military manpower he resembled his fellow Republicans Eisenhower and Nixon. He refused to commit large numbers of U.S. troops to any conflict, preferring instead to rely on covert operations and support for "freedom fighters" like the anti-Soviet insurgents in Afghanistan, a group that included foreign Muslim militants like Osama bin Laden who would later turn against the United States.

The Myth of the Cold War Garrison State

The Cold War began in the late 1940s when Joseph Stalin refused to remove the Red Army from Eastern Europe, imposed communist regimes on the region, began a massive arms buildup, and sponsored communist revolutions throughout the world. The Cold War ended in the 1980s when Mikhail Gorbachev removed the Red Army from Europe, allowed communist regimes to be swept away in free elections, ended the massive Soviet arms buildup, and stopped sponsoring communist revolutions throughout the world. In between the Soviet Union crushed revolts against its rule in Eastern Europe three times, in East Germany in 1950, in Hungary in 1956, and in Czechoslovakia in 1968; Soviet intervention in Poland to crush the Solidarity movement in the early 1980s was narrowly averted by Polish military rule. The Cold War began in Europe and ended in Europe. It was caused by Soviet aggression and it ended with Soviet surrender. The dissolution of the USSR followed the Cold War, but unlike the Soviet evacuation of Eastern Europe this was not necessary for the Cold War to end.

Victory in the Cold War came at a high price in American blood and American treasure, including more than eighty thousand American fatalities in Korea and Vietnam, and vast sums of money spent by American taxpayers on armaments and subsidies to allies and foreign proxies rather than on more productive investments. Even so, the United States achieved both of its goals in the Cold War. It thwarted Soviet hegemony in Eurasia and the world, and did so without sacrificing the American way of life.

It is sometimes claimed that the Cold War, waged to avert the need to create an American garrison state, created one anyway. It is true that some pessimistic defense planners in the late 1940s and early 1950s called for the creation of something like a garrison state. Some proposed massive civil defense projects, including the decentralization of industry and population and universal military training to provide manpower for a standing army capable of fighting and winning a conventional war with the Soviet Union. All of these proposals were rejected as too costly and incompatible with the individualistic American way of life.[18] Even at a time when Americans were most fearful of the Soviet Union, Congress repeatedly defeated bills to create universal military training. Instead, the far-less-intrusive selective-service "lottery" system was adopted in 1948. The unpopularity of the Vietnam War led to the abolition of this limited draft in 1973 in favor of a purely professional military.

As a percentage of GDP, U.S. military spending dropped dramatically after World War II, when half the economy had been in effect nationalized. Peaks during the Korean and Vietnam Wars and the Reagan buildup of the 1980s interrupted but did not stop the long decline in spending on the military, which dropped still further following the end of the Cold War. Military spending after 1945 peaked at 17.5 percent at the height of the Korean War and fell to slightly more than 10 percent during the Vietnam War, before resuming its steady decline. Defense spending rose slightly during the Reagan buildup of the 1980s to a little more than 5 percent of GDP before dropping to around 4 percent by 1994.[19]

By 2000, federal spending on defense was lower than it had been at any time since the 1930s, and as a percentage of the population the number of Americans in active military service was lower than it had been since 1940.[20] The United States spent around 3 percent of GDP on defense, comparable to the percentage of its GDP spent at that time by France. Once the largest item in the federal budget, defense spending had dropped to third, after Social Security and non-defense discretionary spending. With the draft abolished, civil defense exercises long abandoned, and defense spending as a percentage of the economy no more than 3 to 4 percent, the United States at the end of the Cold War was hardly a garrison state, as some critics claimed.

But while the Cold War did not create an American garrison state, it did strain America's republican institutions and its civilian economy. America's democratic republican government is based on checks and balances among the presidency, Congress, and the courts. But the permanent state of emergency in the Cold War inevitably created an "imperial presidency." And the vast sums that the United States spent to defeat the Soviet Union's bid for hegemony were a necessary but tragic diversion of resources from the civilian economy and American taxpayers.

The end of the Cold War, and the prolonged period of great power peace that followed, provided the United States with an opportunity to adopt a more modest and solvent foreign policy. Unfortunately, instead of welcoming the emergence of a peaceful multipolar world, America's bipartisan foreign policy elite in the 1990s and 2000s sought to convert America's temporary Cold War alliance hegemony into enduring American global hegemony, at considerable cost to the American way of life.

Chapter 8

_____

The Cold Peace

We are on the brink of plunging into a cold peace.

—Boris Yeltsin, 1994

SOMEONE WHO FELL INTO A COMA IN 1989, shortly after the fall of the Berlin Wall, and then awakened two decades later would be astonished at how little the strategic map of the world had changed. To be sure, there were more than a dozen new countries, most of them formed from the disintegration of the Soviet Union and Yugoslavia. The Warsaw Pact had vanished, and NATO extended to the borders of a shrunken post-Soviet Russia. But NATO was still commanded by an American. In Europe, Britain and France still had their own nuclear deterrents, but a reunited Germany did not.

In East Asia, Japan, South Korea, and Taiwan were still protectorates of the United States. Japan, like Germany, still lacked nuclear weapons, even though India, Pakistan, and possibly North Korea had joined the nuclear club. Russia and China were still excluded from the American alliance system and treated as rivals by the United States, as during most of the Cold War.

There were new American spheres of influence in the Middle East, where the United States had invaded and occupied Iraq, and in Central Asia, where the United States had invaded and occupied Afghanistan. Even so, a modern Rip Van Winkle awakened from a long sleep might have concluded that the Cold War never really had ended at all, inasmuch as the United States, still the military protector of semi-sovereign Japan and Germany, was still locked in strategic rivalry with Russia and China.

In December 1994 Russian President Boris Yeltsin complained that the West "has not yet freed itself from the heritage of the Cold War. We are on the brink of plunging into a cold peace."[1] The period that began with the end of the Cold War deserves to be known as the Cold Peace.

The Gulf War and the End of the
Post–Cold War Strategic Debate

The end of World War II was accompanied by a vigorous debate over the future of U.S. foreign policy, among isolationists, world federalists, balance of power realists, and anticommunists who disagreed about whether the best U.S. response to Soviet aggression was the "rollback" of Soviet power by force, a strongpoint strategy in which the United States would defend only offshore islands like Japan and Taiwan against the Soviets and their proxies, or containment, defined as resisting further Soviet bloc expansion while waiting for changes in Soviet policy or the Soviet regime. The great debate about U.S. foreign policy after World War II effectively came to an end with the Korean War in 1950. By defending noncommunist South Korea against conquest by the communist North, while avoiding direct war with North Korea's sponsors, the Soviet Union and China, the Truman administration adopted the strategy of containment, which formed the basis of American grand strategy until the end of the Cold War in the 1980s.

Following the Cold War, another great debate took place. In the late 1980s and early 1990s, the future of U.S. foreign policy was the subject of vigorous controversy. Once again, some proposed a strategy of isolationism.[2] World federalists hoped for a global federation of nations under a revitalized UN.[3] Some realists called for the United States to eliminate its Cold War alliance system and to act as an "offshore balancer" in a multipolar world.[4] Some liberal internationalists called for a global concert of power.[5] Yet others, particularly members of the faction known as "neoconservatives," called for the United States to convert its status as the only remaining superpower into American hegemony.[6]

Just as the Korean War effectively ended the great debate about American strategy after World War II in favor of a U.S. grand strategy of containment, so the Gulf War in 1991 effectively ended the great debate about American strategy after the Cold War in favor of a U.S. grand strategy of global hegemony. After the end of the Gulf War, realists, isolationists, world federalists, and others continued to argue for their options. But they had little or no influence on U.S. policy. The advocates of hegemony had prevailed. Under both Bill Clinton, a Democrat, and George W. Bush, a Republican, variants of the U.S. global hegemony strategy guided America's engagement with the world.

Apart from the context provided by the time, the expulsion of Iraq from Kuwait by the United States and its allies in 1991 might not have been a turning point in history. After all, Britain had defeated a similarly aggressive military dictatorship in Argentina in the Falklands War in 1982. And the Iran-Iraq War of 1980–88 had been far more devastating than the Gulf War, without having significant repercussions beyond the region. But the psychological impact of the Gulf War was profound both in the United States and the world.

Televised coverage of the war gave the impression of overwhelming and nearly magical U.S. military power. The mystique of U.S. precision airpower was magnified by the U.S. government, which lied about the success rates of American missiles and missile defenses.[7] The Gulf War also rehabilitated the image of the military in the United States, following a long series of partial successes or total debacles: the stalemate in Korea, the failed war in Vietnam, and a series of minor disasters including the bungled invasion of tiny Grenada under President Reagan and the botched attempt to rescue American hostages in Iran in 1979 under President Carter. Even many liberals began to see clean, swift U.S. military power as a potential tool for achieving idealistic internationalist goals like nation building and combating genocide.

Proponents of American global hegemony claimed that it was a natural fact of the international system, the product of America's disproportionate wealth and military power.[8] But the United States could have been the richest and most powerful state in several conceivable systems of power, unipolar or multipolar. American global hegemony was anything but natural. It was the result of a carefully considered U.S. policy.

Blueprint for U.S. Global Hegemony

In 1992 Paul Wolfowitz, then the third-highest-ranking civilian in the Defense Department headed by Dick Cheney, took the lead role in drafting a "Defense Planning Guidance" that laid out a strategy for turning America's temporary Cold War predominance into indefinite U.S. global hegemony. "The number one objective of U.S. post Cold War political and military strategy should be preventing the emergence of a rival superpower," said the draft. "Our first objective is to prevent the re-emergence of a new rival.

This is a dominant consideration underlying the new regional defense strategy and requires that we endeavor to prevent any hostile power from dominating a region whose resources would, under consolidated control, be sufficient to generate global power. These regions include Western Europe, East Asia, the territory of the former Soviet Union, and Southwest Asia." The draft continued: "There are three additional aspects to this objective: First the U.S. must show the leadership necessary to establish and protect a new order that holds the promise of convincing potential competitors that they need not aspire to a greater role or pursue a more aggressive posture to protect their legitimate interests. Second, in the non-defense areas, we must account sufficiently for the interests of the advanced industrial nations to discourage them from challenging our leadership or seeking to overturn the established political and economic order. Finally, we must maintain the mechanisms for deterring potential competitors from even aspiring to a larger regional or global role."[9] To prevent hostile powers from dominating Western Europe, East Asia, the territory of the former Soviet Union, and Southwest Asia, the United States itself would be the dominant power in Western Europe, the dominant power in East Asia, the dominant power in the territory of the former Soviet Union, and the dominant power in Southwest Asia, for decades or generations to come.

When leaked to the press, the draft Pentagon document caused an international uproar, with its call for permanently subordinating both "potential competitors" like China and "the advanced industrial nations" to the United States. Although the administration of George Herbert Walker Bush publicly distanced itself from the defense guidelines, in practice the leaders of both major parties agreed with the idea that the United States should attempt to use its position as the sole surviving superpower to convert its temporary hegemony over the anti-Soviet alliance into the basis for indefinite U.S. global hegemony.

The hegemony strategy became official U.S. doctrine when Wolfowitz joined the George W. Bush administration in 2001 as the number two civilian official at Donald Rumsfeld's Pentagon and Dick Cheney became vice president. In a 2002 commencement address at West Point, Bush reiterated the strategy in which the United States would remain at the top of the great power pecking order: "Competition between great nations is inevitable, but armed conflict in our world is not . . . America has, and intends to keep, military strengths beyond challenge . . . making the destabilizing arms races of other eras pointless, and limiting rivalries to trade and other pursuits of peace."[10]

Earlier the Clinton administration had preferred the rhetoric of geoeconomics to geopolitics and was far more supportive of international institutions than its successor. Liberals argued that the United States should disguise its hegemony by working through multilateral institutions and alliances like the UN and NATO; conservatives preferred a style of combative unilateralism. But these differences in style disguised a fundamental consensus. Following the Gulf War, the bipartisan foreign policy elite in Washington agreed that a unipolar world was in America's interest and that the United States therefore should try to convert its Cold War alliances in Europe, Asia, and the Middle East into the foundations for enduring U.S. global hegemony. In 2000 Paul Wolfowitz observed with satisfaction: "In 1992 a draft memo prepared by my office at the Pentagon, which proposed a post–Cold War defense strategy, leaked to the press and caused a major controversy . . . Just seven years later, many of these same critics seem quite comfortable with the idea of a Pax Americana."[11]

The Strategic Triad of Hegemony:
Dissuasion, Reassurance, and Nonproliferation

"Benevolent global hegemony" is how two neoconservative writers, William Kristol and Robert Kagan, described "America's international role" in 1996.[12] The grand strategy of U.S. global hegemony that became the new consensus of U.S. foreign policy in the 1990s rested on three policies: dissuasion, reassurance, and nonproliferation.

• Dissuasion meant that the United States would try to monopolize as much of the world's military strength as possible, in order to deter "potential competitors from even aspiring to a larger regional or global role." The Bush administration's National Security Strategy declared: "Our forces will be strong enough to dissuade potential adversaries from pursuing a military build-up in hopes of surpassing or equaling the power of the United States."[13] To this end the United States indefinitely would continue to spend more on defense than most or all other great powers combined. In the words of one neoconservative supporter of U.S. global hegemony, because of its role as benevolent global policeman the United States "must support arms control, but not always for itself. It must live by a double standard."[14]

Reassurance meant that, in return for their agreement not to challenge U.S. global hegemony, the United States would agree to provide security for the other great powers like Japan, China, Russia, and Germany in their own regions and in regions of concern to all of the great powers, like the Middle East: "[W]e must account sufficiently for the interests of the advanced industrial nations to discourage them from challenging our leadership . . . "[15] Every great power in the world would be offered the chance to become an American protectorate on the same terms that Japan and Germany had accepted during the Cold War. In return for giving up its military independence and keeping its military limited and unthreatening, it would have its security provided by the United States.

Coercive nonproliferation was the third element of the strategic triad of U.S. hegemony. In order to deter challengers and reassure deferential allies, the United States had to maintain the ability to threaten or punish threatening states. If those states acquired nuclear weapons and other weapons of mass destruction along with long-range missile capabilities, the costs of U.S. attacks on them would rise and they might be able to threaten U.S. bases and military buildups in regions the United States sought to treat as American spheres of influence. For this reason many American strategic thinkers argued in favor of preventive attacks or wars to prevent proliferation, like Israel's 1981 attack on Iraq's nuclear reactor. Some justified the 1991 Gulf War, as well as the Iraq War in 2003, as a preventive war to stop Saddam Hussein's regime from acquiring weapons of mass destruction that could undermine U.S. military hegemony in the Middle East, even if they did not threaten the United States itself.[16] Even apart from the possibility that proliferation might make it easier for terrorists to acquire weapons of mass destruction, nonproliferation therefore became an obsession with the U.S. government once it had adopted the hegemony strategy.

The Public Rationale for U.S. Global Hegemony: Policing Regional Rogue States

The grand strategy of U.S. global hegemony was the strategy that dared not speak its name. The international scandal produced by the candor of the 1992 Pentagon planning document was a reminder of the perils of candid public discussion of America's post–Cold War strategy. American policymakers could not openly say that the United States, out of fear of great power competitors, sought to keep China and Russia weak, Germany and Japan demilitarized, and the European Union incapable of acting as a coherent entity in foreign policy. A publicly acceptable rationale that could justify permanent U.S. military hegemony in Europe, Asia, and the Middle East was necessary.

By the mid-1990s, the bipartisan U.S. foreign policy elite settled on a public rationale for American grand strategy that disguised the actual U.S. policy of perpetually limiting the independence and strength of all the other great powers of the world. The Gulf War had provided the U.S. foreign policy elite with a new category of enemies that could justify making the Cold War alliances and bases of the U.S. permanent: "rogue states" like Saddam Hussein's Iraq. The term "rogue state" originated as pure propaganda. However, by the mid-1990s this pejorative phrase was being treated as a serious term in the U.S. foreign policy debate. As a result, discussions of U.S. foreign policy during the Cold Peace acquired an oddly propagandistic flavor, reminiscent of ritualized Soviet discussions of world politics in terms of the "camps" of "imperialism" and "socialism."

In the "National Security Strategy of the United States" issued by the Bush administration in September 2002, rogue states were defined as regimes that "brutalized their own people and squander their natural resources . . . display no regard for international law . . . are determined to acquire weapons of mass destruction . . . sponsor terrorism around the globe" and "hate the United States and everything for which it stands."[17] The vagueness of the definition meant that the category of "rogue states" potentially had a great number of members. In practice, however, the United States employed the "rogue state" category selectively as a label for regimes that threatened U.S. primacy or military freedom of action in the three critical regions of Europe, Asia, and the Middle East. That is why the United States focused on Serbia (Europe), North Korea (Asia), and Iraq, Iran, and Syria (the Middle East), rather than on Burma, a horrendous tyranny in Southeast Asia, or on the genocide of more than a million people in Rwanda and Burundi, in sub-Saharan Africa. Although they contained a number of appalling tyrannies, Southeast Asia and sub-Saharan Africa were strategically insignificant regions, irrelevant to the American project of establishing global hegemony.

America's designated "rogue state" enemies were vicious regimes that posed genuine if sometimes exaggerated threats to their neighbors and to

U.S. interests. The United States did not invent the threats of Serbian ethnic cleansing, Iraqi regional aggression, or North Korean and Iranian pursuit of nuclear weapons, although it sometimes exaggerated the dangers. But the United States had a choice of options in responding to these genuine threats in areas important to American security. In each crisis American leaders tended to choose the option that would reinforce U.S. hegemony in a particular region, while ruling out other options that might enhance the independence of regional great powers from the United States.

Reassurance and the Rogue State Wars

Following the Gulf War, the new American grand strategy of global hegemony inspired the United States to fight a series of "rogue state wars." In addition to achieving their immediate goals—ending the bloody wars of the Yugoslav Succession, toppling Osama bin Laden's allies in Afghanistan and the Baathist regime in Iraq—these small wars provided the United States with an occasion to attempt to add Eastern Europe, the Middle East, and Central Asia to its existing military protectorates.

Whatever their other goals, the rogue state wars were all wars of reassurance. By demonstrating its military prowess in their own regions, the United States reassured major regional powers that it had the ability to protect them and their legitimate interests, while reminding them that it also could deter or defeat them if they resisted U.S. regional and global hegemony. The Kosovo War of 1999, for example, was seen as a test of whether the U.S.-controlled NATO alliance, recently expanded into post–Soviet Eastern Europe, could bring peace and order to the region. According to Secretary of State Madeleine K. Albright, whose ultimatum to Milosevic at the Rambouillet Peace Conference in February 1999 provided the occasion for the war, "Belgrade's actions constitute a critical test of NATO, whose strength and credibility have defended freedom and ensured our security for five decades."[18] According to former National Security Adviser Zbigniew Brzezinski, "It is no exaggeration to say that NATO's failure to prevail would mean both the end of NATO as a credible alliance and the undermining of America's global leadership."[19] Senator John McCain observed that "whether we had a strategic interest in the Balkans or not we acquired one the moment we threatened force. Credibility is a strategic asset of the highest order, and well worth fighting to maintain."[20]

The need for the United States to demonstrate its credibility as the defender of the interests of U.S. allies and client states was a common theme both during the Cold War and during the Cold Peace that followed. But the dangers that the U.S. sought to avert were quite different in the two eras.

During the Cold War, the United States feared that the loss of U.S. credibility as their protector might cause rich but weak states like Japan and West Germany to appease the Soviet Union out of fear, informally adding their industrial resources to those of the Soviet bloc by means of trade and investment policies extorted from them by Soviet threats. The defection by appeasement of allies to a superpower rival was not a concern during the Cold Peace. None of the regional rogue states that the United States battled or threatened, including Iraq, Iran, Serbia, and North Korea, was capable of obtaining hegemony in its own region, much less the world. If it had obtained weapons of mass destruction, Iraq might have intimidated Saudi Arabia and the Gulf emirates, but it could not have overawed Iran, Turkey, and Egypt or mastered the Middle East. And Serbian hegemony in Europe or North Korean hegemony in East Asia was as unlikely as Guatemalan hegemony in North America.

The geopolitical danger that the United States sought to avert by means of its interventions in the Balkans, the Persian Gulf, and Northeast Asia was the danger that its allies might increase their military self-reliance, at the expense of U.S. influence in those regions. American leaders feared that the major powers of Europe and East Asia might respond to the threats posed by minor states like Serbia and North Korea by building up their own military forces and power projection capabilities. This would not threaten the United States directly, because the regional military buildups would be directed at regional threats, not the United States. But even if initially they were friendly toward the United States, an independent Europe, an independent Japan, a more powerful China, and well-armed, self-reliant Middle Eastern powers might come into conflict with the United States in the remote future. According to the logic of the hegemony strategy, it was more prudent to keep all other great powers relatively disarmed and dependent on the United States, by proving that the United States was willing and able to protect their security interests in their own European or Asian neighborhoods, as well as in the oil-producing Middle East, a region of concern to all of the great military-industrial powers.

Post–Cold War Europe:
Keeping Germany Down and Russia Out

During the early years of the Cold War, as we have seen, Churchill's military adviser Lord Ismay remarked that the purpose of NATO was to "keep the Americans in, the Russians out, and the Germans down." Following the fall of the Berlin Wall, this reasoning continued to guide U.S. policy toward Europe.[21]

The end of the Cold War changed the strategic landscape by making possible the reunification both of Germany and Europe. Rather than welcoming the demise of the Iron Curtain, American as well as British and French leaders shared alarm in the early 1990s at the prospect of a "Fourth Reich" capable of dominating both Western and Eastern Europe. Ignoring anxious allies in Washington, London, and Paris, Germany's chancellor Helmut Kohl took the initiative and negotiated Soviet consent to the reunification of Germany. Having presented this to his Western allies as a fait accompli, Kohl reassured the United States by agreeing that Germany would be reunified within the U.S.-led NATO alliance. Kohl then reassured France that Germany would not become the hegemon of a large, loose EU by supporting French proposals for further centralization of the European Union. The goal, Kohl assured his allies, was a "European Germany" rather than a "German Europe." Underestimated at the time, Kohl proved to be one of the most creative and successful statesmen in contemporary history.

The reunification of Germany within NATO managed to keep the United States "in" and Germany "down." To keep Russia "out" the United States and its allies extended NATO to the borders of post-Soviet Russia. Russia protested, but it could not effectively resist. To justify punitive policies that took advantage of Russia's military weakness and economic bankruptcy, American policymakers and foreign policy experts exaggerated the danger that a "Weimar Russia" might produce a "Russian Hitler" who would menace Europe and the world.

The eastward expansion of NATO secured the hegemony of the United States in post–Cold War Europe, by ensuring that the former communist countries of Eastern Europe would not become part of a German or Russian sphere of influence. At the same time, their membership in NATO, dominated by the United States, was considered preferable by Washington to their membership in a purely European alliance like the Western European Union (WEU) in which the United States had no say.

In Western Europe, Britain acted as a de facto satellite of the United States in foreign policy, while France, sometimes with German support, favored an independent European military and an independent European foreign policy. In the 1990s, proposals for an independent, common European foreign policy seemed to many to be discredited by the inability of Britain, Germany, and France to agree on policy toward the Balkan War that accompanied the dissolution of the Yugoslav federation. The U.S.-led NATO war against Serbia in 1998, justified by the need to prevent the ethnic cleansing of Albanians by ethnic Serbs in Kosovo, further reasserted U.S. military leadership in Europe.

When France, with the support of Germany, refused to use its vote in the Security Council to authorize the U.S. invasion of Iraq in 2003, the Bush administration's conservative political allies vilified both France and Germany in the U.S. media. By rewarding small NATO states that joined the United States and Britain in the invasion of Iraq, President George W. Bush effectively destroyed NATO as a multilateral alliance and turned the U.S.-European military relationship into a hub-and-spoke system centered in Washington like America's bilateral East Asian alliances. Secretary of Defense Donald Rumsfeld praised America's new client states in Eastern Europe as "new Europe" and contrasted them with the states of "old Europe" like France and Germany. The Bush administration punished Germany for its opposition to the U.S. invasion of Iraq by refusing to support Germany's bid for a permanent seat on the UN Security Council.[22]

The United States consistently favored the enlargement of the EU, on the calculation that the addition of more members and greater cultural diversity would reduce the ability of European countries to agree on a common foreign policy of which the United States might disapprove. To that end, the United States urged the EU to admit Turkey, prompting French President Jacques Chirac to reply that EU–Turkey relations were of no more concern to the United States than U.S.-Mexico relations were to the EU.[23]

The Kosovo War in 1999, waged by the United States on behalf of Albanian Muslim separatists in the Serbian province of Kosovo, sent a strong signal not only to Paris but also to Moscow and Beijing, whose opposition to the war in the UN Security Council led the Clinton administration and its NATO partners to wage the war without Security Council authorization. When Russia unilaterally moved to take part in the occupation of Kosovo, which had been divided into five NATO protectorates, Wesley

Clark, the U.S. general in charge of the NATO campaign, ordered that the Russians be stopped by force. A British general refused to comply with the order, on the grounds that it might start "World War III."[24] Many Chinese were convinced that the accidental U.S. bombing of the Chinese embassy in Belgrade was not a mistake but a deliberate warning on the part of the United States. One Chinese analyst interpreted the U.S.-led war in Kosovo as part of a "python strategy" in which the United States would use "its thickest body to coil tightly around the world and prevent any country from possessing the ability to stand up to it."[25]

Preserving American Hegemony in East Asia

In East Asia after the Cold War, the United States pursued a policy similar to its policy in Europe, with the substitution of Japan for Germany and China for Russia. The decision by the Clinton administration to maintain roughly one hundred thousand troops in East Asia, most of them in Okinawa, Japan, and South Korea, signaled a decision to maintain the Cold War status quo in the region indefinitely. When the need for a massive U.S. military presence in the area was questioned, Japan rather than China was often named as the threat in off-the-record remarks by American officials. For example, one U.S. admiral justified U.S. forces in East Asia as "the cork in the bottle" to prevent the genie of Japanese military power from emerging.[26]

   U.S. fear of an independent Japan, more than the unlikely prospect that North Korean weapons would make their way into the hands of Muslim jihadist terrorists, was the major, if seldom acknowledged, reason for the repeated war scares in Washington over the prospect of North Korea's acquisition of nuclear weapons and other weapons of mass destruction. Even after the end of the Cold War and half a century of liberal democracy (more liberal in the case of West Germany than of Japan), Germany and Japan continued to be discouraged from obtaining nuclear deterrents of their own, even though developing nations like China, India, and Pakistan had joined the United States, Britain, France, Russia, and Israel in the nuclear club. American strategists feared that the acquisition of nuclear weapons by North Korea, even for purely defensive purposes, might frighten Japan and South Korea into obtaining their own nuclear deterrents. Once this occurred, the public in each country might question the purpose of a continuing U.S.

military presence on their territories, and the United States might lose its forward bases in East Asia. Invited politely to leave by Japan and South Korea, the United States overnight might cease to be the dominant military power in East Asia and the western Pacific.[27]

The economic stagnation of Japan in the 1990s, along with the problems caused by the fact that it was the most rapidly aging society in the world, led policymakers in both Beijing and Washington to downgrade their assessments of Japan's potential military power. Fearing Japan less, China and the United States feared each other more.

"Asia 2025," an official report produced in spring 2000 by the Pentagon's Office of Net Assessment under the leadership of Andrew Marshall, who like Paul Wolfowitz was a leading neoconservative strategist, treated Sino-American conflict as inevitable, whether China proved to be strong or weak: "China will be a persistent competitor of the United States. A stable and powerful China will be constantly challenging the status quo in East Asia. An unstable and relatively weak China could be dangerous because its leaders might try to bolster their power with foreign military adventurism."[28] In one scenario, by conquering Taiwan China would coerce Japan and a re-unified Korea into closing their American bases. In "The National Security Strategy of the United States of America" (2002), the Bush administration identified China as a threat: "In pursuing advanced military capabilities that can threaten its neighbors in the Asia-Pacific region, China is following an outdated path that, in the end, will hamper its own pursuit of national greatness."[29]

The Bush administration declared that it considered China a "strategic competitor" rather than a "strategic partner." On April 1, 2001, a U.S. Navy surveillance plane near China's coast collided with a Chinese fighter jet, killing the Chinese pilot and leading to the imprisonment and interrogation in China of the U.S. crew for eleven days.

The mutual threat posed by Muslim militants caused a brief thaw in relations between the two countries after 9/11. But in March 2005, China's legislature passed an Anti-Secession Law as a warning against any effort by Taiwan to seek independence. In July 2005, General Zhu Chenghu warned of possible Chinese nuclear retaliation against the United States in the event of a Sino-American conflict over Taiwan: "If the Americans draw their missiles and position-guided ammunition on to the target zone on China's territory, I think we will have to respond with nuclear weapons."[30] A decade earlier in 1995, another Chinese general, Xiong Guangkai, warned that Americans should be more worried about losing Los Angeles to nuclear weapons than saving Taipei.[31] In response to China's Anti-Secession Law, Japan under conservative nationalist leadership announced for the first time that the fate of Taiwan was of interest to Japan, a move that was interpreted as support in Tokyo for a U.S.-Japanese alliance against China.

Some American advocates of an anti-Chinese policy hoped that India could be enlisted as a counterweight to China along with Japan. India's leaders, however, were careful to improve their relations with the United States and China at the same time. Like China, India was focused on catching up with the United States and the other industrial nations by means of rapid growth and preferred to avoid geopolitical conflict.

The Middle East:
An Exclusive American Sphere of Influence

While the United States sought to prolong its Cold War policies in Europe and Asia with minor modifications, its post–Cold War policy in the Greater Middle East marked a radical departure. In the two decades following the fall of the Berlin Wall, the United States expanded its military presence in the region, which soon eclipsed Europe and Asia as the focus of American foreign policy.

Until the 1960s, Britain was the dominant outside power in the Middle East, a role that it had played, with a supporting role by France, since Britain and France agreed to carve up the former Ottoman Empire in the secret Sykes-Picot Treaty of 1916. As Britain and France reduced their roles during the Cold War, the United States and the Soviets backed rival sides. The United States gained an ally when Egypt, a former Soviet ally, became an American client state with the 1978 Camp David Peace Accords that President Carter brokered between Egypt and Israel. But the United States lost Iran as an important regional ally in 1979, when Islamic revolutionaries led by the Ayatollah Khomeini overthrew the Shah, who had been installed in a 1953 coup supported by the United States and Britain.

During the 1980s the United States pursued a balance of power policy in the region, backing Saddam Hussein's Iraq in the Iran-Iraq War in order to check Iranian power. But in 1991 Saddam's invasion of Kuwait threatened all of the oil-consuming countries, as well as violating the post-1945 bans on aggressive war, territorial conquest, and annexation. All of the members of the UN Security Council agreed to authorize the United States to lead a war against Iraq.

In order to prevent the broad American-led coalition from fraying, President George Herbert Walker Bush limited the goal of the war to the expulsion of Iraq from Kuwait. Saddam's regime was left in control of part of Iraq, while other parts were controlled by the U.S. and British forces, which maintained sanctions and periodically bombed Saddam's armed forces. The state of quasi-war that existed throughout the 1990s between the United States and Iraq justified the retention of massive U.S. Armed Forces in the Persian Gulf.

Jihad Against America

On the morning of September 11, 2001, Muslim terrorists, most of them from Saudi Arabia and Egypt, hijacked four jetliners in the United States for suicide missions. The terrorists crashed two jets into the Twin Towers of the World Trade Center in New York City, murdering around three thousand people, and plunged another into the Pentagon in Arlington, Virginia, killing nearly two hundred. A fourth jet, headed for Washington, D.C., crashed in a field in Pennsylvania.

The worst terrorist attack in the history of the United States was devised by Osama bin Laden, an exiled Saudi prince and a veteran of the resistance against the Soviet Union in Afghanistan in the 1980s who led a group of Muslim radicals known as al-Qaeda, "The Base." Al-Qaeda played a role in the 1993 car-bomb attack on the World Trade Center in New York City, a harbinger of the far deadlier attack in 2001, and in the 1996 bombing of Khobar Towers in Saudi Arabia, where U.S. Marines lived. On February 23, 1998, bin Laden joined the Egyptian radical Ayman al-Zwahiri and others in issuing a call for "Jihad against Jews and Crusaders." It named three grievances: the U.S. military presence in "the holiest of places, the Arabian Peninsula"; the ongoing battles between the United States and Iraq; and Israel's "occupation of Jerusalem and murder of Muslims there." The group issued a "fatwa" or religious edict: "The ruling to kill the Americans and their allies—civilian and military—is an individual duty for every Muslim who can do it in any country in which it is possible to do it, in order to liberate the al-Aqsa mosque [in Jerusalem] and the holy mosque [in Mecca] from their grip, and in order for their armies to move out of all the lands of Islam, defeated and unable to threaten any Muslim."[32]

Six months later, on August 7, 1998, hundreds were killed by car bombs at U.S. embassies in Tanzania and Kenya. On August 20 the United States retaliated by sending cruise missiles to strike an al-Qaeda training camp in Afghanistan and a factory in Sudan that erroneously was suspected of manufacturing chemical weapons for al-Qaeda. Al-Qaeda carried out a suicide attack on the USS *Cole* in a harbor in Yemen on October 12, 2000, and followed it with the devastating attack on the United States itself on 9/11.

Changing the Subject from Terrorism Back to Rogue States

On coming to power in January 2001, the administration of George W. Bush, influenced by veterans of the first Bush administration who had favored "going to Baghdad" during the Gulf War like Vice President Dick Cheney and Deputy Secretary of Defense Paul Wolfowitz, all but ignored al-Qaeda while focusing on the goal of deposing Saddam Hussein and converting Iraq into an American client state. The al-Qaeda attacks on the United States on September 11, 2001, did not lead to a reconsideration of the obsession with Iraq and other "rogue states," once the United States, in a war endorsed by the UN Security Council, toppled Afghanistan's Taleban regime, which had hosted al-Qaeda's terrorist training camps.

In his annual State of the Union address to Congress on January 29, 2002, President Bush changed the subject from the stateless terrorists of al-Qaeda, now deprived of a sanctuary in Afghanistan, to what he called the "axis of evil"—Iraq, Iran, and North Korea. These three states had nothing to do with al-Qaeda or the attacks on the United States; indeed, Osama bin Laden, a Sunni Muslim zealot, was hostile to the secular Baathist regime in Iraq and the Shia theocracy in Iran. But by making the implausible argument that rogue states might give nuclear weapons and other weapons of mass destruction to terrorists like those of al-Qaeda, the Bush administration and much of the American foreign policy elite used the attacks of 9/11 to reinforce the already-existing U.S. focus on rogue states. The existing policy of rogue state containment was simplified and redefined as part of the "Global War on Terrorism (GWOT)," as though the effort of the North Korean dictatorship to deter U.S. attack or invasion by obtaining nuclear weapons was part of the same phenomenon as the efforts of Muslim jihadists to promote theocratic revolutions in the Muslim world.

To justify a second U.S. war against Iraq, a policy supported throughout the Clinton years by many of the neoconservatives who joined the administration of George W. Bush in 2001, the Bush administration manipulated intelligence that purported to show that Saddam had or would soon have weapons of mass destruction and that Iraq was linked to al-Qaeda. Both of these claims were proven to be false, after the United States had invaded in 2003. The pretextual nature of the reasons offered to justify an invasion of Iraq was suggested by a policy document produced by the neoconservative think-tank Project for the New American Century in September 2000, just before the presidential election and a year before the al-Qaeda attacks on September 11, 2001. Entitled "Rebuilding America's Defenses: Strategies, Forces and Resources for a New Century," and drawn up for Paul Wolfowitz, Dick Cheney, Cheney's Chief of Staff Lewis Libby, and Donald Rumsfeld, the document explains: "The United States has for decades sought to play a more permanent role in Gulf regional security. *While the unresolved conflict with Iraq provides the immediate justification, the need for a substantial American force presence in the Gulf transcends the issue of the regime of Saddam Hussein*"[33] (emphasis added).

The neoconservative supporters of the Iraq War hoped that the installation of a pro-American regime in Baghdad would promote several goals. It would allow the United States to move its military bases from Saudi Arabia, where they had provided devout Muslims with a grievance that bin Laden exploited, to intimidate Iran and Syria, and to create a safer environment for Israel. But their scenario in which the Iraqi exile Ahmed Chalabi, a favorite of the neoconservatives, came to power after a brief war whose costs would be paid for by Iraqi oil exports proved to be illusory.

The Iraq War was a military disaster, an economic disaster, a diplomatic disaster, and a moral disaster for the United States. It was a military disaster because the U.S. military, following a quick victory against Saddam's regime, was unable during the occupation that followed to repress Sunni nationalist insurgents and a small number of foreign jihadists. It was an economic disaster because the costs in American taxes and American lives were vastly greater than the Bush administration had promised. It was a diplomatic disaster because, with the exception of America's ally Britain and its protectorate Israel, most major allies of the United States in the Middle East and Europe opposed the American invasion of Iraq; the contrast with the Gulf War, in which the United States led a coalition including Turkey and many Arab states, was striking. And it was a moral disaster, because press stories and photos illustrating the torture by American soldiers and intelligence agents of suspected terrorists and Iraqi insurgents helped to destroy what little remained of America's international reputation as a benevolent superpower.

Ironically, in the memoir he co-authored with his National Security Adviser Brent Scowcroft, President George Herbert Walker Bush had written in 1998: "I firmly believed that we should not march into Baghdad . . . It would have taken us way beyond the imprimatur of international law bestowed by the resolutions of the Security Council, . . . condemning [young soldiers] to fight in what would be an unwinnable guerilla war. It could only plunge that part of the world into even greater instability and destroy the credibility we were working so hard to reestablish."[34]

Protecting the Oil of the Industrial Nations

The Iraq War that began in 2003 did achieve one goal. It put the U.S. military in charge of the country with the fourth-largest proven oil reserves in the world.

Of the three major oil-producing nations in the Persian Gulf, Saudi Arabia remains a U.S. protectorate, Iraq at the time of this writing is occupied by the United States, and Iran is bordered by three U.S. client states that contain significant numbers of U.S. military forces—Iraq, Pakistan, and Afghanistan. "Regime change" in Iran that brought a pro-American regime to power would complete the conversion of several major oil-producing countries into U.S. protectorates. The most populous Arab country, Egypt, has been a subsidized U.S. client state since the Camp David Accords between Egypt and Israel brokered by the United States in 1978.

Many frustrated Americans hoped that U.S. involvement in the Middle East could be reduced if only the United States could liberate itself from dependence on Persian Gulf oil. They did not understand, and America's bipartisan foreign policy elite was careful not to explain, that the United

States was in the Middle East to protect not only its own oil but also that of other great powers, in order to discourage those great powers from building and projecting military power of their own.

By the first decade of the twenty-first century, the United States derived only about one-fifth of its oil from the Middle East. Sixty percent of Middle Eastern oil went to Asia. Half of China's oil came from the Persian Gulf region. The CIA estimated that by 2015 three-quarters of all Middle Eastern oil will go to Asia, with only one-tenth going to Western nations including the United States.[35]

The fact that Japan heavily subsidized the liberation of Kuwait from Iraq by the United States in 1991 was a clue to the bargain between the United States and its major protectorates in the post–Cold War period. Thomas P. M. Barnett, an influential American strategic thinker who taught at the Naval War College, noted that "the West . . . has come to rely less and less on Persian Gulf oil . . . The United States, for example, imports more energy supplies from Canada than from any other nation, and gets the bulk of its imported oil from North and South America." According to Barnett: "In effect, U.S. Naval presence in Asia is becoming far less an expression of our nation's forward presence than our exporting of security to the global marketplace."[36] Barnett argued that "in the end, this is a pretty good deal. We trade little pieces of paper (our currency, in the form of a trade deficit) for Asia's amazing array of products and services. We are smart enough to know this is a patently unfair deal—unless we offer something of great value along with those little pieces of paper. That product is a strong U.S. Pacific Fleet, which squares the transaction quite nicely."[37]

The power to protect by its nature is also the power to threaten. American policymakers did not make this explicit. But "Asia 2025," the alarmist report about China published by the Pentagon in 2000, noted a potential weakness of China, Japan, and the two Koreas, observing that by 2020 Asia might consume three times as much energy as Europe.[38] In a book published by the National Defense University, defense analyst Douglas E. Streusand wrote of "the American geopolitical imperative to retain control— the ability to use and to deny use—of the sea lines of communications between the Middle East and East Asia."[39] According to Streusand: "Asia, including China, depends on the United States, not merely on the actual sellers of the petroleum and natural gas, for its energy and thus for its economic prosperity and growth. The leverage of energy access control can counterbalance the leverage of China's size and proximity on the Pacific Rim. It also offers significant leverage over China itself. From this perspective, the U.S. commitments in the Persian Gulf and Indian Ocean protect not only our own energy supplies but also our status as a global power. Since we are currently engaged in a war against Osama bin Laden, who claims the American presence in Saudi Arabia as the principal justification for his hostility, there is no doubt that the U.S. presence in the Gulf brings painfully expensive baggage. But it is an essential component of the maintenance of global order."[40]

The ability of the United States to cut off oil supplies to Asia did not go unnoticed in Asia. A 2005 report commissioned by the U.S. Defense Department entitled "Energy Futures in Asia" cited the belief of Chinese officials that the United States had the military ability to cut off Chinese oil imports.[41] To reduce its vulnerability to the United States, China sought to provide for its future energy needs by deals with oil-producing countries hostile to the United States, including Iran, Sudan, and Venezuela. In 2005 a bid, later withdrawn, by China's state-owned oil company, the China National Offshore Oil Corporation (CNOOC), to take over the U.S. oil company Unocal, which had large holdings in oil fields and pipelines in Azerbaijan, Georgia, and Turkey, created alarm in the United States. China went on to buy Canada's Petrokazakhstan.[42]

In addition, according to a 2005 Pentagon report, "China is building strategic relationships along the sea lanes from the Middle East to the South China Sea in ways that suggest defensive and offensive positioning to protect China's energy interests, but also to serve broad security objectives." According to the report, China was pursuing a "string of pearls" strategy by building or upgrading naval bases in Bangladesh, Burma, Cambodia, and the South China Sea "to deter the potential disruption of its energy supplies from potential threats, including the U.S. Navy, especially in the event of a conflict with Taiwan" in which the United States might impose a blockade preventing oil imports to China.[43]

With good reason the political scientist Robert A. Pape observed that "U.S. monopolization of Persian Gulf oil would be the single most significant act that the United States could take to increase its relative power, save for taking control of European or Asian resources."[44]

The New Great Game in Central Asia

The U.S. quest for influence in countries with substantial energy resources was not limited to the Middle East. During the Cold Peace of the 1990s and early 2000s the United States engaged in a version of the "Great Game," the strategic competition in Central Asia between the British Empire and Russia in the nineteenth century, which ended only when the common German threat produced an Anglo-Russian rapprochement. First the Clinton administration, then the administration of George W. Bush, sought unsuccessfully to cut off Moscow's links with the former Soviet states of Central Asia by promoting an oil pipeline from Baku in Azerbaijan through Georgia to Turkey that would avoid Russian territory. The U.S. government also sought unsuccessfully to persuade U.S. oil companies to bypass Russia with a pipeline from the Caspian through Ukraine to Poland.[45]

[The U.S. invasion of Afghanistan in the winter of 2001–2, in order to topple the Taleban government and end al-Qaeda's use of Afghan territory as a headquarters and training center for global terrorism, deepened U.S. military involvement in Central Asia] Even before the attacks of September 11 and the war with Afghanistan the Bush administration, on coming into office, began planning a major base realignment that was only made public in August 2004. The large concentrations of U.S. troops in Germany, Japan, and Korea that remained from the Cold War would be drawn down. The new U.S. strategy would depend on the use by small, highly mobile U.S. forces of a spider's web of bases, some of them "lily pads" or jumping points. Most of the new bases were in the Middle East and former Soviet republics in Central Asia, ranging from a massive base in Qatar to U.S. bases in Kyrgyzstan and Uzbekistan.

The unacknowledged purpose of the new ring of U.S. bases in the Middle East and Central Asia, some suggested, was to position the United States for conflict with China, which many American neoconservatives considered inevitable. In a 2004 article James Hogue, the editor of *Foreign Affairs*, noted that "some Bush administration officials remain convinced that the United States and China will ultimately end up rivals." He drew this conclusion: "Militarily, the United States is hedging its bets with the most extensive realignment of U.S. power in half a century. Part of this realignment is the opening of a second front in Asia. No longer is the United States poised with several large, toehold bases on the Pacific rim of the Asian continent; today, it has made significant moves into the heart of Asia itself, building a network of smaller, jumping-off bases in Central Asia. The ostensible rationale for these bases is the war on terrorism. But Chinese analysts suspect that the unannounced intention behind these new U.S. positions, particularly when coupled with Washington's newly intensified military cooperation with India, is the soft containment of China."[46]

The United States was not the only great power seeking bases and allies in Central Asia. Russia countered the U.S. presence in Kyrgyzstan by opening its own base there, and sought to make a temporary base in Tajikistan permanent. In the words of one observer, "the Russo-American struggle for bases is becoming an ever-more open struggle over rival spheres of influence or efforts to deny such to the other side."[47] When the United States sought to deploy mobile troops to safeguard oil and gas pipelines in Georgia and Azerbaijan, a Russian official replied, "To ensure security of oil and gas pipelines by use of foreign military troops is beyond world practice. Azerbaijan has the potential to secure the pipelines itself."[48] China undertook joint maneuvers with the military in Kyrgyzstan and India acquired an air base in Tajikistan.[49] The struggle for bases, oil, and gas among the United States, Russia, China, and India in Central Asia appeared likely to intensify.

Soft Balancing:
The Worldwide Backlash Against American Hegemony

No other great power has been willing or able to risk a direct military confrontation with the United States since the end of the Cold War. Instead of competing with the United States in the military arena, major regional powers including China, Russia, France, and Germany have preferred to try to checkmate the United States in the diplomatic arena by means of what has been called "soft balancing."[50]

In the United Nations, for example, Russia and China prevented the Security Council from authorizing war against Serbia, forcing the United States and its NATO allies to go to war in Kosovo without the UN's blessing. Similarly in 2003 France, Russia, and China, backed by Germany, blocked the Anglo-American push for a Security Council resolution authorizing a U.S.-led invasion of Iraq.

In addition to thwarting the United States in the Security Council, some great powers have sought to enhance their influence and weaken the United

States by constructing regional security and trade organizations from which the United States is excluded. This explains the persistent support of France for a purely European defense organization, in addition to or instead of NATO, in which the United States would play no part. American protests failed to prevent the EU from establishing its own military planning agency, independent of NATO and thus of Washington. Over American objections, the EU insisted on building its own rapid reaction force and developing its own satellite network, Galileo, which ended the monopoly of the U.S. global positioning satellite (GPS) system.

The participation of China in Europe's Galileo project alarmed the American military. But China shared an interest with other aspiring space powers in preventing American control of space for military and commercial uses. Even while it collaborated with Europe on Galileo, China also partnered with Brazil to launch satellites.

Similar efforts to promote the soft balancing of American power were evident in the politics of trade. Afraid of being shut out of Asian trade diplomacy, the United States beginning in the 1990s backed the Asia-Pacific Economic Cooperation (APEC) forum, which included the United States and Australia along with the major Asian countries. China backed the rival ASEAN Plus Three (APT) organization, which includes China, Japan, South Korea, and the ASEAN countries but excludes the United States and its ally Australia. India, by joining, might make the organization ASEAN Plus Four. APT had the potential to be the world's largest trade bloc, dwarfing the EU and NAFTA. The deepening ties of the APT member states represented a major diplomatic defeat for the United States. So did the announcement in 2005 of a South American economic community, which signaled a rejection of the American goal of a Western-Hemisphere free-trade zone dominated by the United States.

Perhaps the most important example of "hard balancing" of the United States on the part of other great powers was provided by China and Russia, which formed the Shanghai Cooperation Organization (SCO). Founded on June 15, 2001, the SCO included China, Russia, Kyrgyzstan, Kazakhstan, Tajikistan, and Uzbekistan. Its dedication to preserving "multipolarity" was a coded reference to the desire of its members to prevent the United States from turning Central Asia into an American sphere of influence. In July 2005, China and Russia persuaded their SCO allies Kyrgyzstan and Uzbekistan to ask the United States to remove its bases from their countries.

Under Russian pressure, Georgia also announced its opposition to permanent U.S. bases in its territory.[51] This was followed by massive Sino-Russian military exercises on the Shantung peninsula in East Asia, which included amphibious landings of the kind that could be used in a Chinese invasion of Taiwan.

The states that were most opposed to U.S. global hegemony were great powers with aspirations to a greater role in their own regions, including China, India, Russia, France, and Germany. Alone among the great powers Japan and Britain were content to defer to the United States in their foreign policy—Japan, out of fear of China and North Korea, and Britain, because the Anglo-American "special relationship" provided British statesmen with a status in world affairs that otherwise they would have lacked. Some small states in Europe and Asia like Poland and South Korea preferred the hegemony of the United States in their regions to that of larger neighbors.

Beyond the Cold Peace

Following the end of the Cold War, the United States sought to fill every power vacuum left by the demise of Soviet power. Lacking any immediate great power threats, the United States justified the expansion of its commitments and its high level of military spending on the basis of speculative danger from remote threats, often described in lurid terms in the press—a "Fourth Reich," "Japanese Militarism," "Weimar Russia," "Wilhelmine China." This was not prudence; it was paranoia. And even though the proponents of perpetual U.S. global hegemony viewed it as a defensive strategy, other countries interpreted the hegemony strategy as evidence that the United States had adopted an aggressive, imperial policy.

A new grand strategy for the United States is needed. A U.S. foreign policy based on an attempt to discourage the self-reliance of other great powers in favor of their perpetual dependence on the U.S. military is too expensive to be sustained without damage to the American way of life. What the United States needs is a strategy that prevents any hostile power from dominating Asia, the Middle East, or Europe, without requiring the United States itself perpetually to dominate all three regions on its own.

PART III

THE FUTURE OF THE AMERICAN WAY OF STRATEGY

Chapter 9

U.S. Hegemony and the American Way of Life

> . . . [A] foreign policy consists in bringing into balance,
> with a comfortable surplus of power in reserve, the nation's
> commitments and the nation's power.
>
> —Walter Lippmann, 1943

THE PURPOSE OF THE AMERICAN WAY OF STRATEGY is to defend the American way of life by means that do not endanger the American way of life. America's civilian, middle-class society, no less than its democratic republican system of government, must be defended not only from enemies but also from excessive costs of defense.

In order to defend the American way of life by keeping the long-term price of national security low, American statesmen have sought to reshape the environment beyond America's borders. The United States has pursued this goal by promoting liberal internationalism, as the basis of world order, and by promoting a series of grand strategies in the realm of power politics. In power politics, American grand strategy since the emergence of the United States as a great power in the late nineteenth century has combined two objectives: preserving U.S. hegemony in North America, and preventing the hegemony of a hostile power in any of the three regions outside of North America with major industrial or energy resources—Europe, Asia, and the Middle East. In both world wars, U.S. leaders sought to prevent hegemony in other regions by means of great power cooperation in a multipolar world, not by means of solitary and exclusive U.S. global hegemony.

Following the collapse of the Soviet Empire, American leaders broke with this tradition. Instead of leading in the establishment of a great power concert, in the 1990s and 2000s U.S. leaders sought to convert the temporary hegemonic alliance system the United States had constructed during the Cold War into the basis of indefinite U.S. global hegemony. In the words of Colonel Mackubin Thomas Owens, associate dean of the Naval War College, "No matter what presidents have declared the policy and strategy of the United States to be, US strategy in practice is best described as primacy, which is predicated on the idea that the key to future peace and prosperity is for the United States to maintain the power position it held at the end of the Cold War. The twin objectives of primacy are to underwrite a liberal world order by providing security, while preventing the emergence of a potential new rival along the lines of the Soviet Union."[1]

Whether it is called hegemony or primacy, this plan for U.S. domination of every region with power resources outside of North America represents a radical departure from America's previous policy of seeking to preserve rather than prevent a diversity of power in the world, while sharing the burdens of preserving the peace with other rich and militarily powerful states.

Hegemony Is Not Empire

After the Cold War, many analysts described the United States as a global empire.[2] Even some supporters of the idea of U.S. global hegemony, particularly the influential faction of neoconservatives on the political right, described the post–Cold War United States as an empire. The neoconservative Robert Kagan described the United States as a "Benevolent Empire."[3] "The United States needs an imperial strategy," Elliot Cohen, a leading neoconservative defense analyst, wrote in 1998. "Defense planners could never admit it openly, of course, and most would feel uncomfortable with the idea, but that is, in fact, what the United States at the end of the twentieth century is—a global empire . . ."[4] Stephen Peter Rosen, another neoconservative thinker, wrote that the United States, "if it is to wield imperial power, must create and enforce the rules of a hierarchical interstate empire . . ."[5] Neoconservative civilian appointees in George W. Bush's Defense Department invited historians to private discussions of alleged lessons that the United States could learn from empires of the past.[6]

In 2001 in the neoconservative journal *The Weekly Standard*, the journalist Max Boot published an essay entitled "The Case for American Empire" in which he argued: "Afghanistan and other troubled lands today cry out for the sort of enlightened foreign administration once provided by self-confident Englishmen in jodhpurs and pith helmets."[7] Boot also published a manifesto calling on the United States to engage in colonial wars around the world, borrowing his title *The Savage Wars of Peace* from "The White Man's Burden," a poem by Rudyard Kipling that praised U.S. imperialism in the Philippines in 1898. Kipling called on Americans to join the British Empire in conquering and ruling nonwhite peoples like the Filipinos against their will: "Take up the White Man's Burden—The savage wars of peace" in order to govern "your new-caught, sullen peoples, / Half-devil and half-child."[8]

The description of the United States as an empire, whether by proponents or critics of U.S. policy, was inaccurate. Traditional empires exploited populations for taxes and tribute and ruled them directly or through subservient intermediaries. A genuine global empire would have been incompatible with the existence of sovereign states, even small and weak ones. Hegemony, by contrast, is compatible with a liberal international system based on the independence of many states. In a global society of sovereign states, a hegemon, as the dominant power, may provide security for other states as well as itself. To this end it may insist that other countries defer to its military primacy in their foreign policies. But this is far from the kind of control over the internal affairs of subject populations exercised by the agrarian empires of the past and by industrial-era empires like National Socialist Germany, Imperial Japan, and the Soviet Union.

Genuine precedents for the U.S. hegemony policy were not to be found in Rome or nineteenth-century Britain. They were to be found in the informal protectorates that the United States established over Western Europe and East Asia during the Cold War, and in the informal sphere of influence that the United States consolidated in North America and the Caribbean in the early years of the twentieth century.

While proponents of the strategy of U.S. global hegemony have used pretexts to justify certain policies, like the invasion and occupation of Iraq in 2003, there is no reason to doubt the sincerity of their belief that the strategy promotes American security. One way for the United States to ensure that no hostile power dominates the resources of Europe, Asia, and the Middle East is for the United States to dominate those regions itself. After all, it can be argued, U.S. hegemony in North America has made the United States safer. Why not U.S. hegemony in the world?

The problem with the hegemony strategy is not with its goal of American safety, which must be that of any U.S. grand strategy, but rather with its preferred method for achieving them: perpetual U.S. military hegemony in each of the critical regions of Asia, the Middle East, and Europe. In arguing that the hegemony strategy is necessary for U.S. security, its defenders invoke the theory of "the security dilemma" as the basis for the claim that the only alternative to U.S. hegemony would be spiraling local arms races and possibly devastating regional wars in Asia, Europe, and the Middle East. In arguing that the hegemony strategy is compatible with the American way of life, its defenders claim that it can be carried out indefinitely at a relatively low cost in terms of American taxes and the lives of American soldiers. Neither of these arguments is persuasive. The truth is that the hegemony strategy is not necessary for U.S. security and it costs too much.

The Security Dilemma and Hegemonic Stability

The U.S. hegemony strategy often has been justified by its proponents on the basis of a highly theoretical version of *Realpolitik*, which leads to extreme pessimism about the prospects for great power peace. The key concept is "the security dilemma." The idea is simple. All sovereign states are naturally suspicious of each other. If any country builds up its military forces for defense, other countries will assume that it will use those forces for aggression and feel compelled to build up their own militaries in response. The result inevitably will be a cycle of arms races that can spin out of control into all-out war.

The only possible way to prevent the security dilemma from producing arms races and wars, according to the hegemony school, is "hegemonic stability." One powerful state, the hegemon, should more or less monopolize military force and provide free security to other countries. In effect, the hegemonic power acts as a de facto government for a regional or global system of sovereign states. In civilized countries individuals do not feel the need to amass weapons in their homes out of fear of their neighbors, because they trust the government to protect them from crime. In the same way, states that trust a benevolent hegemon to protect their existence and interests can relax, reduce their armaments to a minimum, and focus on civilian pursuits like trade.

In *The Case for Goliath: How America Acts as the World's Government in the 21st Century*, the political scientist Michael Mandelbaum invokes American hegemony as the solution to the security dilemma in Asia, Europe, and the Middle East: "Reassurance ensures against what *might* happen, and the need for it arises from the structure of the system of sovereign states. Because no superior power controls relations among them, an attack by one against another is always possible. Governments therefore tend to take steps to prepare to defend themselves . . . But military preparations that one country undertakes for purely defensive reasons can appear threatening to others, which may then take military measures of their own and so set in motion a spiral of mistrust and military buildups."

Fortunately, according to Mandelbaum, U.S. hegemony eliminates this dilemma: "The American military presence in Europe acts as a barrier against such an undesirable chain of events. It reassures the Western Europeans that they do not have to increase their armed forces to protect themselves against the possibility of a resurgent Russia . . . At the same time, the American presence reassures Russia that its great adversary of the first half of the twentieth century, Germany, will not adopt policies of the kind that led to two destructive German invasions in 1914 and 1941."[9] The alternative to U.S. hegemony would be a far more dangerous world: "At best, an American withdrawal would bring with it some of the political anxiety typical during the Cold War and a measure of the economic uncertainty that characterized the years before World War II. At worst, the retreat of American power could lead to a repetition of the great global economic failure and the bloody international conflicts the world experienced in the 1930s and 1940s."[10]

The neoconservative journalists William Kristol and Robert Kagan have made the same argument for perpetual U.S. global hegemony: "The more Washington is able to make clear that it is futile to compete with American power, either in size of forces or in technological capabilities, the less chance there is that countries like China or Iran will entertain ambitions of upsetting the present world order. And that means the United States will be able to save money in the long run, for it is much cheaper to deter a war than to fight one."[11] Mackubin Thomas Owens of the Naval War College agrees: "The basis of [U.S.] primacy is hegemonic stability theory. According to the theory of hegemonic stability, a decline in relative U.S. power could create a more disorderly, less peaceful world."[12]

History and the Security Dilemma

The idea of an inevitable and dangerous security dilemma in Europe and Asia that can only be eliminated if the United States continues to act as the benign hegemon in both regions is interesting. But is it valid? The only way to test theories about international politics is to interpret history. And history does not support the idea of an inevitable security dilemma that forces neighboring states into ever-worsening spirals of destructive competition.

Adherents of the theory of the security dilemma explain the world wars and the Cold War as the tragic and unintended results of defensive strategies of great powers that drifted into conflict more on accident than on purpose. President Bill Clinton was referring to the security dilemma when he justified U.S. interventions in former Yugoslavia including the Kosovo War by repeatedly reminding the American people that World War I started in the Balkans.[13] The implication was that World War I was caused by the uncontrolled escalation of a Balkan conflict, and that the phenomenon might happen again. Clinton's successor as president, (George W. Bush, also endorsed the idea of U.S. hegemony as the solution to the security dilemma in his 2002 West Point commencement address: "Competition between great nations is inevitable, but armed conflict in our world is not . . . America has, and intends to keep, military strengths beyond challenge . . . making the destabilizing arms races of other eras pointless, and limiting rivalries to trade and other pursuits of peace."[14])

But the idea that the global conflicts of the twentieth century were produced by a security dilemma in Europe is simply wrong. The world wars and the Cold War were not accidental results of "destabilizing arms races." They were crimes—premeditated crimes. And they arose, not from the dynamics of the international system, but from the ambitions of aggressive regimes in Berlin and Moscow. To paraphrase a slogan of opponents of gun control, arms races don't cause world wars, great powers do.

Both world wars were deliberately launched by Germany. In neither 1914 nor 1939 was Germany in any peril of unprovoked attack by France, Britain, or Russia, much less the United States. Motivated by ambition rather than insecurity, the rulers of Germany in both world wars wanted their nation to be an awe-inspiring global superpower rather than a medium-sized regional European power, and this required the conquest of Europe and western Eurasia and its transformation into a German Empire. If

Germany's leaders had been content, as Bismarck had been, with Germany's status as first among equals in Europe, there might have been arms races among Germany and its neighbors and small wars in the Balkans. But there probably would have been no world wars, no matter how many archdukes were assassinated.

Nor was the Cold War the accidental result of the collision of defensive security strategies adopted by the Soviet Union and the United States. After World War II ended the United States withdrew most of its troops from Europe and Asia and demobilized them, even though the Red Army remained in Eastern Europe. And Stalin knew from American and British spies that it would be years before American airpower credibly could threaten his domain with atomic destruction. Stalin's postwar attempt to maximize Soviet power, by turning Eastern Europe into a colony, promoting communist revolutions in China, Korea, Vietnam, and elsewhere, and beginning the massive, decades-long Soviet arms buildup, was inspired by a mixture of Marxist-Leninist messianism and great power ambition. Since abandoning communism, post-Soviet Russia has been content with its status as a regional great power.

The security dilemma theory that justifies U.S. hegemony strategy assumes that the nature of a country's government is irrelevant to its foreign policy. It is not necessary to endorse the theory that democracies will never go to war with each other in order to reject the idea that Britain, France, Germany, and Russia, in the absence of U.S. hegemony in Europe, would inevitably become enemies. Germany is not ruled by Junkers or Nazis craving *Lebensraum* (living space) in the East, Russia is not ruled by communists trying to overthrow capitalism, and British policies toward Europe are no longer driven by fears of a continental threat to British colonies overseas.

If the theory of an inevitable security dilemma is mistaken, then the major argument for U.S. hegemony in terms of American national security collapses. This is because the cost-benefit analysis of U.S. hegemony depends on whether the security dilemma exists or not. If the alternative to perpetual U.S. military hegemony in Europe or Asia is a local arms race that might spiral out of control into World War III, then the costs of U.S. hegemony in those regions, including the costs of occasional small reassurance wars by the United States as local policeman, are relatively minor by comparison to the benefits. But if the alternative to perpetual U.S. hegemony in Europe and

Asia is likely to be peace among the local great powers, if only a tense and armed peace, rather than new rounds of Sino-Japanese or Russo-German war, then American taxpayers need to ask their elected leaders why it is necessary to continue to encircle China and Russia, to continue to treat Japan and Germany as U.S. protectorates, and to continue unilaterally to threaten or wage war against lesser states hostile to U.S. hegemony in Asia, Europe, and the Middle East like North Korea, Saddam's Iraq, and Iran.

Is American Hegemony Compatible with the American Way of Life?

If the idea of an inevitable security dilemma is mistaken, then it may be possible for the United States to enjoy security at low cost even if the United States is not the hegemon of Europe, the hegemon of Asia, and the hegemon of the Middle East. The hegemony strategy therefore fails the test of necessity. It is not necessary for U.S. national security.

What about a second test? Is the U.S. hegemony strategy compatible with the American way of life?

As we have seen, the hegemony strategy requires that the United States engage in three policies: dissuasion, reassurance, and coercive nonproliferation. First, the United States will outspend all other great military powers combined, with the goal, in the words of the Pentagon's 1992 Defense Planning Guidance draft, of dissuading or "deterring potential competitors from even aspiring to a larger regional or global role."[15] Second, the United States must be willing to go to war, if necessary, to "reassure" its dependent allies in Asia, Europe, and the Middle East by protecting them against purely local threats, whether or not the United States itself is threatened. To quote the 1992 Defense Planning Guidance again, "Second, in the non-defense areas, we must account sufficiently for the interests of the advanced industrial nations to discourage them from challenging our leadership or seeking to overturn the established political and economic order." The United States indefinitely should provide security for other great powers like Japan, China, Russia, and Germany both in their own regions and in areas of concern to all of the great powers like the Persian Gulf: "[W]e must account sufficiently for the interests of the advanced industrial nations to discourage them from challenging our leadership . . . " Finally, in order to achieve the first two goals, the United States must discourage the proliferation of advanced weapons to hostile countries, in order to maintain maximum freedom of action for the U.S. military to coerce countries in American spheres of influence by threatening them or attacking them at minimal cost to the United States.

These policies are too costly in the long run to be compatible with the American way of life. The policy of outspending all other militaries in the world will harm the U.S. economy over time, if it has not done so already. In addition, an effective sustained strategy of adding Asia, Europe, and the Middle East to the Caribbean and Central America as exclusive U.S. spheres of influence would probably require a level of U.S. military manpower that cannot be obtained without the revival of the draft at a tremendous loss in the liberty of Americans. To be successful, the U.S. hegemony strategy would require so great a mobilization of America's economic resources and manpower for military purposes that the United States would be in danger of becoming a garrison state.

The Hegemony Strategy
and the Lippmann Gap

In his classic study *U.S. Foreign Policy: Shield of the Republic* (1943), Walter Lippmann wrote that "foreign policy consists in bringing into balance, with a comfortable surplus of power in reserve, the nation's commitments and the nation's power."[16] When commitments exceed resources, the result is what Samuel P. Huntington has described as a "Lippmann Gap."[17] The strategy of American global hegemony suffers from a serious and growing Lippmann Gap in two dimensions of power: money and manpower.

In 2004–2005, the United States accounted for 45 percent of global spending on the military.[18] But this was chiefly the result of decisions by other great powers to spend less on defense after the disappearance of the Soviet threat. The United States was able to spend almost twice as much on defense as its NATO allies combined only because the latter had chosen to slash their defense spending following the Cold War. If NATO had continued to spend as much on defense as they had in 1985, U.S. spending would have exceeded theirs only by 10 percent.[19]

"Americans should be glad that their defense capabilities are as great as the next six powers combined," the neoconservative journalists William Kristol and Robert Kagan wrote in 1996. "Indeed, they may even want to enshrine this disparity in U.S. defense strategy. Great Britain in the late 19th century maintained a 'two-power' standard, insisting that at all times the British navy should be as large as the next two naval powers combined, whoever they might be. Perhaps the United States should inaugurate such a two- (or three-, or four-) power standard of its own, which would preserve its military supremacy regardless of the near-term global threats." Kristol and Kagan argued that the United States should perpetually spend as much on defense as it did during the Cold War.[20]

But the U.S. economy is not a limitless cornucopia that can sustain a level of permanent military spending comparable to that of the Cold War without harm. The long-term growth of the U.S. economy depends on public investments in scientific research, infrastructure, and education. Since the end of the Cold War, such public investments have diminished as a percentage of the U.S. federal budget. The main threat to the U.S. budget is escalating health-care costs, followed by entitlements for the elderly, and Pentagon spending. If the percentage of the U.S. economy devoted to health care and pensions rises as the U.S. population ages, spending more of the budget on the military may lead to less long-term public investment in laboratories, schools, and infrastructure. Some Pentagon spending produces useful spin-offs for the civilian economy, like the Internet. But for the most part money spent on weapons and soldiers is money that cannot be used for private and public investments that increase long-term U.S. productivity growth.

The waste involved is illustrated by the example of the Iraq War. Before the war the Bush administration argued that it would cost no more than sixty billion dollars; when White House economic adviser Lawrence Lindsey said that the price tag might be as much as two hundred billion dollars, he was pressured into resigning. The ultimate cost of that "war of choice" to the American taxpayer may be one to two trillion dollars, according to Linda Bilmes, a former secretary of commerce, and Joseph Stiglitz, the former head of the World Bank and a winner of the Nobel Prize in economics: "We conclude that the economy would have been much stronger if we had invested the money in the United States instead of in Iraq. . . . [Avoiding war] would arguably have saved the nation at least $1 trillion—enough money to fix Social Security for the next 75 years twice over."[21]

Even in the absence of conflict with other great powers and small but expensive wars against minor countries like Iraq, the attempt of the United States to maintain its position at the top of the hierarchy by surpassing most or all other great powers in military spending is likely to grow ever-more expensive. If China and other rising powers spend more on the military as their economies grow, the United States will have to spend ever more to keep its solitary military lead, as long as it is unwilling to pool the costs of its defense with allied great powers. It is all but certain that the U.S. public, confronted with a choice between slashing middle-class entitlements, dramatically raising taxes, and limiting military expenditures, will force their elected leaders to limit military expenditures, thereby dooming dissuasion as an element of the hegemony strategy.[22]

Perpetual Wars of Reassurance

To the escalating costs of dissuasion must be added the costs of reassurance. According to theorists of U.S. hegemony, the United States should discourage the great powers of Europe and Asia from exercising military power on their own by reassuring them that the United States will defend them from threats in their own regions. In other words, in order to advance the goal of a near monopoly by the United States of global military power, the United States will volunteer to fight not only America's wars on America's behalf, but also Japan's wars on Japan's behalf, Germany's wars on Germany's behalf, China's wars on China's behalf, and so on.

If the issue honestly were put in this way to the American people, public rejection of the hegemony strategy would be instant and overwhelming. Having learned from the history of the twentieth century, the American public is no longer isolationist. Polls show that Americans support not only military action on behalf of narrow U.S. interests, but also international efforts in which other countries participate. But the bargain proposed by hegemony theorists, by which the United States defends the strategic interests of other great powers, while those powers sit on the sidelines and profit from the sacrifice of American blood and American treasure, goes far beyond what the American public is likely to support. If perpetual small wars on behalf of the security interests of other great powers are the price of a unipolar, America-centered world, then the price is too high.

Military Manpower and the Lippmann Gap

The price of American hegemony is too high in terms of manpower as well as taxes. While no Americans died as a result of combat in Kosovo, in the

Iraq War more Americans have been killed than died in every U.S. military conflict between the end of the Vietnam War in 1975 and the U.S. invasion of Iraq in 2003. The total number of dead is a fraction of the losses suffered by the United States in Vietnam and Korea. But the stakes for the United States during the Cold War conflicts in Asia were far higher than the stakes in Kosovo or in Iraq. In any event, public opinion turned against the Iraq War once the American death toll neared one thousand. An "Iraq Syndrome"—a generation-long reluctance to commit U.S. troops to combat—is likely to follow the war in the same way that the "Vietnam Syndrome" followed that much costlier war.

In itself this might doom the U.S. hegemony strategy. In order to be the hegemon of Asia, Europe, and the Middle East and to reassure other great powers, the United States must be willing to threaten war, and occasionally to wage war, completely on its own if necessary, against states that threaten the peace in those regions. In a period of a decade and a half, the United States fought three reassurance wars—the Gulf War, the Kosovo War, and the Iraq War. (The Afghan War of 2001 by contrast was a war of self-defense against the state sponsor of al-Qaeda, and the U.S. invasion of Panama in 1989 was a traditional if questionable exercise of U.S. hegemony in North America.) At this rate, the United States, in the interest of maintaining its status as the dominant military power in the three critical regions outside of North America, may be fighting a substantial small war on the scale of the wars in Iraq and the Balkans two or three times a decade.

Even before the Iraq War, the United States between 1989 and 1999 engaged in almost four-dozen military interventions, compared to only sixteen during the entire Cold War.[23] No longer worried that U.S. military intervention might trigger a superpower confrontation, American leaders following the Cold War became trigger-happy. Liberals as well as conservatives began to see military force not as a desperate last resort, but as a legitimate tool to achieve goals ranging from preventing weapons proliferation to rebuilding shattered societies. The attitude of much of the U.S. foreign policy elite was illustrated by Clinton's secretary of state, Madeleine Albright, who challenged the reluctance of Colin Powell, chairman of the Joint Chiefs of Staff, to involve the United States in the Wars of the Yugoslav Succession: "What's the point of having this superb military that you're always talking about if we can't use it?" In his memoirs Powell recalled: "I thought I would have an aneurysm. American GIs were not toy soldiers to be moved around on some sort of global game board."[24]

Already, however, the U.S. military is showing the strain placed on it by the simultaneous small wars in Afghanistan and Iraq. Recruitment and re-enlistment rates in America's volunteer military have plummeted. The United States has tried to fill the manpower gap by enlisting forces from allied countries, but with the exception of Britain no allied country has sent more than token forces to assist the United States in Iraq. In desperation, the U.S. government has relied on private contractors or mercenaries, whose ambiguous legal and political status raises serious ethical questions for U.S. foreign policy.[25]

Most disturbing of all, the U.S. government has accelerated the naturalization of immigrants serving in the U.S. military.[26] In effect, the United States is now selling citizenship to foreigners in return for military service. This policy of using hastily naturalized foreigners as cannon fodder in quasi-imperial small wars is completely incompatible with America's democratic republican tradition of the citizen soldier.

The hegemony policy is labor intensive. In the North American sphere of influence of the United States, temporary interventions and some prolonged occupations in the Caribbean and Central America have usually required only the U.S. Marines. But by seeking to add Asia, Europe, and the Middle East to the Caribbean and Central America as exclusive American spheres of influence, the United States multiplied the number of necessary U.S. interventions and the number of soldiers necessary to carry them out.

Recognizing this, some supporters of American hegemony have called upon the United States to reinstitute the draft. But military conscription has always been deeply unpopular among the American people. The U.S. government quickly abolished the draft following the Civil War and the two world wars and revived it, in the limited form of selective service, only reluctantly in the late 1940s in order to check Soviet aggression. The use of conscripts in the Korean and Vietnam Wars was so unpopular that the draft was abolished in 1973. It had no chance of being revived even before Americans were horrified by the carnage of the Iraq War.

Ironically, by calling for the United States to spend far more on the military and reinstate the draft, some leading neoconservative supporters of the U.S. hegemony strategy implicitly concede the existence of a Lippmann Gap.[27] The clear implication is that absent much higher rates of defense spending and the revival of military conscription, the United States will not be able to function as the global hegemon in a unipolar world. This is almost certainly correct.

The Hegemony Strategy
and the U.S. Constitution

The plan for U.S. world domination, then, is too costly. The American way of strategy seeks to secure America by methods that do not impose excessive costs on either the civilian U.S. economy or the liberties of individual Americans. The hegemony strategy fails these tests. Dissuasion, the first part of the hegemony strategy—the requirement that the United States perpetually outspend all other great military powers combined—cannot be sustained in the long run without crippling the U.S. economy by diverting too many resources from civilian to military uses. Reassurance, the second part of the hegemony strategy—the requirement that the United States wage wars of reassurance on behalf of American protectorates in Asia, Europe, and the Middle East—cannot be successful unless the United States increases its military manpower by means of a draft, which would be a major deprivation of the liberty of young Americans. The same objections can be raised to the third element of the hegemony strategy, the requirement that the United States prevent the proliferation of weapons of mass destruction by preventive wars. To draft Americans to defend the United States and its allies against imminent peril is one thing; to draft them merely to defend America's status as the leading military power in Asia, Europe, and the Middle East is quite another.

The damage done to the American way of life by the hegemony strategy cannot be measured solely in terms of the effects of excessive military spending on America's civilian economy and of a revived draft on America's individualistic society. There is intangible damage, too, in the form of the damage done to America's democratic republican constitution of government.

All wars, including small wars, erode the constitutional system of checks and balances among Congress, the courts, and the presidency and concentrate power in the executive branch. If the United States continues on its present course, fighting significant small wars like the Kosovo War and the Iraq War every few years in the service of U.S. global hegemony, the United States will be on a more or less permanent wartime footing and power inevitably will be concentrated in presidents to a degree that America's Founders would have considered dangerous. The world wars and the Cold War created an "imperial presidency."

The end of the Cold War held out the possibility that the role of the president, inflated by decades of superpower struggle, would shrink back to its normal dimensions. But the ambitious project of establishing solitary U.S. hegemony over the rest of the world, even in the absence of the threat of a rival superpower, created a new rationale for the imperial presidency, once the Cold War rationale ceased to be valid.

Fixing the Facts Around the Policy

On July 23, 2002, Richard Dearlove, the chief of British Intelligence, briefed British Prime Minister Tony Blair after returning from a trip to Washington to meet with Bush administration officials. According to the minutes of that briefing, Dearlove told Blair: "Military action was now seen as inevitable. Bush wanted to remove Saddam, through military action, justified by the conjunction of terrorism and WMD. But the intelligence and the facts were being fixed around the policy."[28]

A few months later, on October 7, 2002, in a speech to the American public delivered in Cincinnati, Ohio, President George W. Bush justified the forthcoming invasion and occupation of Iraq that began on March 20, 2003:

> Some citizens wonder: After eleven years of living with this problem [Iraq], why do we need to confront it now?
> There is a reason. We have experienced the horror of September 11. We have seen that those who hate America are willing to crash airplanes into buildings full of innocent people. Our enemies would be no less willing—in fact they would be eager—to use a biological, chemical or nuclear weapon.
> Knowing these realities, America must not ignore the threat gathering against us. Facing clear evidence of peril, we cannot wait for the final proof—the smoking gun—that could come in the form of a mushroom cloud.[29]

In May 2003, after U.S. inspectors failed to find any weapons of mass destruction in Iraq, Deputy Secretary of Defense Paul Wolfowitz, one of the chief architects of the Iraq War as well as of the strategy of U.S. global hegemony, admitted in an interview: "The truth is that for reasons that have a lot to do with the U.S. government bureaucracy we settled on the one issue that everyone could agree on which was weapons of mass destruction as the core reason" for the war. After it was proven that Saddam had no ties with al-Qaeda as well as no weapons of mass destruction, the Bush administration hastily changed its justification for the war, alleging that its main purpose all along had been to bring democracy to Iraq and the Arab world in general. Wolfowitz, however, admitted that bringing democracy to Iraq "is a reason to help the Iraqis but it's not a reason to put

American kids' lives at risk, certainly not on the scale we did it."[30] The strategic thinking behind the U.S. invasion of Iraq was made clear in a document drawn up for Wolfowitz in "Rebuilding America's Defences: Strategies, Forces and Resources for a New Century," the policy document quoted in the previous chapter and published in September 2000 by the Project for the New American Century, the neoconservative think tank affiliated with Wolfowitz, Rumsfeld, Cheney, and other high-ranking members of the Bush administration: "The United States has for decades sought to play a more permanent role in Gulf regional security. While the unresolved conflict with Iraq provides the immediate justification, the need for a substantial American force presence in the Gulf transcends the issue of the regime of Saddam Hussein."[31]

It is hardly surprising that President George W. Bush and his administration manipulated data suggesting that Saddam Hussein had atomic weapons and links to al-Qaeda. And they did it with such success that when the United States invaded Iraq in 2003 almost half of the American public believed that Saddam had played a role in the 9/11 attacks on New York and Washington. The hegemony strategy practically forces even American leaders with the best of intentions to pretend that reassurance wars against minor and limited threats, whose genuine purpose is to reinforce American military hegemony and reassure American client states in the Middle East, Asia, or Europe, as the case may be, are in fact motivated by clear and present dangers to the American people.

In 2000, before joining the administration of George W. Bush, Wolfowitz defended the earlier Gulf War, claiming that "we will never know what might have happened if Saddam Hussein's occupation of Kuwait had not been reversed: Would he, as seems entirely probable, have brought the governments of the Arabian peninsula under his control and, with the wealth that provided, built up his arsenal of conventional and nuclear weapons in preparation for a much bigger war with Iran or Israel? If so, then what President Bush achieved was much more than just the liberation of Kuwait . . . "[32] According to Wolfowitz, who had been a high-ranking Defense Department official during the Gulf War, the United States had been right to sacrifice American lives to contain Saddam in order to avert the need of "Iran or Israel" to sacrifice the lives of their own soldiers and citizens in their own defense. At the time of the Gulf War, however, the American public was not told that its purpose was to protect Iran or Israel.

A Defense Strategy That Cannot Be
Defended in Public

The three elements of the U.S. global hegemony strategy, the policies of dissuasion, reassurance, and nonproliferation, share two characteristics in common. First, all three are essential to the success of the project of establishing and maintaining U.S. global hegemony on the basis of enduring U.S. hegemony in the Middle East, Asia, and Europe as well as North America. Second, none of these three policies can be explained honestly to the American people.

Consider the policy of dissuasion, which requires the United States to monopolize as much of the world's military power as it can, in order to deter other great powers from challenging U.S. hegemony in their regions or the world. Given the premises of the hegemony strategy, the policy of dissuasion is perfectly logical. But its purpose is to seek to forestall a remote and speculative danger that may not ever occur, not to respond to a clear and present danger. American voters would probably reject a policy with such high costs and such speculative benefits, in favor of other uses for their tax dollars. Consequently proponents of the hegemony strategy tend to justify high levels of U.S. defense spending by grossly exaggerating the potential danger that might be posed in the near future by other countries, not only great powers like China but also lesser powers like Iran and North Korea.

Reassurance is another policy essential for the success of the U.S. hegemony strategy whose actual strategic rationale must be concealed from the American public. American leaders cannot tell the voters that the United States must risk war with North Korea in order to "reassure" Japan that it does not need to acquire its own nuclear deterrent and exercise more military and diplomatic independence from its American protector. Therefore the American public is told that North Korea might give nuclear weapons to al-Qaeda to blow up American cities, or that North Korean missiles endanger California.

Coercive nonproliferation by means including preventive war is yet another essential component of the hegemony strategy that American policymakers are unwilling to discuss and defend candidly in public. The main reason for the nonproliferation policy, although not the only one, is to maintain the ability of the U.S. military to invade weak countries at low cost in America's regional spheres of influence, particularly the relatively new U.S. sphere of influence in the Persian Gulf. This rationale would be difficult to sell to American voters. For this reason the possible but highly improbable threat that "rogue states" might equip al-Qaeda or other terrorist groups with weapons of mass destruction, or allow them to be stolen, is presented in public as the chief if not the only rationale for U.S. nonproliferation policy as applied to North Korea, Saddam's Iraq, and Iran, even if the actual motive of those regimes for acquiring weapons of mass destruction has not been to attack the United States or its allies but rather to deter the United States, the local hegemon, from attacking or invading them.

The ultimate purpose of the U.S. hegemony strategy is to make America safe by forestalling the possible emergence of major dangers in the remote future. This is a laudable goal. But support by the American people for the hegemony strategy cannot be generated unless its proponents exaggerate limited threats and treat possible long-term threats as immediate dangers.

"You have to scare hell out of the American people," Senator Arthur Vandenberg is said to have told President Harry Truman early in the Cold War.[33] American leaders have sometimes exaggerated threats or concealed their true objectives, in the service of U.S. grand strategy. But even when the public in earlier eras was deceived about the details of earlier American grand strategies, it understood the strategies themselves, from the strategy to defeat Germany and Japan to the strategy to contain the Soviet Union. That is not the case with respect to the hegemony strategy. "The U.S. national security elite (Democratic and Republican) did, however, settle on a policy of hegemony sometime in the late 1990s," the political scientist Barry R. Posen has observed. "The people of the United States did not play a significant role in this decision, so questions remained about how much they would pay to support this policy."[34]

The U.S. hegemony strategy is the first grand strategy in American history that cannot be explained to the American public for fear that they might not support it. Some champions of the U.S. hegemony strategy are candid enough to admit this. In his book *The Case for Goliath: How America Acts as the World's Government in the 21st Century*, Michael Mandelbaum concedes that the case for U.S. global hegemony might not "persuade the American public, which might well reject the proposition that it should pay for providing the world with government services. American citizens see their country's foreign policy as a series of discrete measures designed to safeguard the interests, above all the supreme interest of physical security, of the United States itself. They have never been asked to ratify their country's status as the principal supplier of international public goods, and if they were asked explicitly to do so, they would undoubtedly ask in turn whether the United States ought to contribute as much to providing them, and other countries as little, as was the case in the first decade of the twenty-first century." Speaking perhaps for many in the U.S. foreign policy establishment, Mandelbaum concludes that it may be necessary to keep the American public in the dark because "the American role in the world may depend in part on Americans not scrutinizing it too closely."[35] In the same cynical spirit, the neoconservative defense analyst Eliot Cohen writes: "The United States needs an imperial strategy. Defense planners could never admit it openly, of course . . . "[36] Yet another neoconservative, Thomas Donnelly, writes of a global strategy allying the United States with Britain, Japan, and India against the other great powers as "the de facto plan of the Bush administration, though officials dare not speak its name."[37]

Nothing could be more repugnant to America's traditions as a democratic republic than a grand strategy that can be sustained only if the very existence of the strategy is kept secret from the American people by their elected and appointed leaders.

Beyond American Hegemony

The three elements of the U.S. hegemony strategy—dissuasion, reassurance, and coercive nonproliferation carried out by means of preventive wars like the war in Iraq—are so costly that they are incompatible with the American way of life. The attempt to ensure that the United States will outspend all other great powers combined in the military realm threatens America's civilian economy in the long run. At the same time, the need to maintain unchallenged U.S. hegemony in other regions by waging regular small wars against minor "rogue states" to reassure local U.S. allies and client states or forestall the proliferation of dangerous weapons probably cannot succeed without the reinstatement of a draft. The hegemony strategy undermines the U.S. constitutional system by putting the United States on a more or less permanent wartime footing, making presidents of both parties virtual dictators. Worst of all, the hegemony strategy is so potentially unpopular that its supporters are compelled to exaggerate or even invent foreign threats in order to justify wars in the service of American hegemony to the American public.

As the symbol of the United States in its pursuit of global hegemony, the bald eagle is less appropriate than the rooster, jealously guarding its preeminence in the barnyard pecking order. The quest for American hegemony is a bad strategy. But its architects and apologists are not bad people. American policymakers and supporters of the U.S. hegemony strategy in the 1990s and 2000s have not been honest with the U.S. public about the larger purposes of American foreign policy. But for the most part they have not had sinister or venal motives. Most if not all have sincerely believed that the United States and the world would be better off if the United States permanently subordinated China, Japan, Russia, and Germany and dominated the oil-producing countries of the Middle East. They have believed that the hegemony strategy is the most prudent and effective way to defend the American way of life. Their analysis can be questioned, but their motives have been honorable.

Good intentions, though, are no excuse for failures of statecraft. What Talleyrand said of Napoleon's execution of a political enemy, the Duc d'Enghien, can be said with equal justice of the hegemony strategy that has provided the basis of U.S. foreign policy since the Gulf War in 1991: "It is worse than a crime. It is a mistake."

Chapter 10

A Concert of Power

> There must be, not a balance of power, but a community
> of power; not organized rivalries, but an organized com-
> mon peace.
>
> —Woodrow Wilson[1]

THE GOAL OF AMERICA'S POST–COLD WAR HEGEMONY STRATEGY has been
legitimate—preventing a hostile power from dominating Europe, Asia, or
the Middle East by intimidation or conquest. While the goal is legitimate,
the cost of the attempt to establish permanent U.S. hegemony in taxes and the
lives of American soldiers is too high.

Even if it were affordable, the plan to establish perpetual U.S. global hegemony would be incompatible with the American way of life. A sounder grand
strategy for the United States in the twenty-first century must be found.

Is Isolationism the Answer?

Like proponents of other strategies, most American isolationists favor U.S.
hegemony in North America. However, for isolationists U.S. hegemony in
the North American quarter-sphere is the beginning and end of American
strategy, not the basis of a policy of U.S. intervention in power politics
beyond North America. An isolationist America would foreswear the use
of force and diplomacy to influence geopolitical outcomes in other parts of
the world.

As we have seen, by the early twentieth century the application of the
industrial revolution to warfare, and particularly the development of
airpower, greatly devalued the security provided to the United States by the
oceans and its remoteness from other great powers. In an age of airpower
and space weapons, any advanced technological power can threaten the

homeland of any other country anywhere on the globe. In the twentieth century, consistent American isolationism probably would have resulted in the domination of the world beyond the Western Hemisphere by a militaristic regime centered in Berlin or Moscow. The capitals of potential global hegemons may be different in the twenty-first century, but the threat they would pose to America's independence and way of life would be the same.

In the future as in the past U.S. security costs will be lowest—and the American way of life will be safest—if no hostile hegemonic power uses its domination of the countries of Asia, Europe, or the Middle East in order to mobilize their human, industrial, or energy resources for military purposes. To dominate any of these crucial regions, an aggressive power need not engage in a campaign of conquest. It might create an "empire of intimidation," using its military power to pressure its neighbors into appeasement and to gain access to their resources through coerced trade agreements that would really be extorted payments of tribute. The United States would then have to choose between appeasing the regional hegemon or building up its arms in self-defense, at the expense of the civilian economy and perhaps civil liberties in the United States. An Asian hegemon would be particularly threatening, in light of Asia's superior industrial resources.

Isolationism, then, should be rejected as a grand strategy for the United States. Preventing the rise of hostile superpowers in Asia, Europe, and the Middle East must remain the major goal of U.S. policy. Without attempting to establish and maintain U.S. global hegemony, the United States can pursue this vitally important objective by means of two alternate strategies from the toolkit of realist power politics: a balance of power and a concert of power.

The United States as Offshore Balancer

One alternative to both hegemony and isolationism is a balance of power strategy for the United States. The political scientist Stephen M. Walt describes America's "traditional role as an 'offshore balancer.'" This strategy assumes that only countries in a few parts of the world are of strategic importance to the United States, such as the industrial nations of Europe and Asia and the oil-producing countries of the Persian Gulf and Central Asia. Instead of controlling these areas directly, the United States would rely on local actors to maintain the regional balance of power. The United States would still stand ready to deploy its power against specific threats to its interests, but it would intervene only when absolutely necessary—when the local balance broke down and vital U.S. interests were clearly threatened by hostile forces."[2]

At the beginning of the twentieth century, Theodore Roosevelt declared: "In fact we are becoming, owing to our strength and geopolitical situation, more and more the balance of power of the whole globe."[3] By this he meant that the United States was now capable of "holding the balance" in different regions and the world as a whole. Like Britain, which had traditionally intervened selectively to maintain a balance of power in a divided Europe, without attempting to conquer Europe itself, the United States would be an unbalanced balancer, a country that can check other powers without being checked itself. To put it another way, the offshore-balancer strategy is a managed balance of power strategy, rather than a pure balance of power system, in which the United States, instead of holding the balance, would be merely one of several powers restrained by shifting coalitions of the others.

The hegemony strategy requires the United States to extend unilateral protection over as many states as possible, with the United States volunteering to provide for their security needs. The offshore-balancer strategy counsels the opposite. Other states should defend themselves, with the United States only intervening if they need reinforcement. As an offshore balancer, the United States would prefer strong, militarily self-reliant allies to demilitarized protectorates whose weakness requires the United States to pay most of the costs of defending them from their enemies.

Both the hegemony strategy and the offshore-balancer strategy seek to maximize U.S. security. But they pursue this goal by different means. The hegemony strategy seeks to maximize U.S. security by maximizing America's share of world power. The offshore-balancer strategy seeks to maximize U.S. security by using alliances to limit a hostile potential hegemon's share of world power. Each strategy, if successful, would lower the security costs of the United States and thereby protect the American way of life from excessive militarization. But the hegemony strategy, in which the United States alone bears the burden of deterring or defeating a hostile great power, is far more expensive than the offshore-balancer strategy, in which the burden of deterring or defeating a hostile great power is shared among the members of a great power alliance to which the United States belongs. The combined power of an anti-hegemonic alliance must be greater than that of the potential hegemon, but the power of each of its individual members, including the United States, need not be.

Offshore Balancing: Pros and Cons

The offshore-balancer strategy makes more sense than a strategy of perpetual U.S. hegemony in Asia, the Middle East, and Europe. However, the offshore-balancer strategy arguably suffers from two flaws.

The first is that according to most versions of offshore balancing the United States would intervene in a region only after the local balance of power had broken down. The problem is that the very absence of American participation in regional power politics might hasten the breakdown of local balances. This was the case in Europe between the world wars. When the United States refused to guarantee the security of France in the 1920s, Britain also refused, for fear of having to confront Germany on its own in the future. In the 1930s, as German power grew, instead of balancing against Hitler many European countries appeased him or even joined him, including the Soviet Union at the time of the Hitler-Stalin pact. If these countries had been certain of American support, they might have balanced against Hitler instead. Balance of power coalitions tend to require an "anchor" power strong enough to convince other states that by joining the coalition they are joining the winning side. The United States could not act as such an anchor power, rallying local states against a local threat, if it stayed out of regional power politics until the moment of maximum danger.

The second defect of the offshore-balancer strategy is diplomatic, rather than military. It is a purely negative strategy. Between crises, the United States would not play a constructive role in shaping the security environment in key regions that affect U.S. security. It is in America's interest, however, to have a place at the Asian table, the Middle Eastern table, and the European table. To use a different metaphor, it is better for Uncle Sam to keep the door half open, and to keep one foot in the door, than to have to knock down a locked door in an emergency.

The offshore balancer strategy is a better plan for the United States than the strategy of unilateral U.S. global hegemony. As a strategy to be followed when a more positive plan fails, offshore balancing has much to recommend it. But it should be Plan B. A far better Plan A is provided by a strategy based on a concert of power.

Some Definite Concert of Power

In his address to the U.S. Senate of January 22, 1917, President Woodrow Wilson announced the concert of power strategy that would replace America's earlier grand strategy of non-entanglement: "In every discussion of peace that must end this war, it is taken for granted that the peace must be followed by some definite concert of power which will make it virtually impossible that any such catastrophe should ever overwhelm us again."[4] More than a decade earlier in his 1905 annual address to Congress, Theodore Roosevelt had endorsed the idea of a concert of power: "Our aim should be from time to time to take such steps as may be possible toward creating something like an organization of the civilized nations, because as the world becomes more highly organized the need for navies and armies will diminish."[5]

A concert is an alliance without a permanent enemy. The members of a concert may take action against one or more states, but the defeat or deterrence of a particular country does not provide the reason for the concert. One important purpose of a concert is to coordinate the action of several great powers in order to minimize the possibility that independent action will bring them into conflict with one another. No coalition, of course, can survive deep conflicts of interest, value, or ambition among states. But a concert of power can minimize avoidable conflicts.

The concert of power strategy also holds out hope that the relative decline of American power in the future need not reduce American security. As other great powers increase their wealth and military might, America's share of world power inevitably will shrink. But the United States need not be less safe or less prosperous, as long as the rising powers share its commitment to the liberal international system. As G. John Ikenberry and Charles A. Kupchan have written, the United States should move "with—rather than against—the secular diffusion of global power. The scope of American primacy will wane as this century progresses; the ultimate objective should be to channel rising centers of power into cooperative partnerships with the United States."[6] The United States may be eclipsed by a greater power or powers one day, in the same way that Britain was eclipsed by the United States in the twentieth century. But as in the case of Britain and the United States, the transition could be peaceful and consensual rather than violent and bitter—the passing on of a torch, rather than the wrestling away of a scepter.

The Concert of Power as Shared Hegemony

A concert of power system can be thought of as a kind of hegemony shared among a number of great powers. This being the case, the strategic imperatives of the concert strategy are identical with those of the hegemony strategy, with the difference that these imperatives must guide the policy of a group of great powers working together rather than by a single great power like the United States acting alone.

No less than a single hegemonic nation, a great power concert must pursue the three policies of dissuasion, reassurance, and nonproliferation. The combined military power of the concert's great power members must be overwhelming enough to dissuade any country or group of countries from challenging the concert's authority. The great-power cartel must reassure lesser states that their legitimate security needs will be provided for, permitting them to disarm and concentrate on trade and the welfare of their citizens. Finally, preventing the proliferation of advanced weapons among lesser states is an imperative for a great power concert seeking to preserve its ability to police a region or the world. A great power combination as well as a solitary hegemon must be able to intervene against threatening minor states at minimal cost.

It is difficult if not impossible for the United States, without bankrupting itself and sacrificing too much of the liberty of American citizens, to carry out the hegemonic strategy by means of the three policies of dissuasion, reassurance, and coercive nonproliferation. But all three policies might far more easily be accomplished by a concert or concerts of great powers that already monopolize most of the world's wealth and military power among themselves.

Can a Great Power Concert Be Sustained?

The most powerful objection to the concert of power strategy may be the argument that it is unrealistic to assume that agreement on a common policy among two or more great powers can be maintained for any considerable length of time.

At first glance, history seems to support this objection. For example, the Concert of Europe, which had managed to moderate intra-European disputes and avert a general European war, collapsed in 1914. And the wartime alliance of the United States, Britain, and the Soviet Union broke down after World War II, instead of being converted into a peacetime concert.

However, in each case, as we have seen, the unprovoked aggression of one great power—Imperial Germany in 1914 and the Soviet Union in the late 1940s—doomed the possibility of concert. If an aggressive great power seeks to attack or intimidate one or more of the others, no concert of power is possible, and an alliance of the threatened powers is necessary to restrain the aggressor.

It is a mistake, then, to argue from the history of the twentieth century that great power concerts are doomed to collapse into dissension. Under different leaders or different regimes, Germany might have continued to be a constructive member of the Concert of Europe, and the Soviet Union might have joined the United States and Britain after 1945 in a global concert to keep the peace.

The Concert of Power: Franklin Roosevelt Versus Woodrow Wilson

Woodrow Wilson identified the idea of a concert of power with the idea of collective security, a system in which all nations in the world, powerful and weak, would unite to punish any aggression by any country anywhere. More realistic American statesmen like Theodore Roosevelt and Henry Cabot Lodge put their hopes for order in a concert of a small number of great powers, chiefly the United States and Britain. In his 1910 Nobel Prize Lecture, Theodore Roosevelt said that "it would be a masterstroke if those great powers honestly bent on peace would form a League of Peace, not only to keep the peace among themselves, but to prevent, by force if necessary, its being broken by others."[7]

Franklin Roosevelt, who had been assistant secretary of the navy under Wilson, was more of a realist like his cousin Theodore Roosevelt than an orthodox Wilsonian. Franklin Roosevelt scoffed at the Briand-Kellogg Pact of 1928 that purported to outlaw war, on the grounds that "war cannot be outlawed by resolution alone."[8] In his mature thinking about the subject, Roosevelt wanted the concert to be restricted to a handful of great powers, and was attracted to the idea of basing global security on regional organizations rather than a universal organization.

According to Wilson, "The equality of nations upon which peace must be founded if it is to last must be an equality of rights; the guarantees exchanged must neither recognize nor imply a difference between big nations and small, between those that are powerful and those that are weak. Right must be based upon the common strength, not upon the individual strength, of the nations upon whose concert peace will depend." Roosevelt repudiated this aspect of Wilson's thought. His idea of great power policing assumed what Wilson called "a difference between big nations and small, between those that are powerful and those that are weak." In Roosevelt's vision, following World War II the United States, Britain, and the Soviet Union, along with Nationalist China, would try to monopolize global military power; small nations would be disarmed. Unlike Wilson, FDR believed that "right" should rest "upon the individual strength, of the nations upon whose concert peace will depend" not upon the "common strength" of all of the nations of the world. The smaller the number of great powers entrusted with policing the world, the easier it would be to get things done, in Roosevelt's view.

By the late 1930s, witnessing the rise of Nazi Germany, Fascist Italy, and Imperial Japan, Roosevelt was putting his hopes in an Anglo-American alliance. He added the Soviet Union and Nationalist China to Britain and the United States to make the "Big Four," which he hoped would police the postwar world. Roosevelt acknowledged that "ostensible" participation for smaller nations might be permitted, to disguise the reality of a great power directorate.[9] The hierarchy of power was illustrated on January 1, 1942, when the United States, Britain, the Soviet Union, and China signed the Declaration of United Nations; the other 22 members of the alliance were not permitted to sign it until the next day.[10]

Roosevelt and Regionalism

The concert of power strategy does not require a single global great power concert. It might be carried out by regional concerts containing different great powers in different combinations.

In his initial thinking about the scope of a future world organization as well as in his substitution of a great power concert for collective security, Franklin Roosevelt broke with Wilsonian orthodoxy. Like his aide Sumner Welles, Roosevelt looked favorably on the idea of a world organization based on regional communities like the Pan-American Union (later the Organization of American States), as an alternative to a global organization of individual states like the League of Nations. When Roosevelt met Churchill in August 1941, three months before the Japanese attack brought the United States into World War II, the president rejected the British suggestion that a plan for a postwar international organization be included in the joint British-American declaration of shared foreign policy goals known as the Atlantic Charter. Roosevelt said that the United States and Britain should act together to police the world for several years after the war ended before considering a new version of the League of Nations.[11] Following the attack on Pearl Harbor and the U.S. entry into the war, Roosevelt privately began referring to the United States, Britain, the Soviet Union, and China as the "Four Policemen" that would be responsible for keeping peace in the world once the Axis alliance had been defeated.[12]

While Winston Churchill resisted Roosevelt's demand for the postwar dissolution of the British Empire, he agreed with Roosevelt about making regional security associations the basis of world order. During a visit to Washington in May 1943, Churchill proposed a Supreme World Council dominated by the great powers that would oversee three regional councils for Europe, the Pacific, and the Western Hemisphere. According to Churchill, the League of Nations had failed because its basis was global, rather than regional. The proponents of the League had failed to understand that "only the countries whose interests were directly affected by a dispute . . . could be expected to apply themselves with sufficient rigor to secure a settlement."[13] Small nations, Churchill argued, should form confederations for their own security.

As the U.S. State Department under Secretary of State Cordell Hull, a devout Wilsonian, worked on planning what became the UN, the distinctively Rooseveltian features were edited out with each draft. For example, in 1943 at the Allied summit meeting in Tehran, FDR described his latest vision of international organization: an assembly to which all states belonged, an executive committee of around ten members made up of the Big Four plus two representatives of Europe, and one representative apiece of

Latin America, the Middle East, the Far East, and the British dominions, which would deal with nonmilitary subjects, and, as a distinct group, "The Four Policemen" who would deal with all military matters. But on December 29, 1943, Hull sent the president an Outline Plan with a General Assembly, a Security Council, a Secretariat and an International Court of Justice.[14] In essence, this was nothing more than the League of Nations reborn. There was no trace of Roosevelt's suggestion that the great power concert and the executive committee be two distinct entities. Gone, too, was Roosevelt's plan for representation of regional groups in the UN.

Unhealthy and distracted by greater priorities, Roosevelt permitted the dilution of his original vision. During the Dumbarton Oaks Conference of 1944, he agreed to the British suggestion that France be included on the Security Council, while suggesting that Brazil too should have a permanent seat.[15] The final missed opportunity came when the United States reluctantly agreed to give all five permanent members of the Security Council a veto. Ironically, in his 1923 essay for the American Peace Award in which he proposed a Society of Nations to replace the League of Nations, Roosevelt had criticized the idea of unanimity: "Common sense cannot defend a procedure by which one or two recalcitrant nations could block the will of the great majority."[16]

It was a tragedy that Wilsonian utopians, with their insistence on a universalist world organization, prevailed in the design of the post–1945 security system. The initial plans of FDR and Churchill for a concert of Europe, a concert of Asia, and a concert of the Americas overseen by a few great powers made far more sense than the UN organization, which, in its final form, had all of the design defects of the original League of Nations. Even the Security Council, which is often described as an innovation, in its final form was an almost exact replica of the Council of the League of Nations, right down to the division between permanent and nonpermanent members. The permanent members of the League Council originally were Britain, France, Italy, and Japan; Germany and the Soviet Union later briefly became permanent council members.

The UN Security Council: Flawed by Design

Soviet intransigence paralyzed the Security Council for most of the Cold war. Following the Cold War, the Security Council functioned as intended when it authorized the Gulf War, a policy on which all five of the permanent members agreed. However, the United States was unable to win Security Council endorsement for the Kosovo War of 1999 or the Iraq War of 2003 and proceeded to wage each war without UN backing.

Any attempt to institutionalize a concert of great powers in a formal organization like the UN Security Council is destined to fail. The world is too fluid. The relative power of particular countries is always changing, as a result of different rates of economic growth and population growth as well as changing political systems and foreign policies. If the great power concert is institutionalized, then fading great powers will cling to their institutional position, while resisting the admission of new, rising great powers. The UN Security Council, dominated by the victors of World War II, and excluding contemporary great powers like Japan and Germany and India, illustrates this problem. Even if the UN Charter were amended to admit new great powers as permanent members of the Security Council, the roster would probably be obsolete by the time the process of amendment was complete.

The unrealistic idea of a formal, institutionalized great power concert ought to be abandoned in favor of an informal, consultative concert whose membership can change over time. The American legal scholar and strategic theorist Philip Bobbitt has proposed that the Group of Eight leading industrial nations (G-8) would be a good model for a new great power concert.[17] A precedent for this can be found in Russia's request to make the G-8 the forum for negotiations to end the 1999 war in Kosovo.[18]

The G-8 system is based on informal summit meetings among heads of state. In that sense, it resembles the system of summit meetings among the Allies during World War II. And the G-8 summit is held in a different part of the world each time. That echoes FDR's early suggestion that the UN, instead of being located in a single city, should hold meetings in different places.

The informal global concert of power might include the United States, Britain, Germany, France, Russia, China, India, and Japan, and, perhaps, one or more powers from other regions. Over time, the informal great power concert might eclipse the UN Security Council in importance. The UN, flawed from its inception, might be allowed to fade away in the manner of the League of Nations, which continued to function for a while after the establishment of the UN before it finally shut its doors. Like the Palais des

Nations of the League of Nations in Geneva, the UN building in New York might stand as a symbol of a fundamentally flawed approach to global governance.

The Case for Regionalism

Like his preference for an informal great power concert, Franklin Roosevelt's ideas about regional security arrangements deserve to be revisited. The wisdom of the emphasis that Roosevelt and Churchill put on regionalism in their early thinking about postwar world order has been confirmed by history since 1945. The least successful international organizations, in both the military and economic arenas, have been global organizations that are universal in both their membership and their scope, like the United Nations and the World Trade Organization. The most successful military and economic institutions have been regional organizations like NATO and the European Union.

The reason is obvious. It is much easier for small groups of nations that share common goals and common values to agree on policies of defense or economic integration than it is for the nearly two hundred sovereign states in the world to find common ground. Regional groups can proceed quickly toward common security or economic policies, while attempts to do so on the global level tend to be stalled.

The challenges of diplomacy rise exponentially as the number of states in an organization increases. If each state has an embassy in every other state, the total number of embassies equals $n(n-1)$, where n is the number of states in the system. As of this writing, there are 191 states in the United Nations, so that 36,290 embassies would be necessary if each state were represented in every other state. Many poor states, however, cannot afford full diplomatic representation in every other world capital. At far less expense, the states of a region can negotiate with each other in common regional forums.[19]

In recent decades, regional trade blocs have proliferated. Among these are the EU, ASEAN, NAFTA, APEC, Asean Plus Three (APT). These loose and informal forums for trade negotiations, with minimal bureaucracies and regular summit meetings among heads of state or government, should be the model for regional security concerts, just as the G-8 summits should be the model for regular summits among the members of an informal global great power concert.

American strategists have always opposed malign regionalism in the form of rival empires and closed trading blocs. But the maintenance of a liberal international system is compatible with benign regionalism, in the form of local security concerts and regional economic blocs like the EU and NAFTA that are relatively open to foreign investment and trade. Most disputes over national security, trade, immigration, and pollution occur among neighbors and are best resolved at the regional level. Global institutions should supplement and reinforce regional security and economic arrangements, not serve as substitutes for them.

An Alliance of Democracies?

It is sometimes suggested that the membership of a peacekeeping concert of power be limited to democracies. This suggestion finds a precedent in the thinking of Woodrow Wilson, who argued that when the short-lived Russian parliamentary government replaced the tsarist regime, Russia became a "fit partner in a league of honor" that united democracies against autocratic Germany and its allies. According to Wilson: "A steadfast concert for peace can never be maintained except by a partnership of democratic nations."[20] However, the Council of the League of Nations that Wilson later championed included autocratic great powers like Japan, Italy, and the Soviet Union as permanent members. And as we have seen, the United States could not have won in World War II or established the United Nations without the cooperation of the Soviet Union, Nationalist China, and other dictatorships.

If the great power club is to be limited to democracies, a problem of definition arises. What exactly is a democracy? Democracy comes in illiberal as well as liberal varieties.[21] Is an Islamic republic a democracy? What about a country in which a freely elected president wields virtually absolute power? Or an Arab monarchy that is partly parliamentary and partly despotic? Or a country in which a majority ethnic group, by free and fair elections, monopolizes political power at the expense of ethnic minorities?

At what point does democracy give way to dictatorship? In the case of a military coup the discontinuity is obvious. But India's Prime Minister Indira Gandhi declared a martial-law regime in the 1970s. If there had been a league of democracies, should India have been expelled? Greece and Turkey experienced transitions from civilian to military rule and back in the second half of the twentieth century. They maintained their membership in the NATO alliance.

Today all of the great powers, including Russia and India, are at least imperfectly democratic except for China, which has abandoned communist radicalism but continues to be ruled by an authoritarian Communist Party. An alliance of democracies today would be interpreted not just as an alliance without China but also as an alliance against China. While this might appeal to some "China hawks" in the United States, it is in the interest neither of the United States nor of the other great powers to treat a rising China as an international pariah state.

The purpose of a great power concert is not to produce liberty, democracy, and the rule of law in every country, but to provide every country with the shared public good of peace and basic order, so that the need to prepare for war does not impair the ability of particular nations to establish liberty, democracy, and the rule of law by their own efforts inside their own borders. As long as it refrains from aggression, including the internal aggression of genocide and ethnic cleansing, and abides by the norms of liberal internationalism in its relations with other countries, a nondemocratic great power can be a legitimate member of an international league to keep the peace.

The Challenges for Regional Concerts

What would regional concerts do? As long as they are not engaged in rivalries with one another, the great powers can find ample challenges in coping with threats to regional and global security.

International terrorism is one. Terrorism is a tactic, not a strategy, and is employed by different groups with different purposes. But terrorism of any kind is a threat to civilization. No cause, no matter how just, can ever justify the deliberate targeting and killing of civilians. The great powers should collaborate to eliminate terrorism in the twenty-first century in the way that the international slave trade and the barbaric custom of waging wars against countries that default on international debts have been abolished.

Another priority of great power concerts should be preventing the proliferation of weapons of mass destruction, preferably by means of diplomatic sanctions rather than preventive war. Doing so effectively would not only make the world safer but also preserve the gap in military capability between the members of a concert and states in regions that they police. Nor should the focus of great power concerts be on nuclear, chemical, and biological weapons alone. The reduction of conventional arms should be a goal of great power cooperation as well. It is folly for great powers, in the pursuit of short-term diplomatic influence or minor commercial gain, to compete with one another to sell military technology of any kind to poor countries. Those weapons might be turned on soldiers sent by members of a great power concert, if joint military interventions are necessary. And it is a crime for the governments of poor countries to invest their limited resources in sophisticated weapons rather than in public goods like education and infrastructure development. For the great powers to form an armaments cartel in the interest of promoting the negotiated disarmament of the majority of the world's countries would be as moral as it would be prudent.

Yet another challenge to cooperative great power governance is provided by campaigns for national self-determination. Most political violence is related to struggles of national independence movements.[22] Yugoslavia, Iraq, and the Soviet Union probably will not be the last multinational states to disintegrate along ethno-national lines. In some cases great power intervention may be necessary to restore a multinational state under a new constitution or to oversee the partition of a country into two or more new nation-states.

Many of today's national independence movements involve Muslim nations ruled by non-Muslim nations: the Palestinians, the Muslims of Kashmir, the Kurds, the Chechens, the Moros of the Philippines, the Uighurs of western China. Jihadists like Osama bin Laden have opportunistically exploited these legitimate Muslim national liberation struggles, but the struggles go back decades or even generations and have nothing in common with each other. Given the number of great powers that are participants in these struggles, including Russia, India, China, and the United States, as the patron of Israel, progress is impossible unless these and other great powers play an enlightened and constructive role. A strategy of resolving Muslim struggles for self-determination should be a supplement to the campaign to destroy jihadist networks and their members using policing, intelligence, and military means, not a substitute for that campaign.

Another challenge that might best be met by great power collaboration is the problem of failed states. The primary way that the liberal international system solves the problem of global policing is not by creating a

global police authority but rather by requiring each sovereign state to police its own territory and population, enforcing international law by means
of its internal police forces and courts. But what if a government is so weak
that its police and armed forces lack the power to enforce both domestic
and international law? In that case, it is a "failed state," a government that
exists in name only in an anarchic territory.

Osama bin Laden's use of Sudan and Afghanistan, failed states with
weak Islamist regimes, as territorial bases for the al-Qaeda movement illustrates one danger that failed states can cause. In addition to hosting terrorist groups, failed states can be sources of crime, waves of refugees spilling
across borders, epidemics, and pollution. Groups of great powers may need
to intervene in failed states to provide temporary governance until effective
local governments can be established. The legitimacy of such interventions
will be highest if several great powers take part, so that the intervention is
not viewed as disguised imperialism on the part of one power.

Great power concerts should also act to end genocide and ethnic cleansing. The prohibition of both crimes is an inescapable implication of the
logic of liberal internationalism. It would make no sense to promote national self-determination, if entire nations could be annihilated or displaced
with impunity. The norms of the society of states should protect an entire
people from murder or exile, and only the great powers have the ability to
enforce those norms.

The challenges of energy policy and the environmental protection cannot effectively be addressed without great power collaboration. Competition by great powers to control diminishing energy resources would be as
dangerous and destructive as refusal to cooperate to reduce carbon-dioxide
emissions and other forms of industrial pollution. Because they consume
most of the world's energy and produce most of the world's pollution, the
United States and a handful of other great powers have the ability to come
up with workable solutions by agreeing on common policies among themselves, even in the absence of participation or agreement by the majority of
countries in the world.

A concert of power strategy, then, is not an excuse for U.S. withdrawal
or isolation. On the contrary, it is a formula for continued U.S. involvement in efforts beyond America's borders to make the world a safer and
better place.

A Community of Power

A concert of power strategy serves American interests better than either an offshore-balancer strategy or a strategy of U.S. global hegemony. As a participant in regional concerts, the United States can play a constructive peacetime role between crises. And, in the event that a hostile power seeks regional hegemony, the other members of the concert could rally around the United States to form an anti-hegemonic alliance, something they might hesitate to do without the certainty of U.S. participation.

A concert of power strategy on the part of the United States is thus far from utopian. By promoting regional concerts, the United States can maintain its influence in strategically important regions outside of North America, without risking a backlash by trying to impose unilateral American hegemony on all three.[23]

Unlike the policy of unilateral U.S. hegemony, the concert of power strategy is compatible with the American way of life. It does not require the United States to outspend all other great powers; rather, the United States can save money by pooling its defense resources with the other great powers in the hegemonic concert. As long as the great power cartel as a whole is stronger than any potential challenger, it is not necessary for the United States by itself to be stronger than any potential challenger.

Furthermore, the concert strategy, unlike the hegemony strategy, does not require the United States to assume the sole responsibility of policing the neighborhoods of all of the other great powers in the world while they watch from the sidelines. The United States can take part in efforts to police Europe and Asia and the Middle East, when necessary. But U.S. security does not require the United States to wage wars like the Kosovo War and the Iraq War, which were almost entirely American efforts, camouflaged by the nominal participation of a few allies.

The hegemony strategy is based on the fear that if the leading European and Asian countries are strong enough to defend themselves against minor threats in their own neighborhoods, they will be so powerful that they threaten the United States. But from the time that it was first proposed in the 1992 draft Defense Planning Guidance, this premise has never been plausible. The idea that the United States can never be safe, unless every other great power is weak and dependent on the United States in its own region, is absurd. As long as other great powers are allied with the United

States in regional concerts, it is in America's interest to encourage their strength, not to encourage their weakness.

If it adopted the concert of power strategy, the United States might need to join other great powers in joint military interventions outside of North America. But any such U.S. military actions as part of the concert strategy should be authorized specifically by Congress in advance. The United States stayed out of the League of Nations because of Wilson's insistence that the League be able to compel its members to go to war, and the United States joined the UN only because the Security Council has the power only to recommend, not command, the use of force by member states. The concert of power strategy should not be used as a new excuse for an imperial presidency to commit the United States to war without specific Congressional authorization in advance. The president of the United States is the commander in chief of the American armed forces, not the commander in chief of the American people.

Of the four grand strategies the United States might adopt—hegemony, isolation, offshore balancing, and a concert of power—the concert of power strategy is most likely to preserve American security at a minimal cost to the American way of life. Working together with the other great powers of the world would cost less in terms of American taxes, American lives, and American liberty than a misguided retreat into isolation or the doomed attempt to establish solitary U.S. world domination.

*

Chapter 11

American Strategy in the Asian Century

> Peace will prevail in international relations, just as order prevails within a nation, because of the righteous use of superior force—because the power which makes for pacific organization is stronger than the power which makes for a warlike organization.
>
> —Herbert Croly, 1909[1]

ADMIRAL AND EUNUCH ARE UNLIKELY SYNONYMS. But Cheng Ho was both. One of thousands of eunuchs trusted by the Ming Emperor Yung-Lo because he could have no ambitions for his children, Admiral Cheng Ho (1371–1435) led the Chinese Navy on seven expeditions to the "Western Oceans" between 1405 and 1433. His treasure ships, each five times the size of one of the Portuguese explorer Vasco da Gama's vessels, brought back tribute from lands along the Indian Ocean, the Red Sea, and the Persian Gulf.

But after 1433 the Chinese treasure fleets were seen no more. Focused on threats to China's land frontier, and hostile to commerce, the Chinese government outlawed trade and destroyed all records of Cheng Ho's voyages. Subsequently, China endured centuries of decline punctuated by foreign intervention and the deaths of tens of millions during upheavals led by the messianic leaders Hong Xiuquan, who led the bloody Taipeng Rebellion in the nineteenth century, and Mao Zedong, whose reign in communist mainland China from 1949 to 1976 produced the death by execution or famine of more than thirty million Chinese. Superior technology, some of it invented in China, permitted Western states to establish first their commercial dominance and then their military hegemony over China, India, and most of Asia.

As the twenty-first century began, high-quality manufactured goods from China began to flood foreign markets. Chinese diplomats and business executives appeared throughout the world, seeking to secure supplies of oil from the Middle East and Central Asia, food from Brazil, and copper from Canada. In 2003 China became the third country after the United States and the Soviet Union to send an astronaut into space. And China began to build a modern ocean-going fleet.

After an absence of nearly six hundred years, Cheng Ho had returned.

The Perils of Prophecy

U.S. strategy must be based on a sound understanding of present and future trends. Unfortunately, predicting the relative power and wealth of different states in the future can be hazardous. In the first half of the nineteenth century, many thinkers predicted that the power politics of the future would be dominated by the two continental states on the periphery of Europe, Russia and the United States. None foresaw the unification of the German-speaking peoples in 1870, which created a potential superpower whose ambitious rulers plunged the world into two world wars. Only after Germany was defeated and partitioned between the American and Soviet blocs did the nineteenth-century prophecy seem to come true. There may be such surprises in the future. Pan-Arabism and Pan-Turkism, like Pan-Germanism in the nineteenth century, could create new great powers, although these movements have failed in the past. Technological revolutions might dramatically enhance the military and economic power of small countries, if only until larger political units catch up.

Despite these uncertainties, it is possible to discuss power politics in the near and intermediate future with some confidence. The roster of great powers at any given time is small. Great power status is determined largely by a combination of economic development and population. These factors change over time, but they tend to change gradually, not suddenly. By examining economic growth and demographic change it is possible to identify the likely great powers of the future and their probable weight in the world.

The Demographic Revolution

Fertility rates around the world have been falling for some time. Between now and the end of the twenty-first century, the world's population, now more than six billion, is expected to grow to nine or ten billion before stabilizing and possibly declining. Almost all of this growth will take place in today's developing countries. In 1950, developing countries outnumbered today's developed countries by a ratio of two to one; by 2050, the same countries will outnumber today's developed countries by a ratio of seven to one.

In 2003 the medium fertility estimations of the UN suggested that in 2050 the most populous nations would be India (1.5 billion) and China (1.4 billion), followed by the United States (400 million), Pakistan (350 million), and Indonesia (300 million). Together India and China would account for roughly one-third of the human race. The United States, with an estimated population of 400 million, would have only one-quarter the population of either India or China.[2]

By 2010 the Chinese economy may be twice the size of that of Germany and it may surpass the world's second largest economy, that of Japan, by 2020.[3] The French International Relations Institute (IFRI) has predicted that by 2050 Greater China (China, Hong Kong, Macao, and Taiwan) will be the leading economic power, accounting for 24 percent of the world economy. Asia would account for one-half of world GDP and China for one-half of Asian GDP or one-quarter of the world total. Within Asia, the importance of Japan and Korea would decline. China would be followed by North America (the United States, Canada, and Mexico), with 23 percent of world GDP.

The U.S. investment bank Goldman Sachs reached similar conclusions, predicting that by 2050 China will have the largest economy in the world, followed by the United States and India. The next tier might be occupied by Russia, Brazil, and Japan, and a third tier would include Germany, Britain, and other once-mighty European economic powers.[4]

In 1500 A.D. Asia accounted for 65 percent of global GDP. But the percentage had dropped to only 18.5 percent by 1950. That percentage doubled in the second half of the twentieth century, during which Asia, particularly Japan and the capitalist "Little Tigers," grew far more rapidly than Europe and North America.[5] The political domination of the West over the rest of the world came to an end in the last century; Western economic domination will come to an end in this one.

Many of these projections are likely to be wrong, as a result of developments that cannot yet be foreseen. It is reasonable to predict, however, that the twenty-first century will be the Asian Century.

America's Share of Global Wealth and Power

The rise of Asian powers, however, need not mean the relative decline of the United States. America's potential share of global economic and military power has been pretty much the same for a century, and may remain pretty much the same for another century or more.

A country's GDP is a useful, though far from perfect, surrogate for its potential military power. According to the World Bank, in 2000 the United States accounted for 27 percent of the world's GDP. But this is nothing new. In 1913 the U.S. share was even larger at 31 percent and larger still earlier, in 1900 (38 percent). As the American political scientist Robert A. Pape points out, "For the past century, the U.S. share of gross world product was often double (or more) the share of any other state: 32 percent in 1913, 31 percent in 1938, 26 percent in 1960, 22 percent in 1980."[6] At the end of World War II, the United States accounted for around half of all world manufacturing—but that was nothing new. As early as 1929, the U.S. share of global manufacturing output was more than 43 percent.[7]

If the United States had decided to convert its economic potential into military power from the beginning, it would have been the dominant global power from the early 1900s onward. Americans deferred doing this as long as possible, in part for the excellent reason that the United States is a liberal, civilian society that prefers not to spend money on the military, and in part because in the two world wars Americans hoped that Britain and other countries could restrain Germany with U.S. aid short of direct U.S. intervention. Even in 1937, when Hitler's Germany spent 23.5 percent of its much smaller economy on the military, the United States dedicated only 1.5 percent of its own GDP to defense. The moment that the United States mobilized its gargantuan economy for war, Nazi Germany and Imperial Japan were doomed. Later, by devoting a relatively small part of its huge economy to defense, the United States was able to spend the far more militarized Soviet Union into bankruptcy.

What about the future? If the estimates of Goldman Sachs are right, then the NAFTA share of global GDP in 2050, at 23 percent, will be roughly what the U.S. share of the world total was seventy years earlier in 1980, when it was 22 percent. The relative size of the United States in the global economy, then, may prove to be astonishingly stable over the 150-year period from 1900 to 2050. Ironically, some neoconservatives tend to underestimate U.S. strength when they compare the United States to endangered Britain in the 1930s. Jihadists notwithstanding, the world is far safer today. But even if today's world were really that dangerous, the real comparison would not be with Britain in 1937 (relative war potential: 10.2 percent of the global total) but rather with the United States in 1937 (41.7 percent of the global total).

But supporters of U.S. hegemony should not take comfort in these statistics. A nation that over the long term is likely to account for about a quarter of world GDP probably cannot buy half of the world's military power for a prolonged period without over-militarizing its economy and risking the fate of the Soviet Union.

The Relative Decline of Europe

The rise of China and India, if it occurs as expected, need not mean the decline and fall of the United States. Instead, the rise to wealth and power of Asia will come at the expense of Europe, whose share of global population, wealth, and power will undergo a dramatic decline.

Europe, which accounted for 22 percent of the world's population in 1945 and 12 percent in 2000, may have only 6 percent in 2050. At that time Iran (105 million) may outnumber Russia (100 million), and Germany with only 79 million would be smaller than Yemen (84 million) as well as Turkey (97 million). According to UN estimates, Morocco, one-third the size of Spain in 1950, will have 60 percent more inhabitants than Spain in 2050. Africa will go from having 8 percent of the world total to Europe's 22 percent in 1945 to three times the number of people in Europe by 2050. The Russian Federation, which had three times the population of Pakistan in 1950, is projected to have only one-third the population of Pakistan in 2050. At that point Pakistan, if it continues to exist as an intact state, with 4 percent of the world's population will have more inhabitants than the United States, with only 3.9 percent.

One estimate projects absolute as well as relative population decline for many of today's European countries. Between now and 2050, without high levels of Immigration, Germany might shrink from 83 million to 79 million, Italy from 58 million to 51 million, and Russia from 143 million to 112 million—a population smaller than that of Japan in 2050.[8]

According to the U.S. Census Bureau, in 2050 the population of Europe would be 360 million, compared to 400 million in the United States (the middle projection) or 550 million (the high projection). Although the combined market of the European Union nations is larger than that of the United States today, by 2050 it will be surpassed by the internal U.S. market of the United States alone, even without counting 140 million Mexican consumers as part of a NAFTA market. Even now, with roughly the same population as the EU, the United States, by devoting 3 to 4 percent of its GDP to the military, spends twice as much on defense as the EU. If the United States continues to attract more immigrants with higher fertility than Europe, then in 2050 the median age in the United States might be 36.2 compared to 52.7 in Europe.[9]

The European share of the global economy may decline from 22 percent today, roughly comparable to that of the United States, to only 12 percent in 2050. According to one study, nothing but a radical and unlikely merger of Europe with its Mediterranean Muslim neighbors and Russia, along with a higher European birthrate, could avert Europe's precipitous decline in relative wealth and power.[10]

Preventing Hegemony in Asia

While they are similar to the United States in their continental scale, China and India differ from the United States in their poverty. Even when their economies are as large as that of the United States in absolute terms, per capita income in China and India will still be far below that of the United States and other developed nations including Japan and the leading countries of Western Europe.

But China and India do not need to match the American standard of living in order to match or surpass the United States in military spending. If China's per capita GDP matched that of contemporary South Korea, its overall GDP would be 1.35 times that of the United States, and if China's per capita GDP were one-half of modern Japan's, its total GDP would be 2.5 times the GDP of the United States.[11] Suppose that only one-tenth of India's estimated 1.5 billion people were to enjoy the per capita income of Americans, Japanese, or Europeans. That elite Indian minority would be the equivalent of a developed nation of 150 million people—a rich country bigger than Japan, embedded in a much larger, poorer country. If one-quarter of the Indian population enjoyed American living standards, that one-quarter might match the entire U.S. population in 2050. The affluent minority in China or India might provide a larger internal market and more scientists and engineers than the United States as a whole.

In the twenty-first century, most of the world's military and industrial might will be concentrated in greater Asia, which includes East and South Asia as well as Southeast Asia. In the long run, it is possible that congruence between population and power might produce a tripolar world centered on China, India, and the United States. In the relevant future, however, the international system will consist of a handful of great regional powers—China, Japan, India, Russia, Germany, France, and Britain, and perhaps others like Iran and Brazil—in addition to the United States, a power that differs from the others not only in the scale of its economic and military potential but also in its global reach.

Regional Concerts

If the United States were to adopt a concert of power strategy based on regional concerts, what might some of those regional concerts be?

The United States should turn NATO from a residual anti-Russian alliance into a pan-European security concert, by inviting Russia to join NATO as a full and equal member. Just as West Germany was integrated into NATO following World War II, so Russia should be integrated into NATO now that the Cold War has receded into history. Russia's democracy is imperfect, but in the past NATO has included imperfect democracies, including Turkey and Greece during periods of military rule. The purpose of a security concert is to coordinate action in foreign policy and prevent potential disputes, not to impose a single standard of human rights and political freedom on all member states, however admirable that standard might be.[12]

In a European concert, the major players would be the major European powers like Germany, France, and Britain plus the United States and Russia. The EU is unlikely to act as a single entity in foreign affairs. European integration has been focused on creating a common economy and currency, while Europe's states have jealously guarded their military independence. The popular rejection of the proposed EU constitution in 2005 discredited the idea that Europe is evolving into a super state capable of acting as a single entity in world politics.

What about Asia? It would be better to speak of "Asias" in the plural. Asia consists of a number of distinct regions, each of which might have its own security concert in which the United States is a member along with a shifting roster of regional great powers and lesser countries. If only great powers are listed for the sake of brevity, then a Northeast Asian concert might include China, Japan, Russia, and the United States; a Southeast Asian concert, China, Japan, India, and the United States; a South Asian concert, India, Pakistan (a significant rival of India if not a great power), and the United States; a Central Asian concert, China, India, Russia, and, perhaps, Iran and Turkey, as well as the United States. European powers would not necessarily participate in these Asian concerts, while representatives of the United States, China, and India would find themselves sitting with one another at most of the summits.

Averting Unnecessary Conflict with China

While promoting peaceful concerts of power in Asia, the United States must be prepared to join with allies to balance China's power if China makes a bid for hegemony by using military power to intimidate its Asian neighbors, including India. But the United States should avoid unnecessary conflict with China. Even a civilian, liberal, and democratic China would aspire to a greater military role in East Asia, at the expense of the United States, whose temporary hegemony in the region is a relic of World War II and the Cold War.

The United States is unlikely to find allies in Asia and the world if it treats either a Chinese drive to reincorporate Taiwan or reasonable Chinese military modernization as evidence that China is on a rampage and must be stopped. Most of the world would view a Chinese invasion of Taiwan, however deplorable, as the last step in Chinese territorial unification, not as the first step in a career of regional or global domination. The reunification of Taiwan and the mainland should come about peacefully, like China's absorption of Hong Kong. But it would be folly for the United States to cripple itself as well as China in a war over Taiwan. The United States did not go to war with the Soviet Union when it invaded Afghanistan; why, then, should the United States go to war if China invaded Taiwan, which the United States recognizes as part of China?

South Korea, with eleven times the economic might of the North, can defend itself from North Korean aggression with limited American help. The United States should maintain its alliance with South Korea to deter the North. But in the event of a second Korean War South Koreans reinforced by U.S. air and naval power, not Americans, should provide most of the manpower. Over time all but a token number of U.S. troops in South Korea should be removed. And the United States should welcome peaceful reunification of Korea, if it were to occur, rather than fret about losing influence over the Korean peninsula.

Erring on the side of caution, the United States should maintain its treaty with Japan. But it would be a mistake for the United States, in the absence of Chinese aggression, to turn the U.S.-Japan alliance into an anti-Chinese alliance. In any event, Japan's wealth and power relative to that of China is dwindling. China's economy is expected to surpass that of Japan by 2020. Between 1950 and 2050 China's population advantage over Japan is expected to have gone from six to one to sixteen to one.[13]

Since the end of the Cold War, some Americans have argued for an Indian-American alliance against China. But it would be a mistake to assume that China is a natural rival of the United States and India a natural ally. During the Cold War, India tilted toward the Soviet Union and used its leadership in the bloc of nonaligned nations to oppose the United States. China, for its part, went from being an ally of the Soviet Union to an ally of the United States against Moscow in the 1970s and 1980s. China remains a one-party dictatorship, while India has been a democracy, albeit one with periods of dictatorship and corrupt one-party rule. But many democratically elected Indian nationalists have been as hostile to the United States as many unelected Chinese nationalists.

An aggressive China that must be balanced is a possibility. But responding to that speculative threat by a premature policy of encirclement and containment would probably backfire by strengthening anti-American forces in China and isolating the United States from other countries in Asia and the world. And the exhaustion of the United States and China in an unnecessary conflict might weaken the ability of the United States to oppose aggressive policies by other great powers.

Rather than end its bilateral security treaties with Japan and South Korea, the United States should offer a comparable bilateral security alliance to China, offering to help China in the event of unprovoked attack. A bilateral

U.S.-China security treaty would cost nothing—neither Japan nor South Korea, much less the United States, is going to attack China without extreme provocation—and it would turn what is now a de facto anti-Chinese alliance into a genuine concert, that is, an alliance for stability without a designated enemy. In the event of Chinese aggression, the concert rapidly could be converted into a defensive alliance, pending a change in Chinese policy and the return of China to the concert as a member in good standing. Bilateral U.S. treaties with all of the countries of Northeast Asia should supplement, not replace, a multilateral Northeast Asian security concert, which might evolve from the Six-Power negotiations convened in recent years to deal with North Korea's attempt to acquire weapons of mass destruction.

Germany, Japan, and the Concert of Power

In a concert of power system, the United States would still play an important role in security in Asia and Europe. But it would no longer seek to be the hegemon in those regions. The United States would be a hegemonic power only in North America.

This means, among other things, that the United States would no longer be the protector of a dependent Japan and a dependent Germany. The long probation of these countries would come to an end. They would be equal and independent great powers, no different in status from China, India, Russia, Britain, France, and the United States itself.

The specters of a "Fourth Reich" or the revival of Japanese militarism are subjects for sensational fiction, not possibilities that should guide U.S. policy. The Federal Republic of Germany has half a century of experience as a stable liberal democracy and a member of NATO and the EU. Unlike Germany, Japan has avoided confronting its aggressive past, and Japanese democracy is illiberal in many respects. But similar criticisms can be leveled against the imperfect democracies of Russia and India and the authoritarian Chinese regime.

Proponents of indefinite U.S. hegemony over Japan and Germany find it difficult to come up with nightmare scenarios that might justify the cost to American taxpayers and soldiers, in the absence of a threat comparable to that posed by the Soviet Union. Michael Mandelbaum, for example, quotes a 1994 U.S. government report that estimates that a second Korean war fought to reassure Japan of America's willingness to defend it "would cost 52,000 U.S. military casualties, killed or wounded . . . at a financial outlay exceeding $61 billion, very little of which could be recouped from U.S. allies."[14] This is the price that the United States should be prepared to pay as part of its one-way offer of free security to Japan in Japan's own neighborhood. And the alternative, if Japan failed to feel "reassured" by the United States and decided to look after its own defense? Possible arms races among Japan and China and other neighbors. Writing of Germany and Japan, Mandelbaum admits: "The acquisition of nuclear weapons by such affluent, democratic, peaceful countries would not, by itself, trigger a war. It could, however, trigger arms races similar to the one between the United States and the Soviet Union during the Cold War."[15]

According to the hegemony strategy, the United States should prepare to wage a second Korean war and also to engage in an arms race with China if necessary to prevent a Sino-Japanese arms race, just as the United States should engage in an arms race with Russia if necessary to prevent a Russo-German arms race. But as long as a Sino-Japanese or Russo-German arms race did not lead to war, its costs would fall on the economies of those four nations, permitting the United States to invest what might be called its "post-hegemony dividend" to enhance U.S. economic growth and the welfare of American citizens. And the United States, no longer striving for global hegemony, could act as an honest broker in hosting multilateral regional disarmament talks. Perpetual U.S. containment of China and perpetual willingness to lose tens of thousands of American soldiers in a war in Korea or over Taiwan is too high a price for the American people to pay for forestalling the possibility of an arms race in Northeast Asia

The United States should not abandon its alliances with Japan and Germany. But it should convert them from hegemonic alliances, in which one power assumes responsibility for the protection of another, into traditional great power alliances, in which an ally promises if necessary to come to the aid of a country that, however, is chiefly responsible for its own defense. For diplomatic reasons Japan and Germany may decide to maintain their present status as non-nuclear signatories of the Nuclear Proliferation Treaty (NPT) indefinitely. But if these two democratic nations choose to join the ranks of the nuclear powers, which today include the United States, Russia, China, Britain, France, Israel, India, and Pakistan, and possibly, North Korea, the United States should not oppose their decisions.

The U.S. protectorates over Japan and Germany, like the U.S. hegemony strategy itself, are anachronistic relics of the Cold War. U.S. hegemony strategists often quote Lord Ismay's quip that the purpose of NATO is to "keep the Germans down, the Russians out, and the Americans in." The purpose of the hegemony strategy is to keep the Germans and the Japanese down and the Russians and Chinese out. By contrast the purpose of a U.S. concert of power strategy would be to keep the Germans, the Japanese, the Russians, and the Chinese in.

The Middle East:
The United States as Offshore Balancer

The concert of power model is not relevant in every region. In the Middle East, extremist regimes and profound hostilities—Iran and the United States lack diplomatic relations, as does Israel with most of its neighbors—makes a concert unlikely in the near future. And the deep hatred of the United States in the region, a hatred exacerbated although not entirely caused by America's uncritical support of Israel and its unprovoked and unnecessary invasion and occupation of Iraq, has doomed the possibility that the people of the Middle East ever will view U.S. hegemony in the area as benign or even tolerable.

The legitimacy of the U.S. role in the region is rejected by an overwhelming majority of its inhabitants outside of Israel. A 2005 poll of Middle Eastern Arabs commissioned by the Brookings Institution in Washington, D.C., revealed that most believed that the United States was in the Middle East for the oil (76 percent), to protect Israel (68 percent), to dominate the region (63 percent), and to undermine the Muslim world (59 percent), rather than to promote democracy (6 percent) or human rights (6 percent). Asked which countries threatened regional peace the most, only 6 percent named Iran while 70 percent named Israel and 63 percent named the United States. Only 7 percent of those polled approved of al-Qaeda's methods, but 36 percent approved of how Osama bin Laden "confronts the U.S." And a majority of the Arabs polled said that they would prefer China to the United States as the world's only superpower.[16] Even Middle Eastern autocracies friendly to the United States, like Egypt and Jordan, cannot ignore public opinion.

In the Middle East the United States should play the largely negative role of "offshore balancer"—discreetly arming and helping Middle Eastern states prevent any one of their neighbors from dominating the Persian Gulf.[17] As the only great power with global power projection capabilities, the United States is uniquely suited to the task of keeping the Persian Gulf open and policing the international sea-lanes to ensure the uninterrupted flow of oil to the industrial nations. The need for secrecy and swiftness in balance of power policies makes the role of an external "holder of the balance" one that can effectively be played only by a single great power rather than by several.

An offshore-balancer strategy in the Middle East would require the United States to keep a low profile, after it has ended its ill-advised occupation of the Arabs in Iraq. To increase its low levels of legitimacy in the eyes of the inhabitants of the region, the United States should be more evenhanded in its treatment of the Palestinians and Israelis. Finally, a U.S. offshore-balancer strategy in the Persian Gulf is more likely to be viewed as compatible with their interests by China and other great military-industrial powers if the United States consults with them, individually or in great power forums like the G-8 and the UN Security Council.

In the long run, the political evolution of Middle Eastern societies and the abatement of old hostilities might permit the emergence of a genuine security concert like those in other regions. In the short run, however, the maintenance of a local balance of power by the United States, acting as offshore balancer, is the least bad of several bad options.

A Special Relationship with Russia

In the event of a great power conflict in Asia, or a major war in the Middle East, a strong U.S. strategic relationship with Russia would be useful. Russia could provide bases and overland supply lines for the United States and allied great powers. And American and allied troops based on Russian territory could project power into the Middle East and Central Asia without inflaming Muslim sensibilities, as American troops based in Muslim countries have done.

Thanks to Anglo-American cooperation in the two world wars and the Cold War, today "the special relationship" refers to U.S. relations with Britain. But Britain has been a U.S. ally only since the two countries put aside their differences in response to the German threat in the early twentieth century. The European great power with which the United States has shared strategic interests for the longest period is Russia.

Americans despised the despotism of Tsarist Russia and the far harsher totalitarianism of Soviet Russia. But for most of two centuries, the United States and Russia, under various governments, had a common interest in opposing the most threatening European or East Asian power of the day. As a land power that could threaten the rear of any potential European or Asian hegemon, Russia was considered a useful counterweight by American statesmen who had no sympathy for Russian political values. Twice Russia, Britain, and the United States united to defeat Germany's bid for regional and global hegemony. In 1919 President Wilson dispatched troops to Siberia as much to dissuade Japan from threatening the territorial integrity of Russia during its civil war as to help the anticommunist side. The United States dreaded the communists who took power in the Soviet Union in Lenin's coup of 1917, and only established diplomatic relations with the Soviet Union in 1933. But notwithstanding Soviet espionage and subversion in the United States, the only prolonged period of confrontation between the United States and Russia took place during the Cold War, when Moscow made its bid for global hegemony and the United States and the Soviet bloc shared a common strategic frontier running through the middle of partitioned Germany.

From the point of view of sound American strategy, the post–Cold War U.S. policy of isolating and containing Russia has been irrational. A solid Russian-American relationship would benefit the United States as a member of great power concerts in Europe and Asia and as an offshore balancer in the Middle East.

The United States and North America

A great power concert is not possible in North America, where the United States is the only great power. In North America, the United States is and should be the hegemon—a benign hegemon, not a bully.

The continued hegemony of the United States in North America is the necessary precondition of a U.S. concert of power strategy and a U.S. balance of power strategy alike. In order to project power effectively to participate in regional concerts or regional anti-hegemonic alliances, the United States must not be tied down along or near its borders. Before and during World War I, Imperial Germany hoped that a war between the United States and Mexico would prevent the United States from coming to the rescue of

Britain and France and allow Germany to conquer Europe and dominate the world. The same geopolitical logic led the Soviet Union to try to tie down the United States in North America, by means of its alliance with Fidel Castro's communist Cuba and its sponsorship of communist revolutionaries in Central America and the Caribbean.

The greatest potential threats in North America are an alliance between Mexico and a hostile great power and a state of chaos that can be exploited by a hostile great power. The potential threat will be greater in the future because Mexico's population is growing and also because the border between the United States and Mexico is far more densely populated than in the past.

But the integration of the two countries by means of trade and immigration may make such conflict unlikely. Together the United States and Mexico could form an immense economic bloc. With an estimated population of 140 million in 2050, Mexico would be the eleventh largest country, in terms of population size, in the world; adding its population to that of the United States, even without counting Canada, would produce a total of 640 million people.[18] The combined population of the NAFTA countries would outnumber the roughly 500 million people of a Europe that includes Russia in the mid-twenty-first century.

A greater degree of formal cooperation between the United States and its neighbors may be desirable. But a North American community modeled on the European Union is not a realistic possibility. Canada will have fewer people than several American states, Mexico will have no more than a third of the United States population and a much smaller fraction of U.S. GDP, and the countries of the Caribbean and Central America are dwarfed by the colossus to their north. There would be nothing like the EU if Europe consisted of Germany, Belgium, and a handful of poor and mostly tiny countries in the Balkans.

South America and Africa

The hegemonic sphere of influence of the United States includes the Central American states as well as the countries of the Caribbean. But South America is a different continent, far more remote from Asia and Europe than North America, and its natural regional hegemon, Brazil, would resist membership in a U.S.-led alliance. While the alliance of Brazil or other South American states with a power hostile to the United States might be a threat, it would not be a mortal danger like a hostile great power's alliance with Mexico or Caribbean or Central American countries.

The misleading idea of "the Western Hemisphere" is deeply enshrined in American consciousness. Generations of Americans have hoped that a line can be drawn down the middle of the Atlantic and the Pacific, severing a virtuous New World from the sinister Old World. But in geopolitical terms the concept of the Western Hemisphere never made any sense. The East Coast of the United States is closer to Europe, and the West Coast to Asia, than either is to the countries of the southern cone.

The inhabitants of Africa may account for one-quarter of the human race by the twenty-second century. But world power is based on military and economic weight, not weight of numbers. There is not a single first-rate military power or industrial economy in the entire continent. While some parts are progressing, much of Africa remains mired in poverty, anarchy, and ethnic strife. The United States and other outside powers may intervene in Africa, for humanitarian reasons or out of concerns for their security. But there can be no African great power concert until there are African great powers.

Freedom of the Global Commons

In October 1941 Winston Churchill observed: "The whole power of the United States, to manifest itself, depends on the power to move ships and aircraft across the sea. Their mighty power is restricted; it is restricted by the very oceans which have protected them; the oceans which were their shield, have now become both threatening and a bar, a prison house through which they must struggle to bring armies, fleets, and air forces to bear upon the common problems we have to face."[19] The United States was able to help defeat Imperial Germany only because German submarine warfare was unable to prevent the United States from transporting troops and equipment across the ocean, and a generation later the Allied victory in the Battle of the Atlantic was the precondition for the Battle of Normandy.

In the future as in the past the United States will only be able to play a role in regional concerts and balance of power alliances if it is able to project power from North America to critical regions elsewhere in the world. Since the end of the Cold War the United States has enjoyed unchallenged supremacy in the "global commons," defined as the envelope of sea, air, and space.[20] However, America's advantage inevitably will erode as rising industrial nations like China and India, as well as lesser powers, translate their economic strength into naval, air, and space power. Just as the United States insisted on an exclusive sphere of influence in the waters near its borders in the early twentieth century, China and India are likely to challenge U.S. naval power in East Asia and South Asia in years to come. In addition, the development of airpower and space power by rising regional great powers will challenge U.S. primacy in those important military realms.

The United States should maintain its primacy in the global commons as long as it can do so for a reasonable cost. But at some point in the future it may be impossible for the United States to maintain its lead, without spending itself into bankruptcy like the over-militarized Soviet Union. Anticipating the day, perhaps decades or generations in the future, when it will lose its dominance of sea, air, and space to another power or combination of powers, the United States should begin working even now for international accords and arms limitation agreements that increase the security of all major powers. An international regime favorable to the power-projection requirements of the United States could outlast the military primacy of the United States, as long as other great powers found it to be in their interest as well.

Leadership, not Domination

The goal of safety for the United States and its allies, which the strategy of unilateral U.S. global hegemony can purchase only at great cost to the U.S. economy, civil liberty, and constitutional government, can be achieved by the concert of power strategy by means compatible with the American way of life. To deter the domination of critical regions by hostile powers, the United States should pool its military power with that of strong regional allies, not volunteer to defend their interests on their behalf in order to spare their treasuries and their soldiers. For the same reason, the United States should seek to bring order if necessary to anarchic regions that are sources of terrorism, crime, or pandemics as a member of a great power concert, not as a solitary world police officer.[21]

The hegemony strategy cannot honestly be explained to the American people, because if they understood it they would reject it, as even advocates of U.S. hegemony concede. The concert of power strategy does not suffer from this defect. It maintains a leading role for the United States in Asia, the Middle East, and Europe, but ensures that any costs in blood and treasure to the American people would be shared equitably with rich and powerful allies.

It is neither in the power nor the interest of the United States to dominate the world. But it is both in America's power and America's interest to lead the world.

Chapter 12

The American Way of
Military Strategy

I do not entertain the thought of some of the statesmen of
1918 that the world can make, or we can help the world to
achieve, a permanently lasting peace—that is a peace which
we would visualize as enduring for a century or more.

—Franklin Roosevelt, 1939[1]

IN HIS CLASSIC STUDY *THE AMERICAN WAY OF WAR* (1973), the historian Russell
F. Weigley argued for the existence of a distinctive "American way of war"
defined by certain tactics, including overwhelming force and a preference
for technology over manpower ("send bullets, not men").[2] Others have
pointed out exceptions to this alleged rule, such as the techniques used by
the U.S. Cavalry in Indian wars and by U.S. Marines in fighting insurgen-
cies in the Caribbean, Central America, and the Philippines.[3] Still others
have argued for the emergence of a "new American way of war" based on
precision firepower and special forces.[4]

As one military analyst has observed, in all of these debates "the American style of warfare amounts to a way of battle more than a way of war."[5]
Any attempt to define an enduring American way of war in terms of particular tactics is doomed, not only by the diversity of situations in which
the U.S. military is deployed, but also by ever-changing technology, which
replaced the cavalry with tanks in the twentieth century and may replace
piloted aircraft with pilotless drones in the twenty-first.

While it is impossible to generalize about battle tactics, it is possible to
learn lessons from history with respect to military strategy at its highest
level, the level at which military and political goals are one and the same.
"War is policy by other means," the Prussian military-thinker Clausewitz
famously wrote. The U.S. military is the instrument of U.S. grand strategy,

which ought to define not only the goals of the military but also its very structure.

The Concert of Power and American Military Strategy

If the United States were to follow a concert of power strategy, it would still have by far the world's strongest military. And many of the missions of the U.S. military would remain the same: deterring attacks on the U.S. homeland; preserving U.S. hegemony in North America; and maintaining U.S. military primacy in the "global commons" of sea, air, and space, a necessity if the United States is to be able to project power in order to come to the aid of allies in other regions of the world.

But the concert of power strategy would permit the United States to enjoy significant savings in defense spending, by providing alternatives to a unilateral U.S. response to a threatening bid for regional or global hegemony by a hostile power. To such aggression the U.S. response, if possible, should be U.S. participation in a great power alliance, a strategy like the one that the United States pursued in World Wars I and II, not the unilateral extension of U.S. protection over other great powers, the far costlier strategy that the United States pursued by necessity in the Cold War. In the future, the burden of restraining a regional aggressor should be shared by the United States with other great powers that have as much or more at stake.

If great power peace not only endures but also permits great power concerts to be established, then one of the chief tasks of the U.S. military would be to participate in regional policing efforts alongside regional great powers. Occasional joint military interventions by the United States and its regional partners might resemble the reassurance wars that the United States fought in the Balkans and Iraq. But they would be genuine multilateral efforts, not unilateral U.S. interventions disguised by token forces from other countries. The regional concert strategy would be most likely to succeed if coalitions for intervention were limited to a handful of great powers, in order to maximize the possibility of consensus and timely action.

What sort of U.S. military forces would the United States need to contribute to regional security concerts? By definition the countries in which the United States and its great power partners would intervene would not be great powers themselves. In most cases they would be relatively weak or might suffer from anarchy created by civil war or wars of national secession. For these contingencies the regional concerts to which the United States belonged would need highly professional constabulary forces, fluent in the local language if possible, rather than forces designed to defeat other great industrial powers in conventional wars. In short, the United States should send the marines, and perhaps the Special Forces as well.

The U.S. Navy, Air Force, and, perhaps, a future U.S. Space Force would play key supporting roles in providing and defending the logistical infrastructure and intelligence, which interventions by regional concerts would require. The role of the U.S. Army in a concert of power strategy is less clear. War among great powers in the future is likely to take the form of missile exchanges. And small-scale military interventions are likely to require limited numbers of versatile, highly skilled professionals who serve in an area for a long time, not generalists trained to smash the mechanized forces of the enemy and then depart. If the United States adopted the concert of power strategy, the winners among the services might be the Marines, the Navy, and the Air Force. The loser might be the U.S. Army.

A new role for a downsized U.S. Army might be its traditional task, before the world wars and the Cold War—the defense of the American homeland. In the aftermath of the devastating Hurricane Katrina of 2005, which destroyed New Orleans and leveled much of the Gulf Coast, the U.S. Army proved to be far more effective than state National Guard units and local and state police and emergency workers. The army might be equally instrumental in providing order and relief following a devastating terrorist attack inside the United States. The deployment of army units along U.S. borders might also be justified, if illegal immigration, a threat to the national security of the United States in an age of terrorism, cannot be halted by a combination of other measures.

The deployment of the army on American soil must be regulated so that it is compatible with civil liberties. But the defense of U.S. territory was the original purpose of the army, and that may become its central mission once again.

If Concert Fails

No concert of power system can function if one or more of the major powers is hostile to the others or if there are profound disagreements about policy. Franklin Roosevelt is often accused of being naïve in hoping that cooperation among the United States, Britain, and the Soviet Union could be maintained after the defeat of their common enemies. But Roosevelt was a realist who foresaw the possibility of the Cold War. In a 1943 interview with Forrest Davis for the *Saturday Evening Post*, Roosevelt speculated that if Russia refused to cooperate after the war, "the Western allies would no doubt be driven back on a balance-of-power system."[6]

Like the Soviet Union after World War II, great powers in the future may refuse to participate in a global concert. They may be revisionist, seeking to enhance their territory or influence by aggressive means. They may also be revolutionary, like Nazi Germany, the Soviet Union, and Mao's China, each of which based its legitimacy on an ideology that was opposed in principle to the liberal international system. The United States and other great powers committed to the society of states might have no choice except to deter or defeat the threatening revisionist or revolutionary state. But the long-term goal should be to restore the offending country to the concert, once it is willing to assume its role as a constructive member of the society of states, following a change of policy or a change of regime.

In the event that great power conflict recurs, there exists a well-defined if insufficiently recognized American way of world war, if a world war is defined as a conflict, including a cold war, that involves most or all of the great powers of a given era. The historic American way of world war, manifest in the two wars against Germany as well as in the four-decade struggle against the Soviet Union, differs strikingly from the "good war" model dear to the American military and the American public alike. The victory of the United States and its allies in each of the three titanic contests of the twentieth century was based on a variant of the same strategy. In most cases the goal was the defeat of the enemy, not the destruction of the enemy regime, and the strategy was one of the economic exhaustion of the enemy by a coalition of great powers whose combined military and economic resources dwarfed those of the enemy.

Defeat of the Enemy, Not Destruction of the Enemy Regime

In the two world wars and the Cold War, the United States did not make regime change or the complete destruction of the enemy government a war aim. The exception was in the case of Hitler's National Socialist regime, a genocidal state so evil that the Allies agreed on its complete eradication. In two of the three Axis powers, the United States accepted surrender without demanding "regime change." The United States ended its insistence on unconditional surrender in Japan and allowed the Japanese monarchy to survive. In 1943 the Italian king dismissed Mussolini and formed a new government led by Marshall Badoglio that switched sides and joined the Allies (the Italian monarchy subsequently was overthrown). Strictly speaking, therefore, World War II was not a war of total regime change except with respect to Germany.

Following the defeat of Germany in World War I, the Kaiser abdicated and a republic was declared in Germany. But neither the abolition of the Hohenzollern monarchy nor the allied Hapsburg monarchy of Austria-Hungary was a war aim of the United States and its allies. Similarly, the Cold War ended when the Soviet Union agreed to allow self-determination for the nations of Eastern Europe and began serious disarmament negotiations. The democratization of the Soviet Union and its dissolution along national lines in 1990–91 followed the Cold War; they were not preconditions for its end.

Rethinking Limited War

Of all the Cold War debates about deterrence, the one that is most relevant today involves what was known as "limited war," which is better described as limited retaliation. The Eisenhower administration, in the interest of controlling military costs, supported what became known as "finite deterrence." The United States would threaten "massive retaliation" against Soviet cities and military sites in the event of a Soviet attack on Western Europe or Japan. In the 1950s and 1960s, many civilian and military analysts argued that massive retaliation might fail, if an aggressor gambled that the United States would not launch all-out nuclear war in response to limited aggression. According to the theorists of limited war, the United States should maintain the ability to respond to limited attacks with limited counterstrikes, either wholly conventional or involving tactical nuclear weapons. In addition, many theorists of limited war argued that constant communication between both sides should be maintained, even during a limited nuclear exchange, so that each side could communicate its limited goals and so that both sides could engage in negotiation to avert escalation to all-out war. This reasoning provided the rationale for the famous "hot line" between Washington and Moscow.

A strategy of limited retaliation is even more relevant in the twenty-first century than it was during the Cold War, for two reasons, one geopolitical and one social.

Limited War in a Multipolar World

The geopolitical reason for a doctrine of limited retaliation is the inevitable emergence of a fully multipolar world in the military realm. (In the economic realm, the world has been multipolar since the 1970s). In a world of several great powers each must be concerned about the relative strength of most or all great powers, not merely that of their rivals of the moment. Because today's enemy might be tomorrow's ally, it may be wise to avoid destroying an enemy's power altogether, even if the enemy begins a conflict with an unprovoked and atrocious attack.

The importance of maintaining a balance of power in key regions, in the event that a regional concert of power policy failed, means that U.S. strategy toward Germany in World War II may not provide a useful model for U.S. strategy in the twenty-first century. The best precedent for U.S. strategy in great power conflicts in the twenty-first century might be found in the early twentieth, when the United States was already a world power, but one of several in a multipolar world. Although President Theodore Roosevelt admired Japan, he feared that the annihilation of Russian power in the Russo-Japanese War of 1904–5 would destroy a balance of power in East Asia and make Japan too powerful. By means of his intervention as the mediator in the Russo-Japanese peace negotiations, for which he won the Nobel Peace Prize in 1906, Roosevelt maintained a good relationship with Japan while ensuring that Russia would continue to provide a check on Japanese power. In Roosevelt's words, Russia should "be left face to face with Japan so that each may have a moderative action on the other."[7]

In addition to seeking to preserve a balance of power in East Asia, Roosevelt recognized that the United States had an interest in preventing Europe from being dominated by Germany or Russia, the only two great powers capable of doing so. Before World War I, Roosevelt told a German friend that if Britain failed in "keeping up the balance of power in Europe," then "the United States would be obliged to step in, at least temporarily, in order to reestablish the balance of power in Europe . . . "[8] But Roosevelt saw America's role in Europe, as in the world as a whole, as that of an external balancer or "holder of the balance," not the solitary hegemon of Europe or the world. After Germany launched World War I, Roosevelt favored U.S. intervention to defeat Germany's bid for European hegemony. At the same time he opposed a complete annihilation of Germany that would create a power vacuum in central Europe that Russia could fill, and argued "that the smashing of Germany would be a world calamity, and would result in the entire western world being speedily forced into a contest with Russia."[9]

The need to avoid completely annihilating the strength of a defeated great power enemy is the geopolitical argument for limiting the objectives of war in a multipolar world. There is also an argument arising from the nature of society in a brittle world.

Limited War in a Brittle World

For the first time in history, a majority of the world's population lives in cities—immense slums in developing countries and increasingly suburban metro areas in the richer nations. As a result modern societies, rich and poor alike, are increasingly "brittle." Urban and suburban populations are far more vulnerable to the destruction of complex sanitation, health, food delivery, electrical, and transportation systems by war than were their rural ancestors. The potential for mass starvation and widespread disease in populous cities that have been disrupted by war may be far greater than in decentralized, agrarian nations with relatively self-sufficient and dispersed villages and farms.

The suffering of enemy civilians might not concern leaders retaliating against conventional or nuclear attacks upon their homelands. But rational statesmen ought to be concerned about the potential global side effects of excessive retaliation. The pulverization of Afghanistan in the proxy war between the Soviet Union and the United States and its allies, like the chaos in Iraq that followed the U.S. invasion in 2003, provided conditions in which foreign terrorist cells established havens and training grounds. Disease is another danger. A global pandemic, originating in the unhygienic squalor of a destroyed state, might sweep the world and devastate the retaliating country. Then there is the danger of industrial pollution. As more nations industrialize, the danger that indiscriminate and excessive bombardment of enemy territory will release toxic chemicals into the soil, water, or atmosphere will grow. Finally, waves of refugees from an aggressor state that has been plunged into anarchy might spill over its borders into neighboring countries.

The argument from geopolitics and the argument from the nature of urban society, then, lead to the same conclusion: the appropriate response even to an unprovoked attack might be limited retaliation, which disarms the aggressor, while avoiding both the creation of opportunities for other great powers and situations of dangerous anarchy.

Why the United States Should Avoid Decapitation as a Tactic

Defeating the policy of the enemy, rather than destroying the government of the enemy and creating anarchy or opportunities for aggrandizement by rival great powers, should be the objective of the United States in all of its military strategy, including its strategies of deterrence and retaliation. Among other things, this means that the United States should rule out "decapitation"—the killing or disabling of the enemy political leadership—as a military tactic, except as a desperate last resort.

The United States began the Iraq War of 2003 with an attempt to assassinate Saddam Hussein and those around him by means of bombing.[10] Similarly, during the Gulf War in 1991, the United States began hostilities with an attempt to assassinate Saddam by dropping four one-ton bombs on the bunker in which he was believed to be hiding (the bunker later turned out not to exist). The failure of the United States to kill Saddam in the Gulf War permitted the United States to end the war on the basis of negotiation with his regime. But in the Iraq War, while the United States failed to kill Saddam, who later was captured by U.S. forces, it all too successfully destroyed the Iraqi government. The result was anarchy throughout Iraq. Instead of engaging in a peaceful postwar occupation, the United States found itself fighting an insurgency that grew over time. Foreign terrorists took advantage of the anarchy to move into Iraq and attack U.S. forces. The population of Iraq suffered horribly as a result of the U.S. invasion and the insurgency and civil war that followed, which destroyed tens of thousands of Iraqi lives and shattered much of the infrastructure of the country.

Something similar had happened forty years earlier in 1963, when the United States had conspired in the decapitation of an ally rather than an enemy. The ally was the South Vietnamese dictator Diem. The United States supported the military coup in which Diem and his brother were murdered, in the hope that a new military junta would be able to prosecute the war against the North Vietnamese–supported communist insurgency more effectively. Instead, the South Vietnamese state, which had been centered on Diem, disintegrated into chaos, just as the Iraqi state, centered on Saddam Hussein, disintegrated following Saddam's flight into hiding and eventual apprehension.

If the United States completely shatters a foreign government, then in order to forestall chaos or the influence of other nations the United States is bound to provide the government itself, at least until a new, native regime can be organized. Given America's limited military manpower, waging war by means of regime change strategies that require prolonged periods of massive U.S. military occupation following the war is imprudent in the extreme. It is far wiser to limit the objectives of the war in the first place to changing regime policy, while leaving the regime in power, as the United States did in the case of its first war against Iraq in the early 1990s.

The avoidance of decapitation as a military tactic has important implications for U.S. nuclear strategy. The Bush administration has argued that the United States needs to develop a new generation of tactical nuclear weapons to be used in "bunker-busting." If the logic of limited retaliation is accepted, however, the United States should want to negotiate rules that would ensure immunity for leaders during wars, to facilitate constant communication and negotiation even after hostilities have commenced. The model would be the Soviet-American "hot line" system used during the Cold War. An attempt to decapitate an enemy state by slaughtering enemy leaders in their bunkers at the beginning of a war—whether with nuclear weapons or with conventional weapons—should be rejected, because if the tactic succeeded it might commit the United States or other countries or international agencies to govern the defeated country for an indefinite period at enormous cost, as in Iraq.

These strategic considerations apply only to policy toward hostile states, not to policy toward stateless terrorist groups. Whenever it is feasible to do so, morality, as well as the rule of law, requires that terrorists should be treated as criminals, arrested, and tried for their crimes. But if terrorists have established bases in lawless territories in which the local government lacks the capacity or the will to arrest and extradite them, then states victimized by the terrorists are justified in using military means to attack them, as the United States did when both the Clinton and Bush administrations launched missile strikes against suspected al-Qaeda bases in Afghanistan, Pakistan, and, by mistake, in Sudan. International law has always recognized that the right of states to defend themselves includes the right to carry out military operations against pirates, criminals, and terrorists in areas where no functioning government exists.[11]

Regime Change Without War

Ruling out regime change by means of war does not mean ruling out regime change by other means. Following the end of the Cold War, democratic governments replaced communist dictatorships throughout the former Soviet bloc and also replaced many military dictatorships in Latin America. In Eastern Europe, Eurasia, and Latin America, the immediate catalyst was the collapse of Soviet power and the consequent worldwide collapse of communism, defense against which had provided many praetorian regimes in Latin America with a public rationale. In all of these regions, the wave of liberalization and democratization had been preceded by decades of gradual social evolution that had created the preconditions of successful liberal democracy, including secularization, widespread literacy, and rising per capita incomes. In none of these cases, with the exception of one nation in Latin America, was democracy installed by the United States following a U.S. invasion.

That one exception in Latin America was Panama. The American invasion of Panama in 1989 set a precedent for subsequent post–Cold War American policy in Iraq and Afghanistan. In all three, the United States sought to destroy, not merely to defeat, a hostile regime. In all three cases the United States, having demolished the existing government, became the government temporarily during a military occupation. And in all three cases the enemy leaders were treated as criminals.

One need have no sympathy for vicious tyrants like Noriega, Hussein, and Milosevic to wonder whether this novel post–Cold War system, combining American invasions and occupations of foreign countries with trials of their former rulers, is a rational way of promoting democracy in other countries. Recent history provides many examples of countries that evolved from dictatorship to democracy, often with U.S. diplomatic support, without any need for U.S. military occupation or public trials of former rulers.

One method has been "people power." Ultimately rooted in the doctrine of nonviolent resistance of Gandhi and Martin Luther King, Jr., "people power" in the form of mass nonviolent popular protests brought about democracy in the Philippines, Boris Yeltsin's Russia, Serbia, and Ukraine.

Dictators are less likely to relinquish power without bloodshed if doing so subjects them to prosecution. For this reason Latin American societies, with long histories of alternation between military and elected regimes, have devised methods for easing rather than dynamiting dictators out of office. One technique is well-funded exile. Another is immunity from prosecution. This is sometimes combined with a policy of allowing a former dictator to remain commander in chief of the armed forces, as in the case of General Augusto Pinochet in Chile. In some former one-party dictatorships like the Soviet Union and South Africa, the former ruling party has been allowed to recreate itself as one of several democratic parties.

Allowing former dictators to escape prosecution for crimes they committed when in power represents a genuine defeat of justice. But even in domestic justice systems, criminals are often granted lenient sentences or even made immune to prosecution if they cooperate with prosecutors. Negotiated regime change, in which a ruler or ruling party abdicates as part of a deal with the successor government, is preferable to revolutions and invasions that cost great numbers of lives.

Why Preventive War
Should Be Prevented

In a multipolar world that is also a brittle world, the legitimate kinds of war, as well as the legitimate methods of war, must be limited. One kind of war that is not legitimate is preventive war.

The UN Charter, codifying older international law, gives all states the right to unilateral or collective self-defense—including pre-emptive military action in self-defense. Forestalling an imminent attack by means of a pre-emptive strike is a legitimate exercise of force in a defensive war. But pre-emptive war is completely different from preventive war. To justify pre-emptive war, a threat must be imminent. A speculative threat is not sufficient. If President Franklin Roosevelt had learned that the Japanese fleet was heading toward Pearl Harbor to bomb it, he would have had every right to send the U.S. Navy to stop it. But President Harding could not have launched an unprovoked attack against Japan in 1920, on the theory that Japan, while it was not a threat at the moment, might attack the United States in 1941.

The traditional American distinction between preventive war and preemptive war was clarified by the *Caroline* incident of 1837. On December 29, 1837, the British-Canadian Navy attacked a U.S. ship, the *Caroline*, which was ferrying supplies to rebels in Canada. The British, after destroying the ship and letting it slide over Niagara Falls, claimed that they were acting in self-defense. After President William Henry Harrison was inaugurated in March 1841, Daniel Webster, his secretary of state, argued that the British attack was unjustified. According to Webster, if a government launches a pre-emptive strike, "It will be for that government to show a necessity of self-defense, instant, overwhelming, leaving no choice of means, no moment for deliberation."[12] In addition, "the act, justified by the necessity of self-defense, must be limited by that necessity, and kept clearly within it." The British admitted that it was a mistake to take action inside American borders and the United States accepted that admission as an apology.

The Iraq War of 2003 was justified in public by President George W. Bush as a preventive war to prevent Saddam Hussein's development of nuclear weapons and other weapons of mass destruction. The war violated both of Webster's tests for legitimate pre-emptive action: There was no "necessity of self-defense, instant, overwhelming" leaving no choice of means, no moment for deliberation." Nor was the U.S. policy "justified by the necessity of self-defense . . . limited by that necessity, and kept clearly within it." Indeed, had the United States permitted UN arms inspectors to work for several more months, they would have revealed the absence of Iraqi weapons of mass destruction.

The adoption by the United States of the theory of preventive war, if only as a public pretext for a war whose actual strategic purposes were concealed from the public, marked a break not only with international law but also with American tradition. During the Truman years, when General Orvil Anderson, commandant of the Air War College, proposed a preventive war against the Soviet Union, President Truman fired him and publicly repudiated the idea. According to Truman, "You don't 'prevent' anything by war . . . except peace."[13] Earlier, Secretary of State Dean Acheson had distanced the administration from a similar suggestion by Secretary of the Navy Francis Matthews.[14] In the next administration, President Eisenhower told a press conference: "A preventive war . . . is an impossibility today . . . I don't believe there is such a thing; and frankly, I wouldn't even listen to anyone seriously that came in and talked about such a thing."[15] During the Cuban Missile Crisis, when a preventive strike against Soviet missiles in Cuba was suggested, Attorney General Bobby Kennedy rejected the proposal as "Pearl Harbor in reverse" and declared: "For 175 years we have not been that kind of country."[16]

Following the devastation of Iraq by the U.S. invasion and occupation, President Bush and his defenders retroactively justified the war by claiming that even though Saddam Hussein had dismantled his weapons of mass destruction on UN orders and had not rebuilt them, he had possessed the intention to acquire them in the future. But the mere intention of a head of state to acquire weapons at some point in the future cannot legitimate preventive wars. If it could, then any country could invade any other country at any time, on the theory that it might be a threat at some point in the future. Indeed, this reasoning caused World War I. The Kaiser and the German military feared that Russia's growing military and economic power would make it the dominant power in Europe in a decade or two. They manipulated the conflict between Austria and Serbia into an excuse for launching a preventive war to cripple Russia before it could grow too powerful.

The Bush administration did not make it clear whether the prerogative to wage preventive war is limited to the United States or whether other countries can wage preventive wars, too. If any country can wage a preventive war, then every country must assume that it might be a target of preventive war by other states seeking to cripple its military or economic capability for fear that it might pose a threat in the near or distant future. Even if actual preventive wars were uncommon, countries would have to prepare themselves for that possibility. The result would be a world of garrison states. Militaries would expand, taxes would go up, commerce would be crippled, civil liberties would be curtailed, and the American way of life would be doomed.

A Great Power Alliance with
Overwhelming Resources

In the three world wars of the twentieth century the victorious alliance to which the United States belonged was capable of a successful strategy of economic exhaustion because its members had overwhelming military and industrial resources compared to their common enemies. Twice aggressive regimes in Germany were doomed to defeat by the decisive factor of America's massive industrial base. During the Cold War, the combined military-industrial resources of the American-led anti-Soviet alliance steadily grew at the expense of the Soviet Union, as the economies of Japan and Western Europe recovered after World War II. In all three conflicts the U.S.-led alliance, if it stayed together, was practically destined to drive its economically inferior enemies to bankruptcy even in the absence of invasion and occupation of the enemy homeland.

In 1913, the United States, Britain, and France, even without Russia, accounted for 51.7 percent of world manufacturing, compared to only 19.2 percent for Germany and Austria-Hungary.[17] The disproportion in economic power of the United States and its allies during World War II was even more favorable. The historian Paul Kennedy observes that "the Allies possessed *twice* the manufacturing strength . . . *three* times the 'war potential,' and *three* times the national income of the Axis powers, even when the French shares are added to Germany's total."[18] According to one estimate of "relative war potential," in 1937 the United States, the Soviet Union, and Britain accounted for 65.9 percent while Germany, Japan, Italy, and France (soon to be conquered by Germany) produced a combined total of only 24.6 percent. Even in 1937, before its mobilization for war, the United States had 41.7 percent of relative war potential, trailed by Germany with 14.4 percent, the Soviet Union with 14.0 percent, Britain with 10.2 percent, and Japan with a mere 3.5 percent.[19]

The combined economic might of the United States and its allies during the Cold War similarly dwarfed that of the Soviet Union and its satellite states. Throughout that long conflict the U.S. economy was roughly twice the size of the Soviet economy. To America's resources were added those of its allies. By 1970, after Western Europe and Japan had recovered from World War II, the Soviet Union, with only 12.4 percent of global GDP, was overshadowed by the United States (23.0 percent), the European Economic

Community (24.7 percent) and Japan (7.7 percent). The combined share of global GDP of the United States, Western Europe, and Japan was thus 55.4 percent to 12.4 percent on the Soviet side.[20] The superior resources of the anti-Soviet alliance allowed the United States and its allies to roughly match Soviet military expenditures while spending a far lower proportion of their national incomes on arms than the Soviets did. The Soviet Union was not defeated by the United States alone; it was defeated by the combined weight of the military and economic resources of the United States, Western Europe, Japan, and China.

The hegemony strategy and the concert strategy both lead to the conclusion that the United States can be safest if a preponderance of the world's military power is organized in its defense. The difference is that according to the hegemony strategy, a purely American preponderance of power is necessary, while according to the concert strategy it is only necessary that a preponderance of power be possessed by the concert or alliance to which the United States belongs.[21]

As this suggests, the emphasis of historians on battles in the three world conflicts of the twentieth century is somewhat misleading. The primary emphasis ought to be on factories. The United States formally entered World War I in 1917 and World War II in 1941. In each case, however, the United States was bolstering combatants with its industrial and financial support well before its formal entry into the war. In the case of the Cold War, decades of economic warfare against the Soviet Union played as important a part as arms races and proxy battles in Korea, Indochina, and Afghanistan.

The Coalition Must Determine the Mission

"The mission must determine the coalition; the coalition must not determine the mission," Secretary of Defense Donald Rumsfeld declared.[22] This is the exact opposite of the reasoning that guided U.S. policy during the three world wars: *the coalition must determine the mission.*

The models for America's strategies for victory in the world wars as well as the Cold War ultimately are found in the history of siege warfare. Sieges have always been accompanied by battles and sometimes bombardments. But victory in a siege ultimately depended on starving the besieged enemy into submission. The greatest fear of the besiegers, and the greatest hope of the besieged, is that the besieging armies will fall out among themselves and abandon the siege. Preserving harmony among the allies, throughout the duration of a long and expensive siege, is not simply one of a number of diplomatic goals; it is the objective upon which military success ultimately depends.

The key to victory in all three world conflicts of the twentieth century was preserving the coalition of the United States and its great power allies long enough for the strategy of economic exhaustion to force the enemy to sue for peace or collapse. During World War II, the United States and Britain had to reassure Stalin that the Western powers would not consider a separate peace with Hitler, in order to deter the Soviets from doing so. During the Cold War, the United States had to keep the anti-Soviet alliance that included Japan and Western Europe intact for four decades, through one crisis after another.

The need to preserve a great power alliance was of such overriding importance that sometimes it justified entire military campaigns or, in the case of the Cold War, entire wars with rationales that were political and diplomatic rather than strictly military. In World War II the United States and Britain invaded North Africa in part to assure Stalin of their commitment to defeating Hitler, while building up forces gradually for the cross-channel invasion that came on D-Day in 1944. The Korean and Vietnam Wars were credibility wars intended to discourage Japan, West Germany, and other American protectorates from appeasing the Soviet Union by proving that the United States had the political resolve as well as the military capability to defend its allies against Soviet attack or intimidation. During the "Euromissile crisis" of the early 1980s, the deployment of U.S. short- and intermediate-range nuclear weapons in response to the Soviet targeting of Western Europe was a move designed to reassure America's European allies and prevent an intimidated Western Europe from choosing appeasement or neutrality out of fear of Soviet power.

Given the overriding imperative of ensuring that military efforts reinforce alliance unity, civilian control of the military is indispensable. For generations, some American military officers have resented civilian management not only of strategy and operations but also of particular campaigns and tactics. But the president of the United States is diplomat in chief, as well as commander in chief, and diplomatic decisions may need to trump narrowly military logic in a global conflict in which victory depends on holding a great power alliance together by means of compromise and concession.

Fighting on the Basis of American Strengths

As a member of an anti-hegemonic alliance of great powers like the grand alliances that prevailed in the world wars and the Cold War, the United States in any future great power conflict should seek to focus on its strengths in making its contribution. As we have seen, there were two broad schools of thought about how the United States should pursue containment of the Soviet Union. The symmetrical containment school, associated with Democrats like Truman, Kennedy, and Johnson, favored countering Soviet and Soviet-sponsored aggression at every level of violence from counterinsurgency through limited war to potential all-out nuclear war—even at enormous cost to the U.S. economy. The asymmetrical containment school, associated with Republicans like Eisenhower, Nixon, and Reagan, sought to achieve the same goals by less costly means that played to America's strengths and avoided America's greatest weaknesses—limited manpower and a high and, over time, growing aversion to military casualties on the part of the American public. Eisenhower's New Look sought to substitute nuclear weapons for American troops; the Nixon Doctrine sought to substitute the troops of allied states for American troops; and the Reagan Doctrine sought to substitute "freedom fighters" or anticommunist insurgents for American troops. The capital-intensive Republican way of cold war proved to be more successful than the labor-intensive Democratic way of cold war, which produced the Americanization of the Korean and Vietnam Wars, at great cost in public support for U.S. foreign policy.

Future cold wars, if they occur, may not resemble the struggle against the Soviet Union in any respect other than their limitation by rival great powers that share a fear of the destructiveness of all-out warfare. It would be a mistake, therefore, mechanically to apply lessons of Cold War I to a future Cold War II or Cold War III. But one prediction is likely to be borne out: in future great power conflicts, either cold or hot, the United States may be at a disadvantage when it comes to manpower. In the case of conflicts involving populous countries like China or India, the disproportion between enemy manpower and American manpower might be striking.

From this, two tentative conclusions can be drawn. The first is that the United States should try to avoid conflict with any populous state except as an ally of one or more other populous states. The second conclusion is that the U.S. role in future anti-hegemonic alliances should be to concentrate on supplying economic aid and arms, while allies supply most of the troops. This would mark a return to the policy of World War II, in which Allied strategy combined American economic aid and military power with Soviet manpower, and a break with the tradition of symmetrical containment of the Cold War, in which the United States sent its own soldiers to fight on behalf of protectorates and client states. Another historical precedent might be found in the practice of Britain from the seventeenth to the nineteenth centuries, when Britain, whose army was always small compared to those of the continental European powers, repeatedly helped to organize European coalitions in which it supplied financial and naval support while its continental allies fielded vast numbers of troops.

In the interest of maintaining its character as a civilian and commercial society, the United States should specialize as the bank and arsenal of anti-hegemonic coalitions, not its manpower agency. Boots on the ground will always be needed, but most of the boots should belong to America's allies. What was called the "Nixon Doctrine" after it was announced on November 3, 1969, by President Richard Nixon should serve as a guide: "[W]e shall look to the nation directly threatened to assume the primary responsibility of providing the manpower necessary for its defense."[23]

The greatest weapon in the American arsenal is America's domestic manufacturing base. Will the U.S. economy be up to the demands of American strategy in the twenty-first century? That is the subject of the next chapter.

Chapter 13

The American Way of Trade

The successful powers will be those who have the greatest industrial base. Those people who have the industrial power and the power of invention and science will be able to defeat all others.

—Leo Amery, 1904[1]

ONE AIRCRAFT EVERY FIVE MINUTES. That is what the United States produced in 1943 and 1944.[2] In 1939 the United States had produced only 5,856 aircraft. After the United States mobilized its economy in World War II, the total rose to 85,898 aircraft per year in 1943 before reaching a peak of 96,318 in 1944. By contrast, Germany produced only 24,807 aircraft in 1943 and 39,807 in 1944; Japan's totals were 16,693 and 28,180. On D-Day, June 6, 1944, against the 12,837 aircraft of the Allies, the Germans could deploy only 319.[3]

To say that democracy defeated fascism in World War II is therefore somewhat misleading. It is more accurate to say that the factories of the democracies, and those of their communist ally, the Soviet Union, defeated the factories of the Fascist states. In World War II, as in World War I, the decisive factor in the final analysis was not the genius of generals or the efficiency of rival sociopolitical systems. It was the monumental scale and quality of American manufacturing and American finance. Similarly, during the Cold War the U.S. economy was always at least twice the size of the Soviet economy. By spending only 7.5 percent of its GDP on defense on average between 1948 and 1989, the United States with the help of its allies was able to bankrupt the Soviet Union, which devoted between one-third and one-half of its much smaller economy to the military.[4]

The United States was a great manufacturing power before it became a great military power. Indeed, it was and is a great military power *because* it is a great manufacturing power. And the United States must remain a great manufacturing power if it hopes to remain a great military power in the years ahead.

Free Trade in Theory and Practice

For most of its history the United States was one of the most protectionist countries in the world. Only after World War II did the United States begin to preach, if not always practice, free trade. Most U.S. economists and politicians today, however, treat freedom of international trade and investment as the ideal, and many Americans erroneously assume that the United States has always supported free trade.

Supporters of global free trade tend to justify the policy on the basis of two theories dating from the late eighteenth and early nineteenth centuries. One is the eighteenth-century British economist Adam Smith's theory of absolute advantage. Countries should specialize in what they can produce most cheaply, on the basis of their natural endowments. The rival theory of comparative advantage, proposed by the British economist Robert Torrens in 1815 and popularized by another British economist, David Ricardo, in 1817, is more subtle. Even if one country can make both of two goods more cheaply than another country, it ought to specialize in making the product of the industry in which it has a "comparative advantage" and allow the other country to specialize in the other product. In Ricardo's example, Britain, even if it could make both cloth and wine, should import wine from Portugal and devote its resources to making cloth, an industry in which Britain had a comparative advantage.

Despite the continuing appeal of these simple theories to academic economists, their application in the modern world is doubtful. In an industrialized world, Adam Smith's theory of absolute advantage is weak or irrelevant, because apart from some extractive and agricultural industries the location of industries is not determined by natural geographic endowments but rather by government policies and private enterprise. David Ricardo's alternate theory of comparative advantage works only if neither labor nor capital is highly mobile between countries. In a world with mobile capital and labor, Ricardo conceded, the result of free trade would not be increased trade in goods between nations that specialize according to their comparative advantages but rather what is today called outsourcing: "It would undoubtedly be advantageous to the capitalists of England, and to the consumers in both countries, that under such circumstances, the wine and the cloth should both be made in Portugal, and therefore that the capital and labour of England employed in making cloth, should be removed to Portugal for that purpose."[5] Even in a world in which immigration controls limit the mobility of labor, the mobility of capital dooms Ricardo's theory of comparative advantage, by replacing international trade with the outsourcing of industry to low-cost countries, two quite different things that Ricardo himself distinguished, even if many contemporary economists fail to do so.

Even if the classic theories of free trade were valid in modern conditions, champions of free markets have always acknowledged exceptions to the rule of free trade. J.S. Mill argued for an "infant industry" exception to free trade—countries seeking artificially to create an industry in their borders could nurture it, by means of tariffs, subsidies, or other methods, although once it became competitive the government should withdraw its support.[6] And Adam Smith, the patron saint of free trade, conceded the existence of conflicts between security and trade when he wrote: "The wealth of a neighbouring nation, though dangerous in war and politics, is certainly advantageous in trade . . . "[7] Smith justified deviations from free-market policies in the interest of national security, acknowledging that "defense, however, is of much greater importance than opulence."[8]

While the United States has sometimes championed liberalization of trade and investment, neither the United States nor any other country has ever committed itself completely to the utopian idea of eliminating all regulations on the flow of labor, goods, or capital. Eliminating restrictions on the flow of labor would require the United States and other countries to end policies of regulating and limiting immigration that serve the interests of security, high wages, and cultural community—something that neither the United States nor any country is likely to do. Considerable liberalization of the flow of goods and capital among countries has been achieved. But all countries, including the United States, continue to favor some domestic industries, by subtle means like favorable regulations or by crude ones like protectionist tariffs, non-tariff barriers, government subsidies, or government ownership.

A borderless global market is unlikely to exist as long as the world is divided among sovereign states. A genuine global market could be established only by a world government. But a voluntary global federation is impossible, because the countries of the world will not voluntarily surrender their sovereignty, while the costs of the sacrifice of sovereignty and freedom under a coercive world empire would outweigh the relatively trivial gains in efficiency that might result from the creation of a single global market.

None of this means that the policy of free trade may not be beneficial in some or even most circumstances. It does mean, however, that in an industrialized world with considerable freedom of international investment the argument that free trade is always and everywhere the best policy cannot be made.

Three American Trade Strategies

From the earliest years of the republic, the United States, even when it has preached free trade, has usually pursued an economic policy that strengthened or at least did not undermine its military capability. At times the United States has been protectionist, at other times it has adopted free-trade policies. But for more than two centuries the United States has been consistent in using foreign economic policy as a tool of a larger grand strategy based on considerations of national security as well as private commercial profit. The American way of trade has always been part of the American way of strategy.

The United States has had three major trade policies in its history: infant-industry protection, foreign market opening, and outsourcing. In the nineteenth century, in order to create the industrial basis for U.S. military power, the United States used protectionist policies to promote its infant industries at the expense of those of Britain, then the leading military-industrial power in the world. From the late nineteenth to the late twentieth centuries, the United States, having become the world's leading industrial power, abandoned its earlier protectionist policy and began to promote free trade in order to gain access to foreign markets for American manufactured exports. Beginning in the late twentieth century, the emphasis in U.S. trade policy shifted from access by U.S. exporters to foreign consumer markets to access by U.S. multinational corporations to foreign low-wage labor pools. In this third and most recent stage of American economic strategy, the purpose of free trade was no longer to export goods made in the United States to foreign consumers, but rather to import goods made in foreign countries by enterprises owned by American companies or American investors to consumers within the United States.

Each of these three successive trade strategies has been intended to strengthen American security as well as to increase American wealth. Infant-industry protectionism in the nineteenth century enabled the United States to catch up with and then surpass Britain as a military power. In the twentieth century American leaders promoted an integrated global trading system not only to obtain consumers for American exports but also to eliminate dangerous rivalries among great powers seeking to establish exclusive economic blocs and spheres of influence. In the late twentieth and early twenty-first centuries, the policy of promoting the expatriation or "outsourcing" of industry to low-wage nations carried with it the risk that the U.S. defense industrial base would become dependent on manufacturers in potential enemy states or unstable countries.

The American Economy and the British Empire

The first phase of American trade policy can be understood only in terms of the rivalry of the United States with Britain—a rivalry in which trade politics was always an instrument of power politics.

The American Revolution was as much about economic independence as political independence. Like other European empires in the seventeenth and eighteenth centuries, Britain practiced a policy of mercantilism, or the promotion of its own industries at the expense of its military and commercial rivals. In the mercantilist system, the role of British colonies was to provide agricultural commodities and raw materials to Britain, which in turn sold manufactured goods to consumers in the colonies. The British parliamentarian Edmund Burke explained the role of Britain's North American colonies: "These colonies were evidently founded in subservience to the commerce of Great Britain. From this principle, the whole system of our laws concerning them became a system of restriction. A double monopoly was established on the part of the parent country: 1. a monopoly of their whole import, which is to be altogether from Great Britain; 2. a monopoly of all their export, which is to be no where but to Great Britain, as far as it can serve any purpose here. On the same idea it was contrived that they should send all their products to us raw, and in their first state; and that they should take every thing from us in the last stage of manufacture."[9]

To prevent the American colonies from developing industries of their own the British imperial government outlawed manufacturing in them. The 1699 Wool Act annihilated an emerging textile industry in America, as well as the existing one in Ireland. In the 1720s, London abolished British import duties on raw materials from the American colonies like timber and hemp and provided the American colonists with "bounties" or export subsidies for these goods. The purpose was to encourage the colonists to specialize in raw-material exports and to discourage them from going into manufacturing.[10] In 1732, to eliminate a threatening American beaver-hat industry, London passed a law banning colonies from exporting hats to one another or to foreign countries, in order to force the colonists to ship the beaver pelts to Britain, where the hats would be manufactured.[11]

After the thirteen colonies formed the United States and won their independence, Britain was no longer able to prevent their industrialization by force. But as the first country to exploit the industrial revolution, Britain had an enormous advantage over all others. By the middle of the nineteenth century, Britain had a per capita level of industrialization equal to the combined level of those of France, Russia, the German states, the Austrian Empire, and Italy, and its manufacturing surpassed the combined output of France and Russia.[12] In order to maintain their monopoly of advanced industry as long as possible, the British tried to persuade the people of the United States and other countries not to compete with them in manufacturing.

In *The Wealth of Nations* (1776), Adam Smith promoted Britain's strategic interests by writing: "Were the Americans, either by combination or by any other sort of violence, to stop the importation of European manufactures, and, by thus giving a monopoly to such of their own countrymen as could manufacture the like goods, divert any considerable part of their capital into this employment, they would retard instead of accelerating the further increase in the value of their annual produce, and would obstruct instead of promoting the progress of their country towards real wealth and greatness."[13] To further promote its goal of denying advanced technology to other nations, the British government passed laws making it a crime to export technological information, such as that found in factory and machine blueprints. The U.S. textile industry was founded by industrial espionage, on the basis of plans that had been smuggled illegally out of Britain.[14]

The preference of the British Empire for a United States with a preindustrial, agrarian economy was shared by most Southern planters, who were content for the United States to export cotton and other farm products to Britain, in return for British manufactured goods. The alliance between British manufacturers and Southern slave owners in favor of free trade grew deeper between 1810 and 1860, when the percentage of Britain's cotton imported from the American South rose from 48 percent to more than 90 percent.[15]

The First American Trade Strategy: Protecting Infant Industries

A non-industrial America of the kind sought by the British and the Southern slaveholders would have been a second-rank military power. Alexander Hamilton, the first U.S. secretary of the treasury, argued in his *Report on Manufactures* (1794) that to enhance its military power the U.S. government ought to promote U.S. industries, at the expense of the free market if necessary. As an aide to General Washington during the war of independence, Hamilton had witnessed how the U.S. military had been crippled by the absence of American manufacturing.

Hamilton's successor as the leading proponent of an anti-British policy of infant-industry protectionism was the Kentucky Senator Henry Clay, whose "American System" built on Hamilton's program for turning the United States into a military-industrial superpower by means of protectionist tariffs, federal investment in canals, railroads and other infrastructure projects, and a rationalized national banking system. Like Hamilton, who had realized the extent of American industrial weakness during the revolution, Clay viewed domestic manufacturing as an essential element of U.S. national security: "He would afford them protection, not so much for the sake of the manufacturers themselves, as for the general interest. We should thus have our wants supplied, when foreign resources are cut off, and we should also lay the basis of a system of taxation, to be resorted to when the revenue from imports is stopped by war."[16]

In the first half of the nineteenth century, Hamiltonians who opposed the "British School" of free trade formed their own "American School" of "national economy" or economic nationalism.[17] According to the economic thinkers of the American School, the United States, having won its political independence from the British Empire, now needed to win its economic independence from the British economy. The most important American School economist was the Pennsylvanian Henry C. Carey, whom Karl Marx and Ralph Waldo Emerson, among others, considered the most important economist the United States had produced.[18]

The Southern planters who dominated the federal government between 1800 and 1860 tended to favor international free trade, which served their interests as exporters of cotton, tobacco, and other agricultural commodities. However, the dependence of the United States on British manufactures revealed by the Napoleonic Wars and the War of 1812 convinced even Thomas Jefferson and many of his Southern allies of the need to promote American industry. In 1810, President Jefferson's secretary of the treasury, Albert Gallatin, issued his own *Report on Manufactures*, which like Hamilton's report recommended tariffs, subsidies, and government loans to U.S. industries. Jefferson himself complained that his praise of free trade in *Notes on the State of Virginia* (1781–82) was being quoted by some "to cover their disloyal propensities to keep us in eternal vassalage to a foreign and unfriendly people [Britain]."[19] Jefferson's successor as president, James Madison, argued for exceptions to free-trade theory in his annual address to Congress in 1815.[20] Another eminent Southerner of the Jeffersonian school, Andrew Jackson, complained after the War of 1812, "We have been too long subject to the policy of the British merchants" and observed that a tariff could "afford us the means of that defense within ourselves on which the safety and liberty of the country depend."[21]

The division between the industrial North, which sought a high tariff to protect America's infant industries, and the agricultural South, which wanted a low tariff, persisted throughout the first half of the nineteenth century. The triumph of the Republican Party during and after the Civil War permitted the administration of Abraham Lincoln, a disciple of Henry Clay who was advised by Henry C. Carey, to put Clay's "American System" into effect. A combination of high tariff walls protecting infant industries with a national market and continental resources allowed the United States to keep out British goods while financing its own industries with British capital.[22] American infant-industry policies enabled the United States to surpass Britain as the world's leading industrial power by 1900.

Friedrich List, a German liberal in exile in the United States between 1825 and 1830, who adopted economic nationalism while studying the policies and theories of Alexander Hamilton and others, spread the "American School" gospel of infant-industry protection to the rest of the world.[23] Imperial Germany, founded in 1871, adopted American-style protectionism, and so did Imperial Japan after the Meiji Restoration of 1866–1869. Like Hamilton and Clay, German and Japanese leaders favored the promotion of national industries for military reasons. In the nineteenth century Fukuzawa Yukichi, one of the leading thinkers of the Meiji Restoration, made the connection between military strength and civilian economic productivity clear: "The fact that England has one thousand warships does not mean that she has one thousand warships only. If there are one thousand warships, there have to be at least ten thousand merchant ships, which in turn require at least one hundred thousand navigators; and to create navigators there must be naval science. Only when there are many professors and many merchants, when laws are in order and trade prospers, when social conditions are ripe,—when, that is, you have all the prerequisites for a thousand warships—only then can there be a thousand warships . . . "[24]

The Second American Trade Strategy: Opening Foreign Consumer Markets to American Exporters

By the beginning of the twentieth century the infant-industry protection policy advocated by Alexander Hamilton and Henry Clay and implemented by President Abraham Lincoln and his successors had succeeded. State-sponsored industrial capitalism had enabled the United States first to catch up with Britain and then to surpass it to become the leading manufacturing power in the world, and, potentially, the leading military power in the world.

Having fulfilled its temporary purpose, infant industry protectionism was now obsolete. Small businesses and unions continued to defend high tariffs. But the focus of American trade policy shifted from protecting U.S. industries from foreign competition to opening foreign markets in order to add foreign consumers to America's continental consumer base. Confident of their own strength in export competition, America's manufacturers in their own interest now joined America's farmers in favor of free trade and opening foreign consumer markets. Following World War II, the United States prevailed in making the reduction of tariffs—first by means of successive GATT negotiations, and then through the mechanism of the World Trade Organization (WTO)—central to global economic negotiations.

What explains the transformation of the United States from the world's leading protectionist nation into its leading proponent of universal free trade? The conventional wisdom holds that American policymakers after 1945 woke up to the fact that free trade is universally beneficial in economic terms, and has the additional advantage of promoting world peace. In reality, the United States in 1945 had everything to gain and nothing to lose by promoting global free trade. In the 1840s, having become the world's leading industrial power, Britain began to promote free trade in its own interest. In the 1940s, having become the world's leading industrial power, the United States began to promote free trade in its own interest. The elimination of closed imperial economic blocs, including the British Empire, which a declining Britain had finally closed by adopting protectionist policies in the 1920s, and the creation of a single global market served American economic interests as well as security interests. A global market served American security interests by preventing hostile powers from using force to monopolize the economic resources of weaker countries. And it served American economic interests because U.S. manufacturers had little to fear from foreign industry, while American investors in other countries profited from imports bought by consumers in the United States.

As early as 1939, the British historian E.H. Carr observed: "Down to 1930, successive revisions of the United States tariff had almost invariably been upward; and American economists, in other respects staunch upholders of laissez-faire, had almost invariably treated tariffs as legitimate and laudable. But the change in the position of the United States from a debtor to a creditor Power . . . altered the picture; and the reduction of tariff barriers has come to be commonly identified by American spokesmen with the cause of international morality."[25]

The Pentagon and American Capitalism

One reason that U.S. industry led the world was the role of the federal government in promoting technological advances in areas vital to American national security, from the beginning of the twentieth century to its end.

In 1919 President Woodrow Wilson ordered Assistant Secretary of the Navy Franklin Roosevelt to use federal funds and contracts to develop U.S. capabilities in the strategically important new industry of radio. The result was the Radio Corporation of America (RCA), a federally created corporation whose founding shareholder was the U.S. Navy. In the words of one scholar, "Subsequently RCA not only took leadership in radio but pioneered television and founded the global consumer electronics industry."[26]

Many American industrial titans were either founded by the U.S. government or established with government support, like Boeing, which began with defense contracts during World War I, or AT&T/Bell Labs, which the United States turned into a regulated monopoly.[27] The U.S. Manhattan Project during World War II invented atomic power, and the Pentagon was the most important early customer for computers.

Ironically, globalization, which many attribute to free trade and free markets, is an indirect product of the U.S. military-industrial complex. To link U.S. campuses engaged in defense-related research, the U.S. Defense Advanced Research Projects Administration (DARPA) established a network of computers called DARPANET. After the U.S. government made the decision to allow others to use it, DARPANET grew into the present-day Internet, which has revolutionized commerce and daily life worldwide.[28]

The European Union and
Japanese Mercantilism

At the Bretton Woods Conference in 1944, U.S. officials and a British delegation including the economist John Maynard Keynes hammered out what became known as the "Bretton Woods" system for postwar international economic management. Conservatives wanted the new global market to be based on laissez-faire principles. Liberals like Keynes and the American New Dealers believed that the rise of Fascism and other radical movements during the Depression showed the importance of an economic safety net for the middle class, like the New Deal in the United States. The international economy needed to be regulated, they believed, so that governments would not be compelled to overcome trade imbalances by measures like severe devaluations or deliberate inflation that wrecked their middle classes.

These ambitious plans for global economic governance were defeated. The dollar, based on gold, became the international currency, as the British pound had been in the nineteenth century. The International Monetary Fund (IMF), designed to help advanced countries deal with financial crises on behalf of their middle-class safety nets, dwindled into an organization focused on lending to developing countries. And the major challenge to the postwar American goal of a single global market came from two sources that the Bretton Woods diplomats failed to foresee—European economic integration and Japanese mercantilism.

European economic integration was driven by politics, not economics. Fearing the military implications of German industrial recovery, the French promoted the European Coal and Steel Community, which provided for joint European control over core industrial resources. This became the nucleus of the European Common Market, based on Franco-German collaboration that allowed France to preserve a share of political control over the German economy while allowing West Germany to recover without alarming its neighbors. The French-led Common Market was as much an instrument for controlling German power as was the American-led NATO alliance.

The European Common Market, renamed the European Union (EU), faced a crisis with the end of the Cold War, when West and East Germany were reunited and when the countries of the former Soviet Empire in Eastern Europe applied for admission. Fearing the dominance of a united Germany in a larger and looser Europe, France, reversing its traditional hostility to European federalism to some degree, pushed for a more centralized European system. However, the proposed European constitution that resulted died when voters in France and the Netherlands, fearing that immigration to their nations by poor Eastern Europeans and Muslims, particularly if Turkey were admitted to the EU, would increase under the new system, rejected it in 2005.

The United States welcomed the early formation of the European Common Market, but tensions arose as it evolved into a rival commercial bloc. Nevertheless, the United States consistently sacrificed the short-term economic interests of particular American rivals of European enterprises to its strategic interest in retaining the NATO alliance as the basis for U.S. military hegemony in Europe.

The same policy of sacrificing American business interests to American security interests was followed in U.S.-Japan relations during and after the Cold War. After World War II, the United States hoped that Japan, a demilitarized civilian power, could recover its prosperity by exporting to China and other Asian countries. However, this option was foreclosed by communist control of China, North Korea, and North Vietnam. Instead, Japan recovered in part by supplying U.S. military efforts during the Korean and

Vietnam Wars but primarily by targeting the U.S. consumer market while protecting its own by means of non-tariff barriers. By the 1970s and 1980s, Japan's mercantilist trade policy, emulated by the smaller East Asian "Little Tigers" that also practiced protectionism at home for companies exporting to the United States, was harming a number of U.S. industries. But whenever the Commerce Department pressed Japan hard, the Pentagon and State Department intervened in the interest of the U.S.-Japan alliance. During the first term of President Bill Clinton, a potential trade war between the United States and Japan was averted when the United States once again appeased Japanese mercantilism. It was more important for the United States to remain the military hegemon of East Asia than to pry open Japan's informally closed markets for the benefit of American exporters and investors.

The Third American Trade Strategy: Opening Foreign Labor Markets to American Investors

From the 1890s to the 1990s, the basic premise of American trade policy was that U.S. manufacturers would export goods produced in the United States to consumers abroad. However, thanks to the commercial potential of the Internet, which grew out of the U.S. military's DARPANET program, multinational corporations increasingly were able to distribute the assembly line and supporting functions among many different nations. Intra-firm trade across borders, in which one subsidiary of a multinational corporation ships products to another in a different country, grew to account for a substantial percentage of global trade. At the same time, the end of the Cold War and liberalizing economic policies in the former communist bloc and the developing countries made billions of low-wage workers, skilled as well as unskilled, available to U.S., European, and Japanese multinationals.

As multinational corporations based in the United States, Europe, and Japan transferred much or all of their manufacturing to foreign countries, the goals of U.S. trade policy changed. Instead of exporting U.S.-made goods to foreign consumers, many corporations now wanted to import foreign-made goods from their foreign plants to U.S. consumers. The United States would export capital to countries with low-wage labor pools, which would export cheap manufactured goods to American consumers. The second

American trade strategy had sought to open foreign consumer markets. The third American trade strategy sought to open foreign labor markets in order to "outsource" tasks to foreign workers who could be paid less than American workers.

Although the third American trade strategy represented a radical departure from previous policy, the old rhetoric of free trade was used to justify it. For example, President Clinton and others claimed that the purpose of the NAFTA treaty was to increase exports from the United States to consumers in Mexico, when its purpose as well as its ultimate effect was to allow U.S. corporations to move their factories to Mexico to exploit low labor costs in making goods that were exported to American consumers. In addition, Clinton and others employed the catch-phrase "globalization" to imply that the liberalization of trade and investment was a historical inevitability rather than a matter of choice.

Opponents of the third American trade strategy included some national manufacturing firms, workers in the dwindling manufacturing sector, and others concerned about the national security implications of U.S. deindustrialization. However, the coalition in favor of the new trade strategy was more powerful. It included not only the shareholders of multinational corporations that sought to outsource operations to foreign labor markets, but also investors with an interest in rapid economic growth in countries like China and India pursuing a development strategy based on exports to the U.S. consumer market. A majority of U.S. workers by the beginning of the twenty-first century worked in the non-traded domestic service sector. Their jobs were not threatened by outsourcing and they benefited from cheap imports from low-wage producers like China. As David Ricardo had observed almost two centuries earlier when speculating about the possible replacement of traditional trade by outsourcing in a world of mobile capital, "It would undoubtedly be advantageous to the capitalists . . . and to the consumers," if not to the workers displaced by outsourcing.

The U.S. Promotion of
Global Financial Liberalization

The third American trade strategy involved access by U.S. investors to foreign capital markets as well as access by U.S.-based multinationals to pools of low-wage foreign labor. American investors sought to buy or merely invest in companies in developing countries that exported goods and services to the United States. The economic growth of some developing nations, like China, was more rapid than that of the United States and promised higher returns to American investors than investments in the United States itself. These considerations explain why the Clinton administration, under the leadership of Secretary of the Treasury Robert Rubin, made the liberalization of foreign capital markets a crusade. The new strategy was the complete opposite of the one envisioned by the New Dealers and Keynesians at the Bretton Woods Conference in 1944, half a century earlier. The goal of Bretton Woods had been a world in which manufactured exports flowed freely across borders, while capital movements were controlled.

Already by the 1990s the international movement of goods was dwarfed by the size of international capital flows. The dangers of this trend became clear when nervous investors in the United States and other advanced nations pulled their money out of Asian economies, causing the Asian economic crisis of the late 1990s, the worst financial panic to hit the region since the Great Depression. China and Malaysia, which had resisted U.S. advice to liberalize their capital markets, weathered the storm much better than those countries that had done what U.S. policymakers suggested.

Along with the failure of "shock therapy" policies designed to promote a rapid marketization of the former communist economies of Eastern Europe, the Asian financial crisis caused a rethinking of the "Washington Consensus" that held that untrammeled capitalism is always good for all parties. By the early twenty-first century, painful experience had taught policymakers once again that financial markets, like other markets, need to be regulated in the national interest.

Myths of Globalization

Unfortunately, exaggerated claims about the impact of "globalization" have made it difficult for Americans to engage in rational and informed discussion of the world economy. The end of the Cold War had profound effects on the world economy, thanks to the abandonment of socialism by the former communist countries and some developing countries, and the integration of enormous pools of skilled and unskilled labor, particularly those of China and India, into a new global labor market. These phenomena inspired a new conventional wisdom that rested on three claims: in the new global economy, any job could be performed anywhere; all students should be well trained in science and math to compete in the global labor market; and countries that hoped to compete in the global economy needed to downsize generous welfare states. All three of these beliefs were widely shared by members of the U.S. foreign policy elite. And all three were wrong.

The idea that in the new global economy any job could be performed anywhere was false, or at best only a half-truth. Even the economies that are most open to international trade, which tend to be those of small countries, not continental states like the United States, have both a traded sector exposed to foreign competition and a non-traded sector that is insulated from it. Manufacturing, agriculture, and some service-sector jobs tend to be in the traded sector. But most services, such as home construction and hospital care, by their very nature must be provided by workers in the same location as their customers.

Paradoxically, the result of globalization often is to reduce the number of workers in the sectors affected by globalization. When jobs in the traded sector are eliminated by outsourcing or foreign competition, unemployed workers tend to find new jobs in the non-traded domestic service sector. The laid-off steelworker may join a construction crew. Workers in the non-traded sector face competition for jobs in the national labor market from immigrants. But they do not compete with workers in other countries in a global labor market.

The idea that most workers must be proficient in science and math in order to compete for jobs in the global labor market is equally false. According to the U.S. Department of Labor, the ten fastest-growing occupations in the United States between 2002 and 2012 are the following: "medical assistants; networks systems and data communications analysts; physician assistants; social and human service assistants; home health aides; medical records and health information technicians; physical therapist aides; computer software engineers, applications; computer software engineers, systems software; physical therapist assistants."[29] In the foreseeable future, nurses will outnumber computer technicians in advanced nations like the United States with service-sector economies and rapidly aging populations.

The third misconception holds that in order to compete in the global economy states must pare back or eliminate generous welfare states. The premise is that generous welfare states prevent high-wage countries like the United States from competing with low-wage countries such as China and India in traded-sector industries. But scaling back or abolishing the American welfare state would do nothing to make the United States more competitive, unless American workers were willing to work for Indian or Chinese wages.

Far from being handicapped by big government, the countries with the world's biggest welfare states are flourishing in the global economy. According to the World Economic Forum's Global Competitiveness Report, the most competitive economies in the world are, in order, Finland, the United States, Sweden, Taiwan, Denmark, and Norway. Government consumes around half of gross domestic product in all of these countries, apart from Taiwan and the United States, in which the combined federal-state share of GDP is slightly more than 30 percent.[30] The U.S.-government share of GDP is much higher, when tax deductions and tax exemptions for public purposes like private health insurance are counted.[31]

Nor do generous welfare states necessarily impede economic growth. From 1990 to 2002, Sweden and Finland had the same per capita growth rate as the United States. A generous social safety net may promote greater international competition. If, as a result of foreign competition, workers can lose their jobs without losing health care, pensions, and other benefits, then a populist backlash against international trade may be less likely.

The conventional wisdom in the United States about the global economy, then, is simply mistaken. In the future, most workers in the United States will be immune from foreign competition because they work in the non-traded domestic service sector. Most will not need specialized training in math or science. And a generous welfare state need not be a hindrance to international competitiveness.

Globalization Versus National Security

None of this is meant to suggest that Americans should not be concerned about maintaining productive industries in the traded sector as well as maintaining a large pool of world-class scientists and engineers. But the most compelling argument for both of these goals is the argument from U.S. national security.

During the Cold War, the U.S.-sponsored creation of a global market was compatible with American national security. The leading capitalist nations of the world in Asia and Western Europe were military protectorates of the United States. As a result their post-1945 recovery and economic growth, even if it harmed some U.S. industries, added to the combined strength of the American-led anti-Soviet alliance. The Soviet Union and China had socialist economies that were largely shut off from the rest of the world. Last but not least, the owners of most multinational corporations were Americans, Western Europeans, or Japanese.

None of this remains true, as a result of globalization following the Cold War. China and India may soon emerge as the largest market societies in the world along with the United States. These are also the only two states that can potentially threaten the global balance of power by becoming hegemons in Asia. Unlike Japan and Western Europe during the Cold War, China and India are not subordinate military allies of the United States. Each might become a strategic rival of the United States. The outsourcing of American manufacturing and even research and development to China and India must therefore be a cause for concern, if not necessarily alarm, on the part of American strategists.[32]

While it benefits many American consumers and investors, globalization is a potential threat to U.S. national security in three areas: foreign ownership of U.S. defense contractors; outsourcing of the U.S. defense industrial base to foreign countries, including potential rivals; and the dependence of U.S. corporations, universities, and the government itself on science and engineering students from foreign countries. This is a situation completely without precedent in American history. It was only the superiority of factories, scientists, and engineers within America's borders that allowed the United States to defeat Germany twice and bankrupt the Soviet Union. It would have been disastrous not only for America but also for the world if, in the 1920s, the United States had allowed U.S. corporations to outsource most American industry to Germany, and had subsidized the higher education of German scientists and engineers who then returned to serve Germany.

The Concert of Power and the Concert of Trade

Trade in the United States is usually discussed with no reference to national security or global power politics. But it is obvious that not all kinds of global economic systems are compatible with all systems of power politics. To name only one example, free trade is obviously impossible in a world of hostile great powers, engaged in cold war or actual war with one another.

Although hegemonic powers do not necessarily pursue free trade, hegemony may provide the most favorable conditions for liberalization of trade and finance.[33] In a unipolar system neither the hegemonic power nor the other states must be anxious that trade, by contributing to the economic growth of other countries, will undermine their own security. The hegemon possesses such overwhelming power that it does not worry that lesser powers will convert their prosperity into threatening military force. For their part the lesser states do not worry about the military implications of the economic growth of their neighbors, because they are confident that the hegemon will protect them even if they fall behind in economic growth. In North America, the hegemony of the United States insures that the response of faster growth in Santo Domingo might be jealousy in Haiti but not a Haitian arms buildup.

In a balance of power system with a number of great powers the situation is the reverse, in the case of the great powers if not of minor states. Each great power is a potential adversary of the rest and therefore must be concerned that any growth in another's wealth might be translated into a military threat. Each great power in a balance of power system must be as self-sufficient as possible with respect to the economic basis of military strength. No great power can afford to become economically dependent on another great power, not even on an ally, because today's ally might be tomorrow's enemy in a balance of power system.

A security system based on a concert of power is intermediate between a hegemonic system and a balance of power system. Unlike the hegemonic system, the concert of power system is multipolar, not unipolar. And unlike the balance of power system, the concert of power system is based on a high, though limited, degree of trust among the great powers.

From this it follows that a concert of power system might support a degree of freedom of trade and investment greater than that likely in a balance of power system—but considerably less than that possible in a hegemonic system. To hedge against the possibility that one or more great powers would become aggressive, each great power in the concert would be compelled to maintain a high degree of self-sufficiency in basic military industries and resources. At the same time, however, the great powers would be sufficiently relaxed about the intentions of the others to permit a higher degree of economic integration than they could afford if they felt immediately threatened.

A completely free global market would be unlikely in a world in which peace was maintained by great power concerts. But the alternative need not be a world divided among autarkic great power trade blocs engaged in economic warfare. The economic system most compatible with a concert of power would be a mixture of free trade in sectors that are not essential to the military and policies of national self-sufficiency in military industries on the part of each great power. The economic corollary to the concert of power might be called the concert of trade.

Reconciling National Security and the Benefits of Trade

In the future, as in the past, national military power will depend to a large degree on national manufacturing power. If world peace is to be preserved on the basis of a concert of great military powers, then it should be not only the prerogative but the duty of each great power to maintain the industrial base that is the basis of its military contribution to the concert. The concert of trade should reinforce the concert of power, by permitting, if not requiring, each great power to be relatively self-sufficient in military industries and the strategic civilian industries on which they depend.

Some methods of maintaining minimal military self-sufficiency are better than others. Tariffs on foreign imports are the crudest and least equitable way to protect the strategic industries of the United States and other great powers. A tariff is a highly regressive tax on the consumer that redistributes income from workers and shareholders in some industries and others. Non-tariff barriers like regulations that discriminate against foreign products and local-content regulations are similar to tariffs in their effect.

More equitable methods of preserving strategic industries include government subsidy, government procurement (a kind of subsidy), or direct government ownership of industries. These methods are fairer to consumers than tariffs, because the direct or indirect subsidy is paid for by all taxpayers, rather than the consumers of imports alone, as in the case of a tariff. And subsidies for producers, while they deviate from the utopian ideal of a perfect free market, can be compatible with a high degree of free trade. Although subsidies in general are preferable to tariffs, there is a danger that the industries that are subsidized will be those that can mobilize voters or finance politicians, not the ones whose survival is necessary for the military strength of the United States and other great powers.

Market-share agreements, like subsidies, provide a way to reconcile the benefits of free trade with the need to prevent some domestic industries from completely disappearing. For decades market-share agreements were used by the United and other nations in the area of textile trade. Although they fell out of favor during the 1990s, a period of utopian optimism about globalization, in the twenty-first century market-share agreements ought to be made the basis of international trade in strategic industrial sectors that every major nation or trading bloc wants to promote—advanced electronics and aerospace today and, perhaps, robotics, photonics, or nanonics, or even more exotic technologies tomorrow. Free-trade purists may not like market-share agreements, but of all of the ways for nations to prevent domestic industries from being eliminated by outsourcing or global competition, market-share globalism may be the one that deviates least from the ideal of free trade.

While the members of great power concerts must be allowed to preserve and foster their own militarily-relevant industries, in order to permit them to play their shared roles in providing security, the same logic does not apply to the lesser powers that are protected by the great powers. If the great powers are effective in providing free security for their weaker neighbors, then those neighbors have less need to be concerned about the effects of international trade and investment on their safety. Great power concerts, if successful, can permit the majority of countries to adopt freedom of trade and investment, if they choose, without endangering their security.

The Arsenal of American Democracy

Even in the United States, where suspicion of government involvement in the economy has always been deep and intense, it has always been recognized that sometimes the government, rather than the private sector, should provide certain public goods that are paid for out of tax revenues. One of those public goods is national defense.

In 1794, after Congress authorized the construction of six ships for the U.S. Navy, President George Washington rejected the idea of hiring private builders to work under federal contract. Instead, Washington decided, it would be cheaper and more efficient for the federal government to build each ship itself—and to build it in a separate port, in the interests both of security and local economic growth.[34] From the eighteenth century until World War II, the U.S. Navy built its own ships in government shipyards, and the U.S. Army manufactured its own weapons in federal arsenals, using private contractors only temporarily during wars. It was only after World War II that the military came to rely on private defense contractors rather than on its own factories during peacetime.[35]

If the outsourcing of industry by U.S. corporations threatens to make the U.S. military dependent on foreign manufacturers and foreign suppliers, the simplest response might be for the federal government to make the U.S. military's weapons and equipment itself. The argument that a return to this venerable American tradition would represent an expansion of government at the expense of the market does not hold up to scrutiny. The government would not be displacing any consumers, because the U.S. government and the governments of its allies are the only consumers of what the military-industrial complex produces. The military-industrial sector of the U.S. economy will be the same size, whether or not the government buys missiles from private defense contractors or makes them in government factories. The federal government could probably save a great deal of money, because the salaries of military and civilian career officials are far below the remuneration packages of executives of private defense firms.

Competition is limited by the small number of private defense contractors. The benefits of competition might be obtained from competition among rival laboratories, factories, and shipyards within the federal defense industrial system. And a great deal of political corruption would be eliminated, because federal civil servants, unlike the highly paid executives of defense contractors, would have no profits that could be used to buy the support of politicians.

In addition to having many suppliers, in order to avoid depending on one or a few, the government, as the final manufacturer of military goods, could choose to buy the majority of strategic supplies from firms located in the United States or North America. The federal government could also use military manufacturing to maintain a minimum workforce of scientists and engineers. According to the National Science Foundation, China could be producing four times as many doctorates in engineering as the United States; already by 2002, China and the United States issued roughly the same numbers of graduate-level engineering degrees.[36] Today American corporations complain that they are forced to outsource science and engineering jobs, because not enough Americans go into those fields. But why would any rational American student spend years training for a science or engineering job in the private sector that is likely to be outsourced to China, India, or another country where individuals with high skills are willing to work for low wages? Careers in a U.S. government military manufacturing and research system, unlike those in the private sector, could be invulnerable to the threat of outsourcing.

The Cold War–era experiment with the privatization of the defense industrial base was a half-century deviation from the American tradition of public ownership of the U.S. arms industry, which lasted from the 1790s until the 1940s. Now that globalization exposes the U.S. defense industrial base to the possible dangers of foreign control and erosion by outsourcing, it is time to reconsider the older American tradition.

Power Politics and Trade Politics

The first two American trade strategies, infant-industry protection and opening foreign consumer markets, enhanced U.S. national security by enhancing the U.S. military-industrial base. By means first of protectionism and then of consumer base expansion, the United States increased the scale and efficiency of domestic manufacturing, which, as the world wars and the Cold War showed, could be transformed quickly into U.S. military power in an age of industrial warfare. By contrast, the third American trade strategy promotes the deindustrialization of the United States, in the interests of American consumers, investors, and multinationals, but at the possible expense of American security.

Can a country that has outsourced most or all of its manufacturing remain the world's only superpower—or even a great power? The question is particularly urgent inasmuch as several of the rising industrial giants to which U.S. corporations and investors are transferring manufacturing, like China and India, are likely to be the rising military giants of the future.

Liberal utopians have claimed for generations that economic interdependence promises to bring about an end to war and great power rivalry for all time. But this remains as doubtful today as in the past. Whatever may be the basis of economic productivity in the future, the subordination of economic policy to the differing national security strategies of individual countries will remain a feature of world politics, as long as no country or bloc succeeds in becoming an enduring global hegemon and permanently subordinating the economic interests of other nations to its own. The historic concern of strategists with the military implications of economic power remains as valid as ever.

The words of George Washington remain as true today as when, in his first annual address to Congress in January 1790, the first president declared, "A free people ought not only to be armed but disciplined" and therefore "their safety and interest required that they should promote such manufactories as tend to render them independent of others for essential, particularly military, supplies."[37]

Chapter 14

The World Order
Which We Seek

The world order which we seek is the cooperation of free
countries, working together in a friendly, civilized society.
—Franklin Delano Roosevelt, 1941

WHEN SEARCHING FOR GUIDANCE IN THINKING ABOUT U.S. FOREIGN POLICY, many
Americans ransack the histories of other countries and other times. Some
hold up Periclean Athens as a model and assert that Americans should
learn the lessons of the Peloponnesian War. Others prefer nineteenth-century
Europe and ponder the statecraft of Bismarck or Metternich. Some, who
think that the United States should dominate the peoples of the Middle
East or Africa in the service of American hegemony or humanitarian be-
nevolence, cite the colonial wars of the British Empire. Others exaggerate
foreign military threats by comparing the United States to Britain at its
hour of maximum peril in 1939 and calling for an American Churchill.

These intellectual masquerades are as entertaining as a Beaux Arts ball,
in which partygoers dress up in togas, horned Viking helmets, or eighteenth-
century wigs, and they are just as frivolous. Whatever may have been the
case in the early 1900s, when the United States was first emerging as a
great power, today American strategists have a century of American great
power theory and practice to guide them. The country whose historical
experience holds the most apt lessons for the United States of today is the
United States of yesterday. U.S. foreign policy should be rooted in the time-
tested American strategic tradition, not in that of Victorian Britain or
Bismarckian Germany or ancient Rome or ancient Greece. When American
leaders have followed the American way of strategy, they have led the
American republic from success to success, and when they have deviated
from it the results have been disastrous.

How Americans Forgot the American Way of Strategy

Unfortunately, in recent generations the American way of strategy has been in eclipse. If a single date must be found for the break with the historic American way of strategy, it was Friday, January 20, 1961. On that date President John F. Kennedy delivered his Inaugural Address, in which he said: "Let every nation know, whether it wishes us well or ill, that we shall pay any price, bear any burden, meet any hardship, support any friend, oppose any foe, in order to assure the survival and the success of liberty."[1]

Pay any price? Bear any burden? Liberty at home or abroad? Most of Kennedy's admirers, along with his critics, interpreted this as a call for a crusade to bring liberty everywhere in the world—a crusade in which the cost to Americans—"we shall pay any price"—was not an object of concern. It is true that, later in his Inaugural Address, Kennedy spoke of "both sides overburdened by the cost of modern weapons." But it was Kennedy's pledge that the United States would "pay any price, bear any burden" on behalf of a vague crusade for "liberty" beyond U.S. borders that was remembered by Americans, including many who later supported Republican presidents like Ronald Reagan and George W. Bush.

Presidents before Kennedy, including Wilson, Roosevelt, Truman, and Eisenhower, had engaged in idealistic rhetoric about the universalization of democracy and human rights. But they also had gone to great lengths to explain how the freedom of Americans at home would be threatened if foreign danger made an American garrison state necessary. Kennedy and his successors by contrast tended to speak as though there were a direct link between the freedom of anyone in any country anywhere and the freedom of Americans at home. This assertion may have been far more inspiring than reasoned arguments about the need to avoid an American garrison state by taking part in international alliances, but it was false. During most of its history, the United States successfully maintained a liberal, civilian, and democratic system even though most of the rest of the world was illiberal, militarist, and undemocratic. Autocratic great powers like Germany and the Soviet Union had threatened American republican liberty by threatening American security, but dictatorship in Latin America, deplorable as it was, had never threatened the American way of life.

By the end of the Cold War, American public discourse about foreign policy had lost touch with the philosophy of democratic republican liberalism that had shaped it as late as the 1950s. The debate tended to be polarized between idealistic internationalists, who spoke of U.S. foreign policy as though it were an endless crusade to share the American way of life with other nations, or even to impose it on them, and isolationists, in whom the healthy American republican suspicion of imperialism was exaggerated by paranoia about the U.S. government.

The idealists and the isolationists were sometimes joined by thinkers of the *Realpolitik* school who tried, not very successfully, to recommend nineteenth-century European power politics as a guide for U.S. foreign policy in the twenty-first century. Many of the theorists of *Realpolitik* were European émigrés, like the German Hans Morgenthau, an influential academic whose appalling ignorance of America's subtle and complex foreign policy tradition is evident in remarks he published in 1952: "Until very recently the American people have appeared content to live in a political desert whose intellectual barrenness and aridity was relieved only by some sparse and neglected oases of insight and wisdom. What passed for foreign policy was either improvisation or—especially in our century—the invocation of some abstract moral principle in whose image the world was to be made over."[2] Morgenthau's proposed alternative to the "intellectual barrenness" of the American foreign policy tradition was the German approach to power politics, which did so much for Germany in the twentieth century.

As the American way of strategy was forgotten by Americans themselves, U.S. foreign policy oscillated wildly between the amoral *Realpolitik* of Richard Nixon and his national security adviser Henry Kissinger and the Kennedyesque rhetoric of George W. Bush in his second Inaugural Address in 2005: "It is the policy of the United States to seek and support the growth of democratic movements and institutions in every nation and culture, with the ultimate goal of ending tyranny in the world." The older American tradition of foreign policy, which combined republican liberal idealism with prudent concern about the effect of a costly foreign policy on the American republic, has been lost. Without the American way of strategy to serve as a compass in uncharted seas, the United States has been adrift.

The American Way of Strategy

America's wisest leaders have always understood that the purpose of American strategy is not only to defend the people and territory of the United

States, but also to defend the American way of life. The goal of American foreign policy is not so much to prevent others from imposing tyranny on us, as to make it unnecessary for us to obtain our security from others by imposing tyranny on ourselves. To repeat an earlier formulation of this idea: *The purpose of the American way of strategy is to defend the American way of life by means that do not endanger the American way of life.*

The American way of life is democratic republican liberalism. It is embodied in civilian government, checks and balances, a commercial economy, and individual freedom. As a response to foreign danger, the American people might abandon their democratic republic in favor of a tributary state, a garrison state, or a castle society. The tributary state temporarily purchases liberty at home by surrendering independence in foreign affairs. The garrison state is characterized by military government, presidential rule, a statist economy, and individual conscription. The castle society is characterized by weak or absent government, a barter economy, and individual self-defense.

Any of these three alternatives to American democratic republicanism can be a response by the American people to foreign danger. The two greatest threats to the United States are foreign empire and foreign anarchy—the domination of the world outside North America by one or a few militarized empires, or the disintegration of much of the world beyond our borders into chaos. The ultimate goal of preserving a democratic republican liberal way of life inside of America's borders requires success in the proximate goal of minimizing the dangers of empire and anarchy beyond America's borders. This proximate goal, in turn, is best achieved by means of the American way of strategy, which minimizes the dangers of empire and anarchy by two means: liberal internationalism as a system of world order and realism as a system of power politics.

The Case for Liberal Internationalism Restated

According to the mainstream tradition in American foreign policy, the best way to minimize the dangers of empire and anarchy in the world is a liberal international system—a world divided into a plurality of sovereign states. The plurality of states checks potential regional and global empires, while the sovereignty of each state over part of the earth's surface limits anarchy and the evils associated with it like transnational terrorism, crime, illegal migration, pollution, and epidemics. All human beings should be policed by a competent but not tyrannical state; and all of the states of the world share an interest in maintaining their sovereignty against aggressors.

Liberal internationalism can protect America's republican way of life even if all sovereign states are not liberal states, much less liberal states that, like the United States, are also democratic republics. Americans have always believed that liberal states are superior in the abstract to illiberal states, and that among liberal states those with democratic republican constitutions are the best. But wise American statesmen have recognized that a liberal society requires the achievement of certain social conditions, and that the preconditions for a democratic republican liberal state are even more difficult to achieve. In the meantime, the priority of the United States is the preservation of the post-imperial society of sovereign states, not crusades for liberalism or democracy.

America's Changing Grand Strategy

The goal of thwarting empire and anarchy, pursued in the realm of world order by liberal internationalism, must also be pursued in the realm of power politics by realism. American statecraft has combined support for liberal internationalism as a set of rules with guidance by realism in the realm of power politics.

U.S. foreign policy has always been influenced to some degree by domestic factors, ranging from economic interest to ethnic lobbies and the power of religious and ideological movements. But the main factor that has shaped the major strategic decisions of the United States has been fear of other great powers. U.S. policymakers have feared that the United States might be encircled in North America by the allies or protectorates of extra-hemispheric powers. And they also have feared that, even if the United States is secure in its domination of North America, a hostile power or alliance might win global domination by controlling the military and economic resources of Europe, Asia, or both, and then proceed to threaten the United States with direct attack or slow strangulation.

The first fear—the fear of a Balkanized North America—inspired the United States to gain control over the mouth and valley of the Mississippi River, the Gulf Coast, and Florida from France and Spain. The United States then denied influence or control of the ports of San Francisco and San Diego to Britain, and divided control of the Strait of San Juan de Fuca with Britain. Similarly, fear of Imperial Germany impelled the United States to build the Panama Canal and assert its hegemony over the Caribbean and Central America, in order to guard the sea approaches to the United States. By achieving hegemony in North America, while avoiding disintegration in the Civil War, the United States ended the threat of a balance of power in North America that might be manipulated by hostile external powers.

The second fear remained—the fear that a hostile power that established hegemony in Europe, Asia, or both would be able to deploy military forces that an isolated and outnumbered United States could not match. To avert that danger, the United States financed and fought in struggles to prevent Germany from dominating Europe, Japan from dominating Asia, and So-viet Russia from dominating both.

Fear of other great powers continued to shape American strategy during the Cold Peace that followed the Cold War. American strategists feared not only a rising China and a revitalized Russia but also the re-emergence of Germany and Japan as independent military powers. To strengthen its po-sition in possible future conflicts with China or Russia, while forestalling the independence of Japan and Germany, the United States expanded its Cold War protectorate system into Eastern Europe and Central Asia while seeking to create an exclusive U.S. military sphere of influence in the oil-producing Middle East, a region of concern to all of the great powers.

The strategy of denying key regions to other great powers has often led the United States into war against minor powers, which in effect have been pawns in great power rivalries. In the Mexican War, the United States con-quered Mexico in order to prevent an independent California from becom-ing a British protectorate or colony. In the Spanish-American War, the United States fought Spain in order to deny Cuba and Puerto Rico to European great powers, particularly Germany; subsequently, the United States con-quered Spain's former Philippine colony in order to deny it to Germany or other great powers.

The United States has also fought small wars in the interest of proving U.S. credibility to countries that the United States has promised to protect. In the Korean and Vietnam Wars the United States fought clients of the Soviet Union and China in order to reaffirm its credibility as the defender of Japan and Western Europe against the communist bloc. In the rogue state wars of the 1990s and 2000s, the United States fought Serbia and confronted North Korea, in order to assert its enduring role in Europe and East Asia. In the Middle East the United States fought Iraq and contained Iran as part of its strategy of acting as the regional policeman, reducing the incentive of the other great powers to protect their interests in the Middle East by developing their own long-distance power projection forces of the kind that the United States sought to monopolize.

The Greatest Strategic Failures of the United States

The traditional formula for American security combines U.S. hegemony in North America with a pattern of power favorable to U.S. interests in the world as a whole. In the nineteenth century, by expanding across the continent and achieving regional hegemony in North America, the United States averted the danger of a North American balance of power, in which a smaller and weaker United States would have been only one of several actors in a Balkanized continent manipulated by extra-hemispheric great powers. From its secure position as the hegemon of North America, the United States in the twentieth century was able successfully to intervene to prevent Germany or Russia from dominating Europe and also to prevent Japan or Russia from dominating Asia.

In addition to enjoying successes, American strategy has also suffered from failures. Since the United States emerged as a great power around 1900, it has undertaken two misguided grand strategies, in two periods of two decades each. In the 1920s and 1930s, the United States retreated into isolation. In the 1990s and 2000s, the United States sought global hegemony. Each of these policies appealed to Americans who did not like the idea of the United States taking part in traditional power politics by collaborating with other great powers in alliances or concerts.

Isolationists hoped to ban traditional power politics from the North American quarter sphere, while those who might be called hegemonists sought to replace traditional power politics with a Pax Americana in which the United States would persuade some great powers to renounce their military independence and dissuade others from seeking to challenge American might. The isolationists and hegemonists both opposed U.S. participation in great power alliances. The isolationists demanded that the United States avoid "entangling alliances" while the hegemonists preferred "coalitions of the willing" or unilateral U.S. efforts disguised by the token participation of weak client states. The post–World War I isolationists were unilateralist because they feared that alliances would force the United States to wage war. The post–Cold War hegemonists were unilateralist because they feared that alliances would not permit the United States to wage war.

The isolationists of the 1920s and 1930s resembled the hegemonists of the 1990s and 2000s in another way. Each group misunderstood the relationship between security and power. The isolationists made the mistake of thinking that security can be achieved without power. The hegemonists made the mistake of thinking that security and power are identical. They failed to understand that maximizing power does not necessarily maximize security. Indeed, the attempt by a state to obtain more power may make it less secure by alarming other states into taking measures against it.

In the 1920s and 1930s, between the two world wars, American isolationists were disdainful of alliances and neglectful of the U.S. military-industrial base. Instead of entering into an alliance with Britain and France to prevent German revanchism, the United States adopted a policy of unilateralism and isolationism. Instead of treating the Soviet Union it as a potential check on a revival of German power, the United States refused to grant diplomatic recognition to Moscow until 1933. In addition, U.S. leaders between the world wars failed to pay for an adequate military. The isolationists paid for their strategic folly when the Japanese attacked Pearl Harbor.

In the 1990s and 2000s, a similar combination of haughty confidence in American unilateralism and neglect of U.S. military-industrial power characterized the hegemonists, neoliberal Democrats and neoconservative Republicans who dominated U.S. foreign policy following the Cold War. While the isolationists had feared that great power allies would draw the United States into conflicts in other parts of the world, the hegemonists feared that great power allies would handicap America in its attempt to establish global hegemony by consolidating its permanent military supremacy in Europe, Asia, and the Middle East. While spending vast sums on the U.S. military, America's bipartisan foreign policy establishment turned a blind eye to the erosion of the U.S. defense industrial base by the forces unleashed in the new global economy. Neither the jihadist attacks of 9/11 nor the debacle of the Iraq War were catastrophes on the scale of the burning of Washington and Pearl Harbor, because no hostile great powers were involved. But the hegemonist strategy of extending unilateral U.S. commitments while outsourcing American manufacturing industry was doomed to collapse even in the absence of a great power attack or a global conflict. With justification, given the existence of less-expensive alternatives like great power concerts and balance of power alliances, the American people will not make the sacrifices in taxes and military manpower necessary for the U.S. hegemony strategy to endure.

In the 1920s and 1930s, the United States did too little. In the 1990s and 2000s, the United States did too much.

Beyond U.S. Hegemony: Regional Concerts of Power

In the twenty-first century, the relative strategic weights of Europe and Asia are the reverse of what they were in the twentieth century. Asia will contain the greatest concentration of military-industrial power and Europe the second-greatest. America's interest in preventing a potentially hostile hegemon from dominating either region remains as vital today as in the past. The third critical region remains the Greater Middle East, which includes the oil-producing countries of Central Asia as well as those of the Persian Gulf.

Unilateral U.S. military domination of these three critical regions is not necessary, and over a prolonged period it is not affordable at an acceptable cost in American taxes and American lives. Instead of continuing a policy of soft containment of China and Russia, combined with perpetual U.S. protectorates over Japan and Germany, the United States ought to involve both former Cold War enemies and former Cold War allies in regional concerts of power in Asia and Europe. In the event of an aggressive policy on the part of one or more regional powers, the regional concert can be converted into an anti-hegemonic coalition in which the United States takes part. The goal of such an anti-hegemonic alliance, if possible, should be to change the aggressive state's policy, in order to restore it to a legitimate role in the regional concert, rather than to destroy its power, thereby creating a power vacuum that might be filled by another major country in the region or by anarchy.

Instead of trying to establish U.S. hegemony over the Middle East, the United States should return to its pre–Gulf War policy of preserving a balance of power among the states of the region, so that no regional power or external power can succeed in dominating the oil-producing countries of the area. In doing so, the United States should cooperate with China, India, Russia, and the major European powers. In addition, the United States and the other great powers should encourage a regional concert of power in the Middle East, while recognizing that success in that project is not likely in the near future.

Woodrow Wilson was not always right about the details of American grand strategy. But he was right about its objective: "There must be, not a balance of power, but a community of power; not organized rivalries, but an organized common peace."[3]

Preserving the American Way of Life

America's wisest leaders have understood that the purpose of American strategy is not only to defend the people and territory of the United States, but also to defend the American way of life. The greatest threat to the American way of life has always been the possibility that the American people reluctantly might jettison their democratic republican government and social order in order to obtain security.

For two centuries, in changing world conditions, the grand strategy of the United States has sought to promote an external environment in which long-term security costs are relatively low so that there is no need for either an American garrison state or an American tributary state and little danger of an American castle society. Americans have used their power to reshape their environment so that they do not have to reshape their society. Instead of adapting their way of life to the world order they found, they adapted the world order they found to their way of life. Most American statesmen would agree with Paul Nitze and his colleagues, who wrote in NSC-68 of "our determination to create conditions under which our free and democratic system can live and prosper."

In promoting a favorable international order that would make an American garrison state unnecessary, the United States has been guided by enlightened self-interest, not altruism. Americans have sought to create a safer world in order to preserve their own way of life, not to bring liberty or democracy or prosperity to other nations. A world safe for American democracy need not be a democratic world. But it will be a world in which more countries can become democratic republics without risking their security.

The politicians on the Fourth of July and the columnists on Memorial Day, then, are correct. Americans have fought at home and abroad so that their relatives and descendants and fellow citizens can continue to be free to enjoy the American way of life. Generations of American soldiers have indeed fought and died for the freedom of Americans at home.

Notes

Chapter 1

1. Woodrow Wilson, "Address at Coliseum, St. Louis, Mo., September 5, 1919," in *The Papers of Woodrow Wilson*, ed. Arthur Link (Princeton, N.J.: Princeton University Press, 1990), 63: 46–47.
2. "NSC 68: United States Objectives and Programs for National Security," April 14, 1950, in Thomas Etzold and John Lewis Gaddis, eds., *Containment: Documents on American Policy and Strategy, 1945–1950* (New York: Columbia University Press, 1978), 401.
3. Dwight D. Eisenhower, "The Chance for Peace, April 16, 1953." *Public Papers of the President of the United States: Dwight D. Eisenhower, January 20–December 31, 1947* (Washington, D.C.: U.S. Government Printing Office, 1960), 179–188.
4. Dwight D. Eisenhower, "Farewell Radio and Television Address to the American People, January 17, 1961." *Public Papers of the President of the United States: Dwight D. Eisenhower, January 1, 1960–January 21, 1961* (Washington, D.C.: U.S. Government Printing Office, 1961), 1035–40.
5. Woodrow Wilson, "Address at Coliseum, St. Louis, Mo., September 5, 1919."
6. See the discussion in Daniel Patrick Moynihan, *On the Law of Nations* (Cambridge, Mass.: Harvard University Press, 1992).
7. John Adams, *A Defence of the Constitutions of Government of the United States of America* (New York: Da Capo Press, 1971 [1787]), 3:160–61.
8. Henry Saint-John Bolingbroke, *Letters on the Spirit of Patriotism* (Oxford: Clarendon Press, 1917), 74–75.
9. See Quentin Skinner, *Liberty Before Liberalism* (Cambridge: Cambridge University Press, 1997); M.N.S. Sellers, *The Sacred Fire of Liberty: Republicanism, Liberalism and the Law* (New York: New York University Press, 1998); idem, *American Republicanism: Roman Ideology in the United States Constitution* (New York: New York University Press, 1994).
10. Samuel P. Huntington, *American Politics: The Promise of Disharmony* (Cambridge, Mass.: Belknap Press, 1981).
11. For an analysis of the distinctive Southern tradition in politics and economics, see Michael Lind, *Made in Texas: George W. Bush and the Southern Takeover of American Politics* (New York: Basic Books, 2003), idem, "Civil War by Other Means," *Foreign Affairs* (September/October 1999). The best discussion of regional political cultures in the United States is David Hackett Fischer, *Albion's Seed: Four British*

Folkways in America (New York: Oxford University Press, 1989). Another informative study is Daniel J. Elazar, *The American Mosaic: The Impact of Space, Time, and Culture on American Politics* (San Francisco: Westview Press, 1994). See also Walter Russell Mead, *Special Providence: American Foreign Policy and How It Changed the World* (New York: Knopf, 2001); Anatol Lieven, *America Right or Wrong: An Anatomy of American Nationalism* (New York: Oxford University Press, 2004).

12. John Adams to James Sullivan, May 26, 1776, in *The Works of John Adams,* ed. Charles Francis Adams (Boston, 1850–1856), 9: 376–77, quoted in Drew R. McCloy, *The Elusive Republic: Political Economy in Jeffersonian America* (New York: W. W. Norton, 1980), 68.

13. Alan F. Zundel, *Declarations of Dependency: The Civic Republican Tradition in U.S. Poverty Policy* (Albany: State University of New York, 2000), 25.

14. Michel-Guillaume St. John de Crevecoeur, *Letters from an American Farmer* (New York: E. P. Dutton, 1957), 51–52.

15. Register of Debates in Congress, 19th Cong., 1st sess., May 16, 1826, 727–28.

16. Quoted in Tony Smith and Richard C. Leone, *America's Mission* (Princeton, N.J.: Princeton University Press, 1994), 123.

17. According to Samuel P. Huntington, the U.S. military prides itself on being professional and apolitical. Samuel P. Huntington, *The Soldier and the State* (New York: Vintage Books, 1957). See also Peter A. Feaver and Richard H. Kohn, *Soldiers and Civilians: The Civil-Military Gap and American National Security* (Cambridge, Mass.: MIT Press, 2001); Thomas M. Langston, *Uneasy Balance: Civil-Military Relations in Peacetime America Since 1783* (Baltimore: Johns Hopkins University Press, 2003); Charles J. Dunlap, Jr., "The Origins of the American Military Coup of 2012," *Parameters* (winter 1992–93): 2–20.

18. See the discussion in Daniel Patrick Moynihan, *On the Law of Nations* (Cambridge, Mass.: Harvard University Press, 1992).

19. Harold B. Lasswell, "The Garrison State," *The American Journal of Sociology* 46 (1941): 455–68; Lasswell, "The Garrison-State Hypothesis Today," in Samuel P. Huntington, ed., *Changing Patterns of Military Politics* (New York: The Free Press of Glencoe, 1962), 51–70. See also Aaron D. Friedberg, "Why Didn't the United States Become a Garrison State?" *International Security* 16, no. 4 (1992): 109–37; idem, *In the Shadow of the Garrison State* (Princeton, N.J.: Princeton University Press, 2000).

20. Alexander Hamilton, "Federalist 8," in Robert Scigliano, ed., *The Federalist: A Commentary on the Constitution of the United States* (New York: The Modern Library, 2001), 42.

21. John C. Calhoun, *A Disquisition on Government and Selections from the Discourse,* ed. C. Gordon Post (Indianapolis: Hackett Publishing, 1995), 41.

22. Franklin D. Roosevelt, "The Arsenal of Democracy: Introducing Lend-Lease, December 29, 1940," in Russell D. Buhite and David W. Levy, eds., *FDR's Fireside Chats* (Norman: University of Oklahoma Press, 1992), 163–73.

23. Franklin D. Roosevelt, "Annual Message to Congress, January 6, 1941," in Stamford Parker, ed., *The Words That Reshaped America: FDR* (New York: HarperCollins, 2000), 157–66.

24. Rudyard Kipling, "Dane-Geld: A.D. 980–1016," in *Rudyard Kipling: Complete Verse: Definitive Edition* (New York: Anchor Books, 1989 [Doubleday, 1940]), 716–17. The term "tributary state" is used by Alexander Hamilton in "Federalist 7," in connection with the possibility that the disintegration of the United States might lead to the domination of some of the successor states by others: "The opportunities which some States would have of rendering others tributary to them by commercial regulations would be impatiently submitted to by the tributary States." Alexander Hamilton, "Federalist 7," in Hamilton, Jay, and Madison, *The Federalist,* 37. In "Federalist 3," John Jay describes how a powerful state can humiliate a weak one: "In the year 1685, the state of Genoa having offended Louis XIV, endeavored to appease him. He demanded that they should send their *Doge,* or chief magistrate, accompanied by four of their sena-

tors, to *France*, to ask his pardon and receive his terms. They were obliged to submit to it for the sake of peace. Would he on any occasion either have demanded or have received the like humiliation from Spain, or Britain, or any other *powerful* nation?" John Jay, "Federalist 3," in Hamilton, Jay, and Madison, *The Federalist*, 17.

25. Ex parte Milligan, 4 Wallace 2 (1866).
26. James Madison, "Political Reflections," in David B. Mattern, J.C.A. Stagg, Jeanne K. Cross, and Susan Holbrook Perdue, eds., *The Papers of James Madison. Volume 17: 31 March 1797–3 March 1801, with a Supplement, 22 January 1778–9 August 1795* (Charlottesville: University Press of Virginia, 1991), 242

Chapter 2

1. Woodrow Wilson, "War Message, April 2, 1917," 65th Congress, 1st Session. Senate Doc. No. 5, Serial No. 7264, Washington, D.C., 1917: 3–8.
2. Among others who have made this point are G. John Ikenberry and Charles A. Kupchan, "Liberal Realism: The Foundations of a Democratic Foreign Policy," *National Interest* 77 (fall 2004): 38–49.
3. See Robert Jackson, *The Global Concert: Human Conduct in a World of States* (New York: Oxford University Press, 2000).
4. Hedley Bull, *The Anarchical Society: A Study of Order in World Politics*, 3rd ed. (New York: Columbia University Press, 2002 [1977]). Along with Martin Wight and Adam Watson, Bull belonged to the "English School" of international relations theory that promoted a conception of international society sometimes described as "Grotian" after Hugo Grotius, the seventeenth-century Dutch theorist of international law. See Martin Wight, *Power Politics* (New York: Holmes & Meier, 1978); idem, *International Theory: The Three Traditions* (New York: Holmes & Meier, 1992); Adam Watson, *The Evolution of International Society: A Comparative Historical Analysis* (New York: Routledge, 1992). See also Barry Buzan, *From International to World Society?: English School Theory and the Social Structure of Globalization*, Cambridge Studies in International Relations (Cambridge: Cambridge University Press, 2004). Notwithstanding its name, the English School has much in common with traditional American liberal internationalism from the eighteenth century to the present. See Michael Lind, "Toward a Global Society of States," *The Wilson Quarterly* 26, 3 (August 2002): 59–70.
5. George W. Bush, Second Inaugural Address, "President Sworn-In to Second Term," News and Policies, January 2005, www.whitehouse.gov/news/releases/2005/01/20050120-1.html.
6. Hamilton to the Marquis de Lafayette, January 6, 1799, *The Papers of Alexander Hamilton*, ed. Harold C. Syrett and assoc. ed. Jacob E. Cooke (New York: Columbia University Press, 1961–87), 22: 404.
7. Adams to James Lloyd, March 27, 1815, *The Works of John Adams, second President of the United States, With a life of the author, notes, and illus. by his grandson, Charles Francis Adams* (Freeport, N.Y.: Books for Libraries Press, 1969), 10: 145–49.
8. Adams to Richard Rush, May 14, 1821, *The Works of John Adams*, 10: 397.
9. Jefferson to Joseph Fay, March 18, 1793, *The Papers of Thomas Jefferson*, Julian P. Boyd, ed., Lyman Butterfield et al., assoc. eds. (Princeton, N.J.: Princeton University Press, 1950–2004), 25: 402.
10. Jefferson to William Short, January 3, 1793, *The Papers of Thomas Jefferson*, 25: 14–16.
11. Thomas Jefferson, "War, Revolution, and Restoration: To Lafayette, Monticello, February 14, 1815," *The Writings of Thomas Jefferson*, ed. H. A. Washington (New York: Derby and Jackson, 1859), 6: 421–27.
12. Thomas Jefferson, "Letter to John Adams, September 4, 1823," *The Writings of Thomas Jefferson*, ed. H. A. Washington (Washington, D.C.: Taylor and Maury, 1854), 7: 807–9.

13.   Martin Malia, *Russia Under Western Eyes: From the Bronze Horseman to the Lenin Mausoleum* (Cambridge, Mass.: Belknap Press, 1999), 57–59.

14.   Woodrow Wilson, "Self-Government in France," *The Papers of Woodrow Wilson*, ed. Arthur S. Link (Princeton, N.J.: Princeton University Press, 1966–1994), 1: 515–38.

15.   Woodrow Wilson to Daniel Coit Gilman, April 15, 1889, *The Papers of Woodrow Wilson*, 6: 169–72.

16.   Woodrow Wilson, "The Modern Democratic State," *The Papers of Woodrow Wilson*, 5: 85.

17.   George Washington, "Letters to General Lafayette, December 25, 1798," in *The Writings of George Washington*, ed. Jared Sparks (New York: Harper & Brothers, 1848), 382.

18.   Woodrow Wilson, "Address of the President of the United States to the US Senate, January 22, 1917," in Albert Fried, ed., *A Day of Dedication: The Essential Writings and Speeches of Woodrow Wilson* (New York: Macmillan, 1965), 281–87.

19.   Walter Lippmann, *U.S. Foreign Policy: Shield of the Republic* (Boston: Little, Brown, 1943), 36.

20.   Dwight D. Eisenhower, "Toward a Golden Age of Peace, April 16, 1953," in *Peace With Justice* (New York: Columbia University Press, 1961), 34–44. The insistence by the United States on the decolonization of the European colonial empires following World War II is analyzed in William Roger Louis, *Imperialism at Bay: The United States and the Decolonization of the British Empire, 1941–1945* (New York: Oxford University Press, 1978).

21.   Eric Hobsbawm, *The Age of Extremes: A History of the World, 1914–1991* (New York: Pantheon, 1994), 109–12.

22.   Franklin D. Roosevelt, "Annual Message to Congress, January 6, 1941," in Stamford Parker, ed., *The Words That Reshaped America: FDR* (New York: HarperCollins, 2000), 157–66.

23.   Roy P. Basler, ed., *The Collected Works of Abraham Lincoln* (New Brunswick, N.J.: Rutgers University Press, 1953), hereinafter *Lincoln CW*, 7: 18–19.

24.   Basler, *Lincoln CW*, 2: 4.

25.   Quoted in David C. Hendrickson and Robert W. Tucker, "The Freedom Crusade," *The National Interest* 85, 13 (fall 2005): 13.

26.   John Quincy Adams, *An Address . . . Celebrating the Anniversary of Independence, at the City of Washington on the Fourth of July 1821* (1821), 32, quoted in Arthur M. Schlesinger, Jr., *The Cycles of American History* (New York: Houghton Mifflin, 1999), 89.

27.   The idea that liberal states, whether or not they are democratic, will be peaceful and prefer commerce to war has a long ancestry. Recent restatements of liberal peace theory include Anne Marie Slaughter, "International Law in a World of Liberal States," *European Journal of International Law* 6 (1995): 503, and Andrew Moravcsik, "Taking Preferences Seriously: A Liberal Theory of International Politics," *International Organization* 51 (1997): 513.

28.   Immanuel Kant argued that republics were unlikely to go to war, at least with each other, in "Perpetual Peace," reprinted in Carl J. Friedrich, ed, *The Philosophy of Kant: Immanuel Kant's Moral and Political Writings* (New York: Modern Library, 1949), 430–76. For contemporary examples of democratic peace theory, see Bruce Russett, *Grasping the Democratic Peace: Principles for a Post-Cold War World* (Princeton, N.J.: Princeton University Press, 1993); Miriam Fendius Elman, ed., *Paths to Peace: Is Democracy the Answer?* (Cambridge, Mass.: MIT Press, 1997); and Spencer R. Weart, *Never at War: Why Democracies Will Not Fight One Another* (New Haven, Conn.: Yale University Press, 2000). For an argument that emerging democracies tend to be aggressive, see Edward D. Mansfield and Jack Snyder, *Electing to Fight: Why Emerging Democracies Go to War* (Cambridge, Mass.: MIT Press, 2005).

29.   Woodrow Wilson, "For Declaration of War Against Germany," in *The Public Papers of Woodrow Wilson*, ed. Ray Stannard Baker and William E. Dodd (New York: Harper and Bros., 1927), 5: 12.

30. "Excerpts from President Clinton's State of the Union Message," *New York Times*, January 26, 1994, A17.

31. "Independence Day Address Delivered at the Home of Thomas Jefferson," in *Public Papers of the President of the United States: Harry S. Truman, January 1 to December 31, 1947* (Washington, D.C.: U.S. Government Printing Office, 1963), 323–26.

32. Alexander Hamilton, "Federalist 6," in Robert Scigliano, ed., *The Federalist: A Commentary on the Constitution of the United States* (New York: The Modern Library, 2001), 30.

33. Mark E. Pietrzyk, *International Order and Individual Liberty: Effects of War and Peace on the Development of Governments* (Lanham, Md.: University Press of America, 2002), 56. For older statements of this thesis, see Alexander Hamilton, "Federalist 8," in Scigliano, ed., *The Federalist*, 41–47; Otto Hintze, "Military Organization and the Organization of the State" (1906) in Felix Gilbert, ed., *The Historical Essays of Otto Hintze* (New York: Oxford University Press, 1975), 178–215.

34. See Jonathan Haslam, *No Virtue Like Necessity: Realist Thought in International Relations Since Machiavelli* (New Haven, Conn.: Yale University Press, 2002). See also E. H. Carr, *The Twenty Years' Crisis: An Introduction to the Study of International Relations* (New York: Palgrave Macmillan, 2001 [1939]); Hans J. Morgenthau, *Politics Among Nations*, 6th ed. (New York: Knopf, 1985); Kenneth N. Waltz, *Man, The State, and War* (New York: Columbia University Press, 1965); John J. Mearsheimer, *The Tragedy of Great Power Politics* (New York: W. W. Norton, 2001).

35. Francois Genoud, ed., *The Testament of Adolf Hitler,* trans. from the German by R. H. Stevens, with an introduction by H. R. Trevor-Roper, 2nd edition (London: Cassell, 1961), 100.

36. Thucydides, *History of the Peloponnesian War*, trans. Richard Crawley (Mineola, N.Y.: Dover, 2004 [1910]), 33.

Chapter 3

1. Quoted in Samuel Flagg Bemis, *John Quincy Adams and the Foundations of American Foreign Policy* (New York: Knopf, 1965), 181.

2. "Declaration and Resolves of the First Continental Congress, October 14, 1774," The Avalon Project at Yale Law School, *Yale Law School*, www.yale.edu/lawweb/avalon/resolves.htm.

3. Thomas Jefferson, "A Summary View of the Rights of British America" (1774), in *The Complete Jefferson*, ed. Saul K. Padover (New York: Tudor Publishing Company, 1943), 5–9.

4. Thomas Jefferson, "Original Rough Draught," *The Papers of Thomas Jefferson, Volume 1: 1760–1776* (Princeton, N.J.: Princeton University Press, 1950), 423–28.

5. George Washington, "Reply to the French Minister, January 1, 1796," *The Writings of George Washington from the Original Manuscript Sources, 1745–1799*, ed. John C. Fitzpatrick, vol. 34, October 11, 1794–March 29, 1796 (Washington, D.C.: U.S. Government Printing Office, 1940), 413–14.

6. George Washington, "Circular to the States, June 8, 1783," in *The Writings of George Washington*, ed. Fitzpatrick, vol. 26, January 1, 1783–June 10, 1783, 483–96.

7. Alexander Hamilton, "Federalist 8," in Robert Scigiliano, ed., *The Federalist: A Commentary on the Constitution of the United States* (New York: The Modern Library, 2001), 46.

8. Ibid., 43–44.

9. George Washington, "Farewell Address, September 17, 1796," in *The Writings of George Washington*, ed. Fitzpatrick, vol. 35, March 30, 1796–July 31, 1797, 214–38.

10. Thomas Jefferson, "Letter to John Taylor," in *The Complete Jefferson*, ed. Padover, 5–19.

11. Roy P. Basler, ed., *The Collected Works of Abraham Lincoln* (New Brunswick, N.J.: Rutgers University Press, 1953), hereinafter *Lincoln CW*, 5: 527-29.

12. John Jay, "Federalist 4," in Scigliano, ed., *The Federalist Papers*, 22.

13. Hamilton, "Federalist 7," in Scigliano, ed., *The Federalist Papers*, 40.

14. Quoted in Samuel Flagg Bemis, *John Quincy Adams and the Foundations of American Foreign Policy* (New York: Knopf, 1965), 181.

15. James P. Jacobs, *Tarnished Warrior: Major General James Wilkinson* (New York: Macmillan, 1938).

16. Edward Everett, *Orations and Speeches on Various Occasions* (Boston: Little, Brown, 1885), 4: 624.

17. William Ware, *Sketches of European Capitals* (Boston: Phillips, Sampson, 1851), quoted in William L. Vance, *America's Rome*, vol. 2, *Catholic and Contemporary Rome* (New Haven, Conn.: Yale University Press, 1989), 201.

18. Basler, *Lincoln CW*, 4: 426.

19. Frederick Jackson Turner, *Sections in American History* (New York: Henry Holt, 1932), 289.

Chapter 4

1. *Charles Sumner: His Complete Works* (Boston: Lee and Shepard, 1900), 15: 41-43.

2. Thomas Jefferson, "Thomas Jefferson to John Clarke, January 27, 1814," *The Writings of Thomas Jefferson*, ed. H. A. Washington (New York: Derby and Jackson, 1859), 6: 307-8.

3. Thomas Jefferson, "Thomas Jefferson to Thomas Lieper, January 1, 1814," *The Writings of Thomas Jefferson*, 281-84.4.

4. George Washington, "Farewell Address, September 17, 1796," *The Writings of George Washington from the Original Manuscript Sources, 1745-1799*, ed. John C. Fitzpatrick (Washington, D.C.: U.S. Government Printing Office), vol. 35, March 30, 1796-July 31, 1797, 214-38.

5. Thomas Jefferson, "Letter to Archibald Stuart, Jan. 25, 1786," *The Papers of Thomas Jefferson*, ed. Julian P. Boyd and Mina R. Bryan (Princeton, N.J.: Princeton University Press, 1954), 217-19.

6. Thomas Jefferson, "Letter to the US Minister to France (Robert Livingston) April 2, 1802," *Writings* (New York: Literary Classics of the United States, Inc., 1984),1104-7.

7. Thomas Jefferson, "Second Inaugural Address, March 4, 1805," *The Complete Jefferson*, ed. Saul K. Padover (New York: Tudor Publishing Company, 1943), 410-15.

8. Thomas Jefferson, "To the Secretary of War (Henry Dearborn), August 12, 1808," *The Papers of Thomas Jefferson*, ed. Paul Leicester Ford (New York: G. P. Putnam's Sons, 1905), 11: 42-45.

9. Julius W. Pratt, *Expansionists of 1812* (New York: Macmillan, 1925), 73-74.

10. Ibid., 140-41.

11. Annals of Congress, 12th Cong., 1st sess., I, 426, December 9, 1811, quoted in Thomas A. Bailey, *A Diplomatic History of the American People*, 10th ed. (Englewood Cliffs, N.J.: Prentice-Hall, 1970), 138.

12. Thomas Jefferson, *The Writings of Thomas Jefferson*, ed. Paul Leicester Ford (New York: G. P. Putnam's Sons, 1895-98), 9: 366.

13. "Jefferson to Toronda Coruna, Dec. 14, 1813," *Writings of Thomas Jefferson*, 6: 273, cited in Pratt, *Expansionists of 1812*, 244.

14. Domestic Letters, XVI, 234 (State Department MSS), quoted in Pratt, *Expansionists of 1812*, 246.

15. Jefferson to Madison, May 30, 1812, Madison Papers, quoted in Paul A. Varg, *Foreign Policies of the Founding Fathers* (East Lansing: Michigan State University Press, 1963), 290.

16. Speech on Portugal, House of Commons, December 12, 1826, quoted in K. Bourne, ed., *The Foreign Policy of Victorian England, 1830–1902* (Oxford: Clarendon Press, 1970), doc. 3, quoted in Jonathan Haslam, *No Virtue Like Necessity: Realist Thought in International Relations Since Machiavelli* (New Haven, Conn.: Yale University Press, 2002).

17. Quoted in H. Temperley, *The Foreign Policy of Canning, 1822–1827: England, the Neo-Holy Alliance, and the New World* (Hamden, Conn.: Archon Books, 1966), 553.

18. Alexander Hamilton to Lafayette, January 6, 1799, quoted in John Lamberton Harper, *American Machiavelli: Alexander Hamilton and the Origins of U.S. Foreign Policy* (Cambridge, UK: Cambridge University Press, 2004), 232.

19. Thomas G. Paterson, ed., *Major Problems in American Foreign Policy: To 1914* (Lexington, Mass: D.C. Heath, 1989), 1: 183–84.

20. James Monroe, "Seventh Annual Message, December 2, 1823," in Stanislaus Murray Hamilton, ed., *The Writings of James Monroe*, vol. 4, *1817–1823* (New York: G. P. Putnam's Sons, 1902), 325–42.

21. David Urquhart, *Annexation of Texas: A Case of War Between England and the United States* (London: James Maynard, 1844).

22. Ephraim Douglass Adams, *British Interests and Activities in Texas, 1838–1846* (Gloucester, Mass: Peter Smith, 1963; originally published by Johns Hopkins University Press, 1910), 15.

23. Justin H. Smith, *The Policy of England and France in Reference to the Annexation of Texas* (New York: Baker and Taylor, 1911), 384.

24. Jackson to Aaron V. Brown, February 12, 1843, Niles' Register, March 30, 1844, quoted in Norman A. Graebner, *Empire on the Pacific: A Study in American Continental Expansion* (New York: The Ronald Press, 1955), 17.

25. Ashbel Smith, *Reminiscences of the Texas Republic*, 15 December 1875, www.tamu.edu/ccbn/dewitt/smithasbel1.htm, 11.

26. Justin H. Smith, *The Policy of England and France*, 400.

27. Graebner, *Empire on the Pacific*, 31.

28. Frederick Merk, *The Monroe Doctrine and American Expansion, 1843–1849* (New York: Knopf, 1966), 65.

29. Ibid., 65–66.

30. Adams, *British Interests and Activities in Texas*, 234.

31. Ibid., 237–40.

32. Ibid., 243.

33. Ibid.

34. Ibid., 248.

35. John O'Sullivan, "Annexation," *The United States Magazine and Democratic Review* 17 (July 1845): 5–10.

36. Graebner, *Empire on the Pacific*, 30.

37. James K. Polk, First Annual Message to Congress, December 2, 1945, in J. Richardson, ed., *A Compilation of the Messages and Papers of the Presidents, 1789–1907* (Whitefish, Mont.: Kessinger Publishing, 1908), 398.

38. Merk, *The Monroe Doctrine and American Expansion*, 73–74.

39. David L. Dykstra, *The Shifting Balance of Power: American-British Diplomacy in North America, 1842–1848* (Lanham, Md.: University Press of America, 1999), 105.

40. Graebner, *Empire on the Pacific*, 82.

41. Ibid., 76–77.

42. Adams, *British Interests and Activities in Texas*, 262.

43. Merk, *The Monroe Doctrine and American Expansion*, 75.

44. Dykstra, *The Shifting Balance of Power*, 99.

45. Ibid., 99–100.

46. Quoted in D. W. Meinig, *The Shaping of America: A Geographical Perspective on 500 Years of History*, vol. 2, *Continental America, 1800–1867* (New Haven, Conn.: Yale University Press, 1993), 144.

47. Graebner, *Empire on the Pacific*, 87.
48. Ibid., v–vi.
49. Meinig, *The Shaping of America*, 203.
50. Merk, *The Monroe Doctrine and American Expansion*, 289.
51. Quoted in Jasper Ridley, *Maximilian and Juarez* (London: Phoenix Press, 1992), 104.
52. Charles d'Hericault, *Maximilien et le Mexique* (Paris: Garnier Fréres, 1869), 399, quoted in Ridley, *Maximilian and Juarez*, 283.
53. Michael Lind, "Let's Appease Russia! Why the Left- and Right-Wing Hawks Are Wrong," *The New Republic* 212, nos. 2/3 (January 9, 1995–January 13, 1995).
54. Quoted in Meinig, *The Shaping of America*, 544.
55. *Charles Sumner: His Complete Works*, with an introduction by Hon. George Frisbie Hoar (Boston: Lee & Shepard, 1900), 15: 41–43.
56. *Inaugural Addresses of the Presidents of the United States* (Washington, D.C.: U.S. Government Printing Office, 1974), 105.
57. Quoted in Meinig, *The Shaping of America*, 205.
58. Quoted in John Mearsheimer, *The Tragedy of Great Power Politics* (New York: W. W. Norton, 2001), 5.
59. David Ramsay, *An Oration on the Advantages of American Independence* (Charleston, S.C., 1778), 20, quoted in Drew R. McCloy, *The Elusive Republic: Political Economy in Jeffersonian America* (New York: W. W. Norton, 1980), 90.
60. Jefferson to the president and legislative council, the speaker and house of representatives of the territory of Indiana, December 28, 1805, Jefferson Papers, Library of Congress.
61. Roosevelt to Cordell Hull, January 11, 1941, in *F.D.R.: His Personal Letters 1928–1945*, vol. 2 (New York: Duell, Sloan, and Pearce, 1950): 1104–5.
62. For the history of American racism and its influences on changing conceptions of American national identity, see Michael Lind, *The Next American Nation* (New York: The Free Press, 1995).
63. Frederick Merk, *Manifest Destiny and Mission in American History* (New York: Random House, 1963), 210.
64. Ibid., 255.
65. Eric Wolf, *Europe and the People Without History*, 6, quoted in Meinig, *The Shaping of America*, 217.
66. Meinig, *The Shaping of America*, 216.
67. Walter Lippmann, *U.S. Foreign Policy: Shield of the Republic* (Boston: Little, Brown, 1943), 16.
68. Richard Olney to Thomas F. Bayard, July 20, 1895, in *Foreign Relations of the United States, 1895*, pt. 1 (Washington, D.C.: U.S. Government Printing Office, 1896), 558.

Chapter 5

1. Wilson to House, *Woodrow Wilson Papers*, 30: 432, quoted in John B. Judis, *The Folly of Empire* (New York: Simon and Schuster, 2004), 98.
2. Alexander Hamilton, "Federalist 8," in Robert Scigliano, ed., *The Federalist: A Commentary on the Constitution of the United States* (New York: The Modern Library, 2001), 44–46.
3. "Statement of a Proper Military Policy for the United States, Prepared by the War College General Staff Corps in Compliance with Instructions of the Secretary of War," March 1915 (Washington, D.C.: Government Printing Office, 1916), 1.
4. Alfred Vagts, "Hopes and Fears of an American-German War, 1870–1915," *Political Science Quarterly* 54, no. 4 (1939): 514–35 and 55, no. 1 (1940): 53–76; Holger Herwig, *The Politics of Frustration: The United States in German Naval Planning, 1889–1941* (Boston: Little, Brown, 1976); Hans-Jurgen Schroder, *Confrontation and*

Cooperation: Germany and the United States in the Era of World War I, 1900–1924 (Providence, R.I.: Berg, 1993).

5. Holger Herwig and David Trask, "Naval Operations Plans between Germany and the United States of America, 1898–1913: A Study of Strategic Planning in the Age of Imperialism," *Militargeschichtliche Mitteilungen* 2 (1970): 42.

6. Quoted in Howard K. Beale, *Theodore Roosevelt and the Rise of America to World Power* (Baltimore: Johns Hopkins University Press, 1956), 339.

7. Herwig and Trask, "Naval Operations Plans between Germany and the USA, 1898–1913," in Paul M. Kennedy, ed., *The War Plans of the Great Powers, 1880–1914* (London: George Allen & Unwin, 1979), 42; L. P. Shippee, "Germany and the Spanish-American War," *American Historical Review* 30 (July 1925): 754–77.

8. Thomas A. Bailey, *A Diplomatic History of the American People,* 10th ed. (Englewood Cliffs, N.J.: Prentice-Hall, 1970), 515. See also Thomas Bailey, "Dewey and the Germans at Manila Bay," *Hispanic American Historical Review* 45 (October 1939): 59–81.

9. Quoted in Beale, *Theodore Roosevelt and the Rise of America to World Power,* 336. See also John A. Moses and Paul Kennedy, eds., *Germany in the Pacific and Far East, 1870–1914* (St. Lucia, Australia: University of Queensland Press, 1977).

10. A. Grenville, "Diplomacy and War Plans in the United States, 1890–1917," in Paul M. Kennedy, ed., *The War Plans of the Great Powers, 1880–1914* (London: George Allen & Unwin, 1979), 24.

11. Philip C. Jessup, *Elihu Root* (New York: Dodd, Mead and Company, 1938), 1: 314; quoted in Bailey, *A Diplomatic History of the American People,* 548.

12. Elihu Root, interview, November 10, 1930, quoted in Edmund Morris, *Theodore Rex* (New York: Random House, 2001), 681.

13. "General MacArthur's Fear of War with Germany," *New York Times,* December 11, 1903, 1, quoted in Peter Overlack, "German War Plans in the Pacific," *Historian* 60, 3 (spring 1998). See also Edward Parsons, "The German-American Crisis of 1902–1903," *Historian* 33 (May 1971): 436–52; John Clifford, "Admiral Dewey and the Germans, 1903: A New Perspective," *Mid-America* 49 (July 1967): 214–20.

14. Overlack, "German War Plans," 578–93.

15. Ibid. See also Friedrich Forstmeier, "Deutsche Invasionsplane gegen die USA um 1900," *Marine-Rundschau* 68 (June 1971): 344–51.

16. Herwig and Trask, "Naval Operations Plans between Germany and the United States of America, 1898–1913," 5–32; John Maurer, "American Naval Concentration and the German Battle Fleet, 1900–1918," *Journal of Strategic Studies* (June 1983): 147–81.

17. Quoted in Beale, *Theodore Roosevelt and the Rise of America to World Power,* 91.

18. Quoted in ibid., 226–27.

19. Royal Cortissoz, *The Life of Whitelaw Reid* (New York, 1921), 2: 332; quoted in Bailey, *A Diplomatic History of the American People,* 561.

20. Overlack, "German War Plans," 578–93.

21. Richard A. Von Doenhoff, "Biddle, Perry, and Japan," *US Naval Institute Proceedings* 92, no. 11 (1966), 78; Roger Pineau, ed., *The Japan Expedition 1852–1854: The Personal Journal of Commodore Matthew C. Perry* (Washington, D.C.: Smithsonian Institution, 1968), 92.

22. For examples of U.S. interest in overseas naval bases between the Civil War and the Spanish-American War, see Fareed Zakaria, *From Wealth to Power* (Princeton, N.J.: Princeton University Press, 1999).

23. Quoted in Frederick Merk, *Manifest Destiny and Mission in American History: A Reinterpretation* (New York: Alfred A. Knopf, 1863), 263.

24. Quoted in Richard Franklin Bensel, *Sectionalism and American Political Development: 1880–1980* (Madison: University of Wisconsin Press, 1984), 99; "Downes v. Bidwell," http://law.dn.edu/sterling/content/ALH/downes.pdf.

25. Theodore Roosevelt, "Letter to William Howard Taft, August 21, 1907," in *The Letters of Theodore Roosevelt,* ed. Elting E. Morison (Cambridge, Mass.: Harvard University Press, 1951), 5: 762.

26. Mark E. Pietrzyk, *International Order and Individual Liberty: Effects of War and Peace on the Development of Governments* (Lanham, Md.: University Press of America, 2002), 67.

27. William Graham Sumner, "The Conquest of the United States by Spain," in Albert Galloway Keller, ed., *War and Other Essays,* (New Haven, Conn.: Yale University Press, 1919), 295–334.

28. David Fromkin, *Europe's Last Summer: Who Started the Great War in 1914?* (New York: Alfred A. Knopf, 2004), 92, 104–9. See also Fritz Fischer, *Germany's Aims in the First World War* (New York: W. W. Norton, 1967); idem, *War of Illusions: German Policies from 1911 to 1914* (London: Chatto & Windus, 1967); idem, *From Kaiserreich to Third Reich: Elements of Continuity in German History, 1871–1945,* trans. Kim Traynor (Leamington Spa, UK: Berg, 1985); John C. G. Rohl, *The Kaiser and His Court: Wilhelm II and the Government of Germany* (Cambridge, UK: Cambridge University Press, 1994); H. W. Koch, "Social Darwinism as a Factor in the New Imperialism," in H. W. Koch, ed., *The Origins of the First World War: Great Power Rivalry and German War Aims* (Basingstoke, UK: Macmillan, 1972).

29. Quoted in Fischer, *Germany's Aims in the First World War,* 103.

30. Fischer, *Germany's Aims in the First World War,* 104.

31. Quoted in Barbara Tuchman, *The Zimmerman Telegram* (New York: Macmillan, 1966), 89.

32. Overlack, "German War Plans," 578–93.

33. Ibid.

34. Tuchman, *The Zimmerman Telegram,* 43.

35. Tuchman, *The Zimmerman Telegram,* 48–50. See also Thomas Baecker, "The Arms of the *Ypiranga*: The German Side," *Americas* 30 (1973): 1–17.

36. Tuchman, *The Zimmerman Telegram,* 53.

37. See also James Sandos, "German Involvement in Northern Mexico, 1915–1916," *Hispanic American Historical Review* 50 (February 1970): 70–88; Friedrich Katz, *The Secret War in Mexico: Europe, the United States, and the Mexican Revolution* (Chicago: University of Chicago Press, 1981).

38. Joseph Patrick Tumulty, *Woodrow Wilson As I Knew Him* (Garden City, N.Y.: Doubleday, Page and Company, 1921), 159.

39. Quoted in Hans Schmidt, *The United States Occupation of Haiti* (Piscataway, N.J.: Rutgers University Press, 1995), 58; Lansing memorandum, July 11, 1915, in Robert Lansing, *War Memoirs of Robert Lansing* (New York: Bobbs-Merrill, 1935), 19–21.

40. Schmidt, *The United States Occupation of Haiti,* 57.

41. Quoted in Robert O. Work, "Winning the Race: A Naval Fleet Platform Architecture for Enduring Maritime Supremacy," March 1, 2005 (Washington, D.C.: Center for Strategic and Budgetary Assessments), 46.

42. Schmidt, *The United States Occupation of Haiti,* 35.

43. Ibid., 34–35.

44. Ibid., 94–95.

45. Quoted in Schmidt, *The United States Occupation of Haiti,* 118. See, generally, Brenda Plummer, *Haiti and the Great Powers, 1902–1915* (Baton Rouge: Louisiana State University Press, 1988).

46. Quoted in Robert Leckie, *The Wars of America,* vol. 2 (New York: HarperCollins, 1992), 628.

47. *New York Times,* July 12, 1916; quoted in Tuchman, *The Zimmerman Telegram,* 98, 226.

48. Tuchman, *The Zimmerman Telegram,* 52.

49. Quoted in Leckie, *The Wars of America,* 583.

50. Quoted in Beale, *Theodore Roosevelt and the Rise of America to World Power,* 382.

51. Robert Lansing and Louis F. Post, "A War of Self-Defense?" *War Information Services* 5 (August 1917).

52. Quoted in John Spencer Bassett, *Our War with Germany* (New York: Alfred A. Knopf, 1919), 95.

53. Walter Lippmann, *U.S. Foreign Policy: Shield of the Republic* (Boston: Little, Brown, 1943), 34–36.

54. Robert J. Art, *A Grand Strategy for America* (Ithaca, N.Y.: Cornell University Press, 2003), 182.

55. Wilson to House, *Woodrow Wilson Papers*, vol. 30, 432, quoted in Judis, *The Folly of Empire*, 98. See also Frank Ninkovich, *Modernity and Power: A History of the Domino Theory in the Twentieth Century* (Chicago: University of Chicago Press, 1994), 53: "For one thing, the menace as Wilson defined it was less Germany's capacity for world conquest, which was at best questionable, than the grave side-effects of measures that would have been necessary to prevent it, in effect Prussianizing the country and turning it into a garrison state."

Chapter 6

1. Franklin D. Roosevelt, "Annual Message to Congress, January 6, 1941," in Stamford Parker, ed., *The Words That Reshaped America: FDR* (New York: HarperCollins, 2000), 157–66.

2. Philip Bobbitt, *The Shield of Achilles: War, Peace, and the Course of History* (New York: Knopf, 2002), 7.

3. Woodrow Wilson, "Address of the President of the United States to the US Senate, January 22, 1917," in Albert Fried, ed., *A Day of Dedication: The Essential Writings and Speeches of Woodrow Wilson* (New York: Macmillan, 1965), 281–87.

4. Alfred Lord Tennyson, "Locksley Hall," *The Poems of Tennyson*, ed. Christopher Ricks, 2nd ed. (Berkeley: University of California Press, 1987), 2: 126.

5. Theodore Roosevelt, "Address to the Senate and the House of Representatives, December 5, 1905," in Franklin D. Roosevelt and Cortelle Hutchins, eds., *State of the Union Addresses: Theodore Roosevelt* (New York: Kessinger Publishing, 2004), 4: 157.

6. Edward Mandell House, *The Intimate Papers of Colonel House, Arranged as a Narrative by Charles Seymour*, vol. 4, *The Ending of the War, June, 1918–August, 1919* (Boston: Houghton Mifflin, 1928), 26.

7. Ibid., 24.

8. Robert Lansing, *War Memoirs of Robert Lansing, Secretary of State* (Indianapolis: Bobbs-Merrill, 1935), 202.

9. Ray Stannard Baker, *Woodrow Wilson and World Settlement* (New York: Doubleday, Page and Co., 1922), 1: 93.

10. Ray Stannard Baker and William E. Dodds, eds., *The Public Papers of Woodrow Wilson: War and Peace* (New York: Harper and Brothers, 1925–1927), 1: 259.

11. "Charter of the United Nations," June 26, 1945, Office of the High Commissioner on Human Rights, United Nations, www.unhchr.ch/html/menu3/b/ch-cont.htm.

12. Memorandum of March 18, 1919, quoted in Blanche E. Dugdale, *Arthur James Balfour* (London: Hutchinson, 1936), 204.

13. House, *The Intimate Papers of Colonel House*, 394.

14. Ibid.

15. Ibid., 395.

16. Henry Cabot Lodge, *The Senate and the League of Nations* (New York: Charles Scribner's Sons, 1925), 154.

17. William R. Keylor, "The Rise and Demise of the Franco-American Guarantee Pact, 1919–1921," in *The Legacy of the Great War: Peacemaking, 1919* (Boston: Houghton Mifflin, 1998), 109.

18. Lodge, *The Senate and the League of Nations*, 156.

19. John Maynard Keynes, *A Revision of the Treaty being a sequel to the Economic Consequences of the Peace* (San Diego, Calif.: Simon Publications, 2003), 186.

20. *Hitler's Secret Book*, trans. Salvator Attanasio, with an introduction by Telford Taylor (New York: Grove Press, 1961), 209.

21. Hugh Trevor-Roper, *Hitler's Secret Conversations, 1941–1944* (New York: Farrar, Straus & Giroux, 1972), 155.

22. Quoted in Michael Burleigh, "Nazi Europe: What If Nazi Germany Had Defeated the Soviet Union," in Niall Ferguson, *Virtual History: Alternatives and Counterfactuals* (London: Picador, 1997), 343.

23. Trevor-Roper, *Hitler's Secret Conversations*, 147.

24. Richard Overy, *The Dictators: Hitler's Germany, Stalin's Russia* (New York: W. W. Norton, 2004), 455; W. Deist, *The Wehrmacht and German Rearmament* (London: Allen Lane, 1981), 81–84.

25. Quoted in William L. Shirer, *The Rise and Fall of the Third Reich: A History of Nazi Germany* (New York: Simon and Schuster, 1960), 879.

26. Holger H. Herwig, *The Politics of Frustration: The United States in German Naval Planning, 1889–1941* (Boston: Little, Brown, 1976), 241.

27. James P. Duffy, *Target: America: Hitler's Plan to Attack the United States* (Westport, Conn.: Praeger, 2004), 46–47.

28. Duffy, *Target: America*, 83, 105.

29. Ibid., 122.

30. Quoted in Burleigh, "Nazi Europe," 340–41.

31. Douglas Miller, *You Can't Do Business with Hitler* (Boston: Little, Brown, 1941), 211.

32. Ibid., 141.

33. Ibid., 85.

34. Ibid., 87.

35. Ibid., 210.

36. Quoted in William Appleman Williams, *The Tragedy of American Diplomacy* (New York: Dell, 1959), 198.

37. Conference, January 31, 1939 (Extra Confidential), quoted in Thomas H. Greer, *What Roosevelt Thought: The Social and Political Ideas of Franklin D. Roosevelt* (East Lansing: Michigan State University Press, 2000), 180–182.

38. Franklin D. Roosevelt, "Address at the University of Virginia-Charlottesville, June 10, 1940," in *The Roosevelt Reader: Selected Speeches, Messages, Press Conferences, and Letters of Franklin D. Roosevelt*, ed. Basil Rauch (New York: Rinehart, 1957), 252–54.

39. Franklin D. Roosevelt. "Annual Message to Congress, January 6, 1941," in Stamford Parker, ed., *The Words That Reshaped America: FDR* (New York: HarperCollins, 2000), 157–66. Frank Ninkovich describes Roosevelt's view: "If Germany and Japan succeeded in militarily reorganizing the world system into closed regions, the necessity of creating a 'garrison state' would utterly transform the American polity and economy in a totalitarian direction." Frank Ninkovich, *Modernity and Power: A History of the Domino Theory in the Twentieth Century* (Chicago: University of Chicago Press, 1994), 120. In October 1940, Roosevelt received a secret report of the economic and financial committee of the Council on Foreign Relations, which argued that in order to maintain its economic self-sufficiency, if Japan dominated mainland Asia and Germany dominated Europe, the United States would need to create a bloc called the "Grand Area" uniting the Western Hemisphere, the British Empire and most of the Pacific; in addition, the United States would have to engage in massive rearmament.

Lawrence H. Shoup and William Minter, *Imperial Brain Trust: The Council on Foreign Relations and United States Foreign Policy* (New York: Monthly Review, 1977), 135–40.

40. Charles A. Lindbergh, Speech, NBC, June 15, 1940, in Charles A. Lindbergh, *The Radio Addresses of Col. Charles A. Lindbergh, 1939–1940* (New York: Scribner's Commentator, 1940), quoted in Justus D. Doenecke, *Storm on the Horizon: The Challenge to American Intervention, 1939–1941* (Lanham, Md.: Rowman & Littlefield, 2000), 114.

41. Charles A. Lindbergh, Speech, May 19, 1940, in Lindbergh, *Radio Addresses*, quoted in Doenecke, *Storm on the Horizon*, 130.

42. *New York Times*, July 30, 1941, quoted in Doenecke, *Storm on the Horizon*, 130.

43. Hamilton Fish, Congressional Record, June 16, 1940, 8536, quoted in Doenecke, *Storm on the Horizon*, 121.

44. Graeme K. Howard, *America and a New World Order* (New York: Charles Scribner's Sons, 1940), 77, 97. See also John M. Muresianu, *War of Ideas: American Intellectuals and the World Crisis, 1938–1945* (New York: Garland, 1988); Manfred Jonas, *Isolationism in America, 1935–1941* (Chicago: Imprint Publications, 1990).

45. Trevor-Roper, *Hitler's Secret Conversations*, 396.

46. Russell F. Weigley, *The American Way of War: A History of United States Military Strategy and Policy* (Bloomington: Indiana University Press, 1973), 270–71.

47. Corelli Barnett, *The Collapse of British Power* (London: Eyre Methuen, 1972), 272.

Chapter 7

1. "NSC 68: United States Objectives and Programs for National Security," April 14, 1950, in Thomas Etzold and John Lewis Gaddis, eds., *Containment: Documents on American Policy and Strategy, 1945–1950* (New York: Columbia University Press, 1978), 401.

2. Norman Friedman, *The Fifty-Year War: Conflict and Strategy in the Cold War* (Annapolis, Md.: Naval Institute Press, 1999), 12–14.

3. Quoted in Tony Smith and Richard C. Leone, *America's Mission: The United States and the Worldwide Struggle for Democracy in the Twentieth Century* (Princeton, N.J.: Princeton University Press, 1994), 143.

4. Aaron Friedberg, *In the Shadow of the Garrison State: America's Anti-Statism and Its Cold War Grand Strategy* (Princeton, N.J.: Princeton University Press, 2000).

5. Robert A. Taft, *A Foreign Policy for Americans* (Garden City, N.Y.: Doubleday, 1951).

6. James A. Burnham, *Containment or Liberation? An Inquiry Into the Aims of United States Foreign Policy* (New York: John Day, 1953).

7. The containment strategy was laid out in "X" [George Kennan], "The Sources of Soviet Conduct," *Foreign Affairs* 25 (July 1947): 566–82.

8. Steve W. Hook and John Spanier, *American Foreign Policy Since World War II*, 15th ed. (Washington, D.C.: Congressional Quarterly Press, 2000), 44. According to George Kennan in a 1948 address to the National War College, "only five centers of industrial and military power in the world which are important to us from the standpoint of national security"—the United States, Britain, Germany, Japan, and the Soviet Union. George Kennan, National War College Lecture, "Contemporary Problems of Foreign Policy," September 17, 1948, George F. Kennan Papers, Princeton University, Box 17. The term "double containment" is used to describe U.S. policy toward West Germany and the Soviet Union during the Cold War in Wolfram Hanrieder, *Germany, Europe, and America* (New Haven, Conn.: Yale University Press, 1989).

9. Quoted in Robert Jervis, "Domino Beliefs and Strategic Behavior," in Robert Jervis and Jack Snyder, eds., *Dominoes and Bandwagons* (New York: Oxford University Press, 1991), 33.

10.   See Michael Lind, *Vietnam: The Necessary War* (New York: The Free Press, 1999).

11.   Lyndon Baines Johnson, "Why We Are in Vietnam, April 7, 1965," *Public Papers of the Presidents of the United States: Lyndon B. Johnson, 1965* (Washington, D.C.: U.S. Government Printing Office, 1966), 394–97.

12.   John McNaughton, "Proposed Course of Action Re Vietnam," March 24, 1965, in George C. Herring, ed., *The Pentagon Papers*, abridged ed. (New York: Oxford University Press, 1993), 115–19.

13.   H. Schuyler Foster, *Activism Replaces Isolationism: U.S. Public Attitudes, 1940–1975* (Washington, D.C.: Foxhall Press, 1983), 324–25, 332–33, cited in Thomas M. Langston, *Uneasy Balance: Civil-Military Relations in Peacetime America Since 1783* (Baltimore: Johns Hopkins University Press, 2003), 162, 189 n. 32.

14.   Paul Kennedy, *The Rise and Fall of the Great Powers: Economic Change and Military Conflict from 1500 to 2000* (New York: Random House, 1987), 368–69.

15.   Kennedy, *The Rise and Fall of the Great Powers*, Table 43, 436.

16.   Quoted in John Lewis Gaddis, *Strategies of Containment: A Critical Appraisal of Postwar American National Security* (New York: Oxford University Press, 1982), 280.

17.   Richard Nixon, "Address to the Nation on the War in Vietnam, November 3, 1969," *Public Papers of the Presidents of the United States: Richard Nixon, 1969* (Washington, D.C.: U.S. Government Printing Office, 1971), 901–9.

18.   See Friedberg, *In the Shadow of the Garrison State*.

19.   Herbert Stein and Murray Foss, *The New Illustrated Guide to the American Economy*, 2nd ed. (Washington, D.C.: AEI Press, 1995), 206–7.

20.   Andrew J. Bacevich, *American Empire: The Realities and Consequences of U.S. Diplomacy* (Cambridge, Mass.: Harvard University Press, 2002), 155–56.

Chapter 8

1.   Scott Sullivan and Karen Breslau, "Plunging into a Cold Peace," *Newsweek*, December 19, 1994, 39

2.   Patrick Buchanan, "America First—and Second, and Third," *The National Interest* 19 (spring 1990): 77–82; Eric Nordlinger, *Isolationism Reconfigured: American Foreign Policy for a New Century* (Princeton, N.J.: Princeton University Press, 1995).

3.   Strobe Talbott. "The Birth of the Global Nation," *Time Magazine*, July 20, 1992, 70.

4.   Christopher Layne, "The Unipolar Illusion. Why New Great Powers Will Rise," *International Security* 17, no. 4 (spring 1993): 5–51; idem, "From Preponderance to Off-shore Balancing: America's Future Grand Strategy," in Michael E. Brown, Owen R. Cote, Jr., Sean M. Lynn-Jones, and Steven E. Miller, eds., *America's Strategic Choices*, rev. ed. (Cambridge, Mass.: MIT Press, 2000), 99–137; John J. Mearsheimer, "The False Promise of International Institutions," *International Security* 19, no. 3 (winter 1994–1995): 5–49; idem, *The Tragedy of Great Power Politics* (New York: W. W. Norton, 2001).

5.   James Chace and Nicholas Rizoupolos, "Toward a New Concert of Nations: an American Perspective," *World Policy Journal* 16 (fall 1999): 2–10; Charles A. Kupchan and Clifford A. Kupchan, "Concerts, Collective Security, and the Future of Europe," in Brown et al., eds., *America's Strategic Choices*, 218–65; idem, "Concerts, Collective Security, and the Future of Europe: A Retrospective," in ibid., 266–70; idem, "After NATO: Concert of Europe," Op-Ed, *New York Times*, July 6, 1990; John Mueller, "A New Concert of Europe," *Foreign Policy* 77 (winter 1989–90): 3–16; Sherle Schweininger, "America's New Solvency Crisis," *World Policy Journal* 12, no. 2 (summer 1995); idem, "World Order Lost: American Foreign Policy in the Post–Cold War World," *World Policy Journal* 16, no. 2 (summer 1999): 1–24, 42–71.

6.   Charles Krauthammer, "The Unipolar Moment," *Foreign Affairs* 70, no. 1 (1990/1991): 23–33; idem, "Democratic Realism: An American Foreign Policy for a Unipo-

lar World," 2004 Irving Kristol Lecture, American Enterprise Institute, Washington, D.C., February 10, 2004; William Kristol and Robert Kagan, "Toward a Neo-Reaganite Foreign Policy," *Foreign Affairs* 75, no. 4 (July/August 1996): 20-31; idem, eds. *Present Dangers: Crisis and Opportunity in American Foreign and Defense Policy* (San Francisco: Encounter Books, 2000).

7. Tom Wicker, "An Unknown Casualty," *New York Times*, March 20, 1991, A29; Eric Schmitt, "U.S. Details Flaws in Patriot Missile," *New York Times*, June 6, 1991, A9.

8. William Wohlforth, "The Stability of a Unipolar World," *International Security* 24, no. 1 (summer 1999): 4-41.

9. "Excerpts from Pentagon's Plan: 'Prevent the Re-emergence of a New Rival,'" *New York Times*, March 8, 1992, A14; Patrick E. Tyler. "U.S. Strategy Plan Calls for Insuring No Rivals Develop In A One-Superpower World: Pentagon's Document Outlines Ways to Thwart Challenges to Primacy of America," *New York Times,* March 8, 1992, 1; Barton Gellman, "Keeping the U.S. First: Pentagon Would Preclude a Rival Superpower," *Washington Post*, March 11, 1992; Barton Gellman, "Pentagon Abandons Goal of Thwarting U.S. Rivals," *Washington Post*, May 24, 1992.

10. George W. Bush, "Commencement Address at the United States Military Academy in West Point, New York, June 1, 2002," News and Policies, The White House, www.whitehouse .gov/news/releases/2002/06/20020601-3.html.

11. Paul Wolfowitz, "Remembering the Future," *The National Interest* 59 (spring 2000): 35-45.

12. Kristol and Kagan, "Toward a Neo-Reaganite Foreign Policy," 20-31.

13. "The National Security Strategy of the United States of America," September 17, 2002, The National Security Council, The White House, www.whitehouse.gov/nsc/nss.html.

14. Quoted in Owen Harries, "The Perils of Hegemony: Washington Learns That Democracy Is Not Made For Export," *The American Conservative*, June 21, 2004, www.amcon mag.com/2004/2004-06-21/article.html.

15. Tyler, "U.S. Strategy Plan," 1.

16. "Deputy Secretary Wolfowitz Interview with Sam Tannenhaus, Vanity Fair," U.S. Department of Defense, May 9, 2003, www.defenselink.mil/transcripts/2003/ tr20030509-depsecdef0223.html.

17. "The National Security Strategy of the United States of America," September 17, 2002.

18. House Committee on Appropriations Defense Subcommittee, Hearing: Supplemental Appropriations for Military Operations in Kosovo, April 21, 1999.

19. Quoted in "The National Interest," *The Weekly Standard*, April 26, 1999, 18.

20. Senator John McCain, McCain Speech to the National Association of Broadcasters Convention, Congressional Press Releases, Washington, D.C., April 20, 1999.

21. See Christopher Layne, "America as European Hegemon," *The National Interest* 72 (summer 2003): 17-30.

22. "US rebuffs German bid for UN Security Council Seat: report," *Agence France-Presse,* June 9, 2005. According to Barry R. Posen and Andrew L. Ross, the purpose of the expansion of NATO was less to deter Russia than "to forestall even a hint of an independent German foreign policy in the east." Barry R. Posen and Andrew L. Ross, "Competing Visions for U.S. Grand Strategy," *International Security* 21, no. 3 (winter 1996/97): 5-53, repr. in Brown et al., eds., *America's Strategic Choices*, 3-51.

23. Stephen Castle, "Chirac tells Bush to mind his own business over Turkey's EU bid," *The New Zealand Herald,* June 29, 2004, www.nzherald.co.nz/section/story .cfm?c_id=2&objectid=3575342.

24. "Confrontation over Pristina Airport," *BBC News* (Europe), March 9, 2000, http:// news.bbc.co.uk/2/hi/europe/671495.stm.

25. Cheng Guangzhong, "Kosovo War and the U.S. 'Python' Strategy," *Ta Kung Pao* (Hong Kong), June 2, 1999, www.myholyoke.edu/acad/intrel/chengThun, quoted in T. V. Paul, "Soft Balancing in the Age of U.S. Primacy," *International Security* 30, no. 1 (summer 2005): 62.

26. In 1990, Major General Henry C. Stackpole, III, then the commander of U.S. Marine Corps bases in Japan, said, "No one wants a rearmed, resurgent Japan. So we are the cap in the bottle, if you will." Quoted in Sam Jameson, "A Reluctant Superpower Agonizes over Military," *Los Angeles Times*, August 1, 1995, H4.

27. See, for example, the concern expressed by Zbigniew Brezinski, *The Grand Chessboard: American Primacy and Its Geostrategic Implications* (New York: Basic Books, 1997). Michael Mastanduno writes: "The U.S. effort to thwart North Korea's nuclear ambitions was consistent with U.S. nonproliferation strategy in general, and also with the regional strategy of reassuring Japan and discouraging it from having to acquire nuclear capabilities itself." Michaael Mastanduno, "Preserving the Unipolar Moment," in Brown et al., eds., *America's Strategic Choices*, 328.

28. Quoted in Robert J. Kaiser, "2025 Vision: A China Bent on Asian Dominance; Group Bids to Forecast Strategic Challenges," *Washington Post*, March 17, 2000, A25.

29. "The National Security Strategy of the United States of America," September 17, 2002, The National Security Council, The White House, www.whitehouse.gov/nsc/nss.html.

30. Alexandra Harney, Demetri Sevastopulo, and Edward Alden, "Top Chinese General Warns US over Attack," *Financial Times*, July 14, 2005, Asian Pacific Section, 9.

31. Barton Gellman, "US and China almost came to blows in '96: Tension over Taiwan prompted repair of ties," *Washington Post*, June 21, 1998, A1.

32. "Jihad against Jews and Crusaders: World Islamic Front Statement, February 23, 1998," Intelligence Resource Program, Federation of American Scientists, www.fas.org/irp/world/para/docs/980223-fatwa.htm.

33. Neil Mackay, "Bush planned Iraq 'regime change' before becoming President," *Sunday Herald* (Glasgow, Scotland), September 15, 2002, 1.

34. George Bush and Brent Scowcroft, *A World Transformed* (New York: Knopf, 1998), 464.

35. "US Military Tries to Plan for Rise of Asia," *Christian Science Monitor*, April 14, 2001.

36. Thomas P. M. Barnett, "Asia's Energy Future: The Military-Market Link," in Sam J. Tancredi, ed., *Globalization and Maritime Power* (Washington, D.C.: Institute for National Strategic Studies, National Defense University, 2002).

37. Ibid. Another scholar notes that "U.S. policy has been dedicated to dissuading Japan from becoming a 'normal' great power . . . The U.S.-led war in Iraq [the Gulf War] served multiple purposes, one of which was to maintain predictable access to Persian Gulf oil, on which Japan depends far more for its economic prosperity than does the United States." Michael Mastanduno, "Preserving the Unipolar Moment," in Brown et al., eds., *America's Strategic Choices*, 328.

38. "1999 Summer Study: Asia 2025," Office of Net Assessment, Department of Defense; Uwe Parpart, "Bush's lone military superpower vision, Part 2: The enemy is China," *Asia Times Online,* February 17, 2001, www.atimes.com/editor/CB17Ba01.html.

39. Douglas E. Streusand, "Geopolitics versus Globalization," in Tancredi, ed., *Globalization and Maritime Power*.

40. Ibid.

41. Bill Gertz, "China Builds Up Strategic Sea Lanes," *Washington Times*, January 18, 2005, A1.

42. Richard Orange, "CNOOC planning a second power play," *Knight Ridder/Tribune Business News,* November 13, 2005; Andrew Kramer, "Chinese Company's Bid for PetroKazakhstan Is Approved," *New York Times,* October 27, 2005, C6.

43. Gertz, "China Builds Up Strategic Sea Lanes."

44. Robert A. Pape, "Soft Balancing Against the United States," *International Security* 30, no. 1 (summer 2005): 31.

45. John Helmer, "Putin's Hands on the Oil Pumps," *Asia Times*, August 26, 2005.

46. James F. Hoge, Jr., "A Global Power Shift in the Making," *Foreign Affairs* 83, 4 (July/August 2004): 2–7.

47. Stephen Blank, "Central Asia's great base race," *Asia Times Online* (Central Asia), December 19, 2003, www.atimes.com/atimes/Central_Asia/EL19Ag01.html.

48. Ibid.

49. Ibid.

50. See the symposium entitled "Balancing Acts" in *International Security* 30, no. 1 (summer 2005), which includes Robert A. Pape, "Soft Balancing Against the United States," 7–45; T. V. Paul, "Soft Balancing in the Age of U.S. Primacy," 46–71; Stephen G. Brooks and William C. Wohlforth, "Hard Times for Soft Balancing," 72–108; Keir A. Lieber and Gerard Alexander, "Waiting for Balancing: Why the World Is Not Pushing Back," 109–39.

51. Blank, "Central Asia's great base race."

Chapter 9

1. Mackubin Thomas Owens, "A Balanced Force Structure to Achieve a Liberal World Order," *Orbis* 50, no. 2 (March 2006): 307–25.

2. See, for example, William E. Odom and Robert Dujarric, *America's Inadvertent Empire* (New Haven, Conn.: Yale University Press, 2004); Andrew Bacevich, *American Empire: The Realities and Consequences of U.S. Diplomacy* (Cambridge, Mass.: Harvard University Press, 2004); Chalmers Johnson, *The Sorrows of Empire: Militarism, Secrecy, and the End of the Republic* (New York: Metropolitan Books, 2004); Niall Ferguson, *Colossus: The Price of America's Empire* (New York: Penguin, 2004).

3. Robert Kagan, "The Benevolent Empire," *Foreign Policy*, no. 111 (summer 1998): 24–35.

4. Eliot Cohen, "Calling Mr. X," *New Republic*, January 19, 1998, 17–19.

5. Stephen Peter Rosen, "An Empire If You Can Keep It," *The National Interest* 71 (spring 2003): 51–62.

6. Evan Thomas, "The 12 Year Itch," *Newsweek*, March 31, 2000, 54; Michiko Kakutani, "How Books Have Shaped U.S. Policy," *New York Times*, April 5, 2003, D7.

7. Max Boot, "The Case for American Empire," *The Weekly Standard* 7, no. 5 (October 15, 2001).

8. Max Boot, *The Savage Wars of Peace: Small Wars and the Rise of American Power* (New York: Basic Books, 2002).

9. Michael Mandelbaum, *The Case for Goliath: How America Acts as the World's Government in the 21st Century* (New York: Public Affairs, 2005), 34–35. For an argument that U.S. hegemony in Europe is necessary to dissuade Germany from remilitarizing, see Robert J. Art, "Why Western Europe Needs the United States and NATO," *Political Science Quarterly* 111, no. 1 (spring 1996): 1–40. See also Michael Mandelbaum, "Preserving the New Peace," *Foreign Affairs* 74, no. 3 (May/June 1995): 9–13. A similar argument for U.S. reassurance of Japan is made in Aaron L. Friedberg, "Ripe for Rivalry: Prospects for Peace in a Multipolar Asia," *International Security* 18, no. 3 (winter 1993/94): 31–32.

10. Mandelbaum, *The Case for Goliath*, 224. The term "security dilemma" was first used in John H. Herz, "Idealist Internationalism and the Security Dilemma," *World Politics* 2, no. 2 (January 1950): 157–80. For a discussion of hegemonic stability theory, see Robert Gilpin, *War and Change in World Politics* (Cambridge, UK: Cambridge University Press, 1981).

11. William Kristol and Robert Kagan, "Towards a Neo-Reaganite Foreign Policy," *Foreign Affairs* 75, no. 4 (July/August 1996): 26.

12. Owens, "A Balanced Force Structure to Achieve a Liberal World Order," 307–25.

13. "Excerpts from Clinton Address," Federal Document Clearing House, *Washington Post*, March 24, 1999, A20.

14. George W. Bush, "Commencement Address at the United States Military Academy in West Point, New York, June 1, 2002," News and Policies, The White House, www.whitehouse.gov/news/releases/2002/06/20020601-3.html.

15. "Excerpts from Pentagon's Plan: 'Prevent the Re-emergence of a New Rival,'" New York Times, March 8, 1992, A14.

16. Walter Lippmann, U.S. Foreign Policy: Shield of the Republic (Boston: Little, Brown, 1943), 9.

17. Samuel P. Huntington, "Coping with the Lippmann Gap," Foreign Affairs, America and the World 66, 3 (1987/88): 453–77.

18. Stockholm International Peace Research Institute, SIPRI Yearbook, 2005: Armaments, Disarmament, and International Security (Oxford: Oxford University Press, 2005); T. V. Paul, "Soft Balancing in the Age of U.S. Primacy," International Security 30, no. 1 (summer 2005): 52.

19. Keir A. Lieber and Gerard Alexander, "Waiting for Balancing: Why the World is Not Pushing Back," International Security 30, no. 1 (summer 2005): 117–18.

20. Kristol and Kagan, "Towards a Neo-Reaganite Foreign Policy," 18–32: "In 1978, before the Carter-Reagan defense buildup, [defense spending] was about 23 percent [of the federal budget]. Increases of the size required to pursue a neo-Reaganite foreign policy today would require returning to that level of defense spending—still less than one-quarter of the federal budget" (25).

21. Linda Bilmes and Joseph Stiglitz, "War's Stunning Price Tag," Los Angeles Times, January 17, 2006.

22. For the contrary argument that U.S. hegemony is sustainable for the foreseeable future, see William C. Wohlforth, "The Stability of a Unipolar World," in Michael E. Brown, Owen R. Cote, Jr., Sean M. Lynn-Jones, and Steven E. Miller, eds., America's Strategic Choices: An International Security Reader, rev. ed. (Cambridge, Mass.: MIT Press, 2000), 273–309.

23. U.S. Commission on National Security/21st Century, New World Coming: The United States Commission on National Security/21st Century (Washington, D.C.: The Commission, 1999), 128.

24. Colin Powell with Joseph Persico, My American Journey (New York: Random House, 1995), 576.

25. William D. Hartung, "Outsourcing Is Hell," The Nation 278, no. 22 (June 7, 2004): 5–6, 22; Deborah Avant, "Think Again: Mercenaries," Foreign Policy, no. 143 (July/August 2004): 20–22, 24, 26, 28.

26. Anne E. Kornblut and Bret Ladine, "Bush trims route from service to citizenship; West Virginia speech taps patriotic themes," The Boston Globe, July 5, 2002, A2.

27. Tom Donnelly, "Underwhelming Force," The Weekly Standard 9, no. 10 (November 17, 2003).

28. James Risen, State of War: The Secret History of the CIA and the Bush Administration (New York: The Free Press, 2006).

29. George W. Bush, "Remarks by the President on Iraq, October 7, 2002," Cincinnati, Ohio. News and Policies, The White House, www.whitehouse.gov/news/releases/2002/10/20021007-8.html.

30. Sam Tanenhaus, interview with Paul Wolfowitz, Vanity Fair, May 2003.

31. Neil Mackay, "Bush planned Iraq 'regime change' before becoming President," Sunday Herald (Glasgow, Scotland), September 15, 2002, 1.

32. Paul Wolfowitz, "Statesmanship in the New Century," in Robert Kagan and William Kristol, eds., Present Dangers: Crisis and Opportunity in American Foreign Policy and Defense Policy (Encounter Books, 2000), 315.

33. Richard M. Freeland, The Truman Doctrine and the Origins of McCarthyism (New York, 1985); Frank Kofsky, Harry S. Truman and the War Scare of 1948 (New York: Palgrave Macmillan, 1993).

34.   Barry R. Posen, "Command of the Commons: The Military Foundation of U.S. Hegemony," *International Security* 28, no. 1 (summer 2003): 5, n. 2.

35.   Michael Mandelbaum, *The Case for Goliath: How America Acts as the World's Government in the 21st Century* (New York: Public Affairs, 2005), 223–24.

36.   Cohen, "Calling Mr. X."

37.   Thomas Donnelly, "Rising Powers and Agents of Change," AEI Online, posted January 5, 2006, www.aei.org/publications/pubID.23644/pub_detail.asp.

Chapter 10

1.   Woodrow Wilson, "Address of the President of the United States to the US Senate, January 22, 1917," in *A Day of Dedication: The Essential Writings and Speeches of Woodrow Wilson*, ed. Albert Fried (New York: Macmillan, 1965), 281–87.

2.   Stephen M. Walt, "Taming American Power," *Foreign Affairs* 84, 5 (September/October 2005): 18. For other defenses of a grand strategy of offshore balancing, see Christopher Layne, "From Preponderance to Offshore Balancing: America's Future Grand Strategy," *International Security* 19 (summer 1997); John J. Mearsheimer, *The Tragedy of Great Power Politics* (New York: W. W. Norton, 2001).

3.   Quoted in Herman Hagedorn, *The Bugle That Woke America* (New York: John Day, 1940), 9.

4.   Woodrow Wilson, "Address of the President of the United States to the US Senate, January 22, 1917," in *A Day of Dedication*, ed. Albert Fried, 281–87.

5.   Theodore Roosevelt, "5th Annual Message, December 5, 1905," in James D. Richardson, ed., *A Compilation of the Messages and Papers of the Presidents 1789–1908* (Washington, D.C.: Bureau of National Literature and Art, 1908), 11: 1131–81.

6.   G. John Ikenberry and Charles A. Kupchan, "Liberal Realism: The Foundations of a Democratic Foreign Policy," *The National Interest* 77 (fall 2004): 38–49.

7.   Theodore Roosevelt, "Nobel Lecture, May 5, 1910," in Joseph Bucklin Bishop, ed., *Theodore Roosevelt and His Time, Shown in His Letters* (New York: Charles Scribner's Sons, 1920), 2: 422.

8.   Franklin Delano Roosevelt, "Our Foreign Policy," *Foreign Affairs* 6 (July 1928): 585; Willard Range, *Franklin D. Roosevelt's World Order* (Athens: University of Georgia Press, 1959), 166.

9.   Range, *Franklin D. Roosevelt's World Order*, 173.

10.   Townsend Hoopes and Douglas Brinkley, *FDR and the Creation of the UN* (New Haven, Conn.: Yale University Press, 1997), 71.

11.   Ibid., 39.

12.   Ibid., 46.

13.   Ibid., 72.

14.   Ibid, 111.

15.   Range, *Franklin D. Roosevelt's World Order*, 176.

16.   Hoopes and Brinkley, *FDR and the Creation of the UN*, 11.

17.   Philip Bobbitt, "Better Than an Empire," *Financial Times*, March 12, 2004.

18.   Rebecca J. Johnson, "Russian Responses to Crisis Management in the Balkans," *Demokratizatziya* 9, no. 2 (spring 2001): 298–99; T. V. Paul, "Soft Balancing in the Age of U.S. Primacy," *International Security* 30, no. 1 (summer 2005): 61.

19.   The equation for diplomatic representation is found in George Modelski, *Principles of World Politics* (New York: Free Press, 1972), 188.

20.   "For Declaration of War Against Germany," in Ray Stannard Baker and William E. Dodd, eds., *The Public Papers of Woodrow Wilson* (New York: Harper and Row, 1927), 5: 12.

21.   Fareed Zakaria, *The Future of Freedom* (New York: W. W. Norton, 2003).

22. Robert A. Pape, *Dying to Win: The Strategic Logic of Suicide Terrorism* (New York: Random House, 2005).

23. For an earlier version of this argument, see Michael Lind, "Opportunity Missed," in Ted Halstead, ed., *The Real State of the Union* (New York: Basic Books, 2004).

Chapter 11

1. Herbert Croly, *The Promise of American Life* (Boston: Northeastern University Press, 1989 [1909]), 312.

2. Population Division of the Department of Economic and Social Affairs of the United Nations Secretariat, *World Population Prospects: The 2004 Revision and World Urbanization Prospects: The 2003 Revision*, http://esa.un/org/unpp. See also Joseph Chamie, Director of the UN Population Division, "The New Population Order," *New Perspectives Quarterly* (spring 2001).

3. James F. Hoge, Jr., "A Global Power Shift in the Making," *Foreign Affairs* 83, 4 (July/August 2004): 2–7.

4. Dominic Wilson and Roopa Purushothaman, "Dreaming with BRICS: The Path to 2050," Global Economics Paper No: 99, Goldman Sachs, October 1, 2003.

5. Angus Maddison, *The World Economy: A Multinational Perspective* (London: Development Centre of the Organisation for Economic Co-operation and Development, 2002), 142.

6. Robert A. Pape, "Soft Balancing against the United States," *International Security* 30, no. 1 (summer 2005): 7–45

7. Michael Lind, "The American Century Shows No Sign of Ending," *Financial Times*, February 17, 2006.

8. Joel E. Cohen, "Human Population Grows Up," in *Crossroads for Planet Earth*, *Scientific American* Special Issue, September 2005, 50.

9. "Half a Billion Americans?" *The Economist*, August 22, 2002.

10. "Le Commerce Mondiale au XXIe siecle [World Trade in the 21st Century]. Scenarios for the European Union," Institut Francais des Relations Internationales (IFRI), 2002; Martin Walker, "French Study Says Europe Fading," United Press International, May 14, 2003.

11. John J. Mearsheimer, *The Tragedy of Great Power Politics* (New York: W. W. Norton, 2001), 398.

12. For a discussion of "cooperative security" in Europe, see Charles A. Kupchan and Clifford A. Kupchan, "Concerts, Collective Security, and the Future of Europe" and "Concerts, Collective Security, and the Future of Europe: A Retrospective," in Michael E. Brown, Owen R. Cote, Jr., Sean M. Lynn-Jones, and Steven E. Miller, eds., *America's Strategic Choices: An International Security Reader*, rev. ed. (Cambridge, Mass.: MIT Press, 2000), 218–65.

13. Alan Dupont, "The Schizophrenic Superpower," *The National Interest* 79 (spring 2005): 43–51.

14. Michael Mandelbaum, *The Case for Goliath: How America Acts as the World's Government in the 21st Century* (New York: Public Affairs, 2005), 237, n. 40.

15. Ibid., 190.

16. James Zogby, "Attitudes of Arabs: 2005," *Zogby International* (December 2005): www.saudi-us-relations.org/fact-book/polls/arab-attitudes-2005.pdf.

17. Robert A. Pape, *Dying to Win: The Strategic Logic of Suicide Terrorism* (New York: Random House, 2005).

18. United Nations, Population Division "World Population Prospects: The 2002 Revision," February 26, 2003, www.un.org/esa/population/publications/wpp2002/WPP2002-HIGHLIGHTSrev1.pdf.

19. Quoted in Robert O. Work, "Winning the Race: A Naval Fleet Platform Architecture for Enduring Maritime Supremacy" (Washington, D.C.: Center for Strategic and Budgetary Assessments, 2005), 71.

20. Barry Posen, "Command of the Commons: The Military Foundation of U.S. Hegemony," *International Security* 28, no. 1 (summer 2003): 5–46.

21. See Joseph S. Nye, Jr., *The Paradox of American Power: Why the World's Only Superpower Can't Go It Alone* (New York: Oxford University Press, 2002); Michael Hirsch, *At War With Ourselves: Why America Is Squandering Its Chance to Build a Better World* (New York: Oxford University Press, 2004).

Chapter 12

1. Franklin D. Roosevelt to William Allen White, December 1939, in *F.D.R., His Personal Letters,* 4 vols., ed. Elliott Roosevelt (New York: Duell, Sloan, & Pearce, 1947–50), 3, (1928–45), 967; quoted in Willard Range, *Franklin D. Roosevelt's World Order* (Athens: University of Georgia Press, 1959), 47.

2. Russell F. Weigley, *The American Way of War* (Bloomington: University of Indiana Press, 1973). See the critique in Brian M. Linn, "The American Way of War Revisited," *Journal of Military History* 66, no. 2 (April 2002): 501–30, and Russell F. Weigley, "Response to Brian McAllister Linn," *Journal of Military History* 66, no. 2 (April 2002): 531–33.

3. U.S. Marine Corps, *Small Wars Manual* (Philadelphia: Pavilion Press, 2004); Keith Bickel, *Mars Learning: The Marine Corp's Development of Small Wars Doctrine, 1915–1940* (Boulder, Colo.: Westview Press, 2000).

4. Max Boot, "The New American Way of War," *Foreign Affairs* 82, 4 (July/August 2003): 27–40.

5. Antulio J. Echevarria II, "Toward an American Way of War," Strategic Studies Institute Monograph, March 2004, www.carlisle.army.mil/ssi.

6. Forrest Davis, "Roosevelt's World Blueprint," *Saturday Evening Post*, April 10, 1943.

7. Quoted in Walter LaFeber, *The Clash: A History of U.S.–Japan Relations* (New York: W. W. Norton, 1997), 82.

8. Hermann Hagedorn, *The Bugle That Woke America* (New York: John Day, 1940), 9.

9. Ibid., 17.

10. Associated Press, "U.S. Can't Find Hussein Bunker," *Washington Post*, May 30, 2003.

11. Alfred P. Rubin, *The Law of Piracy* (Newport, R.I.: Naval War College Press, 1988).

12. Daniel Webster, "Letter from Mr. Webster to Lord Ashburton, August 6, 1842," cited in Lori F. Damrosch et al., *International Law: Cases and Materials* (Cleveland, Ohio: West Publishing, 2001), 923.

13. Quoted in "Senator Edward M. Kennedy's Induction Remarks," The American Academy of Arts and Sciences, Cambridge, Mass., October 5, 2002.

14. Norman Friedman, *The Fifty-Year War: Conflict and Strategy in the Cold War* (Annapolis, Md.: Naval Institute Press, 2000), 141.

15. Quoted in McGeorge Bundy, *Danger and Survival* (New York: Random House, 1988), 252.

16. Quoted in "Senator Edward M. Kennedy's Induction Remarks," The American Academy of Arts and Sciences, Cambridge, Mass., October 5, 2002.

17. Paul Kennedy, *The Rise and Fall of the Great Powers: Economic Change and Military Conflict from 1500 to 2000* (New York: Random House, 1987), Table 24, 271.

18. Ibid., 355.

19. Ibid., 332, Table 32.

20. Ibid., 436, Table 42.

21. On this element in U.S. strategy during the Cold War, see Melvyn P. Leffler, *A Preponderance of Power: National Security, the Truman Administration, and the Cold War* (Stanford, Calif.: Stanford University Press, 1992).

22.   Quoted in G. John Ikenberry, "America's Imperial Ambition," *Foreign Affairs* 81, no. 5 (September/October 2002): 44–62.

23.   Richard Nixon, "Address to the Nation on the War in Vietnam, November 3, 1969," *Public Papers of the Presidents of the United States: Richard Nixon, 1969* (Washington, D.C.: U.S. Government Printing Office, 1971), 901–9.

Chapter 13

1.   Leo Amery, comment on H. J. Mackinder, "The Geographical Pivot of History," *Geographical Journal* 23, no. 6 (April 1904): 441.

2.   Paul Kennedy, *The Rise and Fall of the Great Powers: Economic Change and Military Conflict from 1500 to 2000* (New York: Random House, 1987), 355.

3.   Ibid., 354, Table 34.

4.   Norman Friedman, *The Fifty-Year War: Conflict and Strategy in the Cold War* (Annapolis, Md.: Naval Institute Press, 2000), 121.

5.   David Ricardo, "On the Principles of Political Economy and Taxation," chapter 7 in Piero Sraffa, ed., *The Works and Correspondence of David Ricardo*, vol. 1 (Cambridge: Cambridge University Press, 1952).

6.   J. S. Mill, *Principles of Political Economy*, in J. M. Robson, ed., *Collected Works of John Stuart Mill* (Toronto: University of Toronto Press, 1963-1991 [1848]), 918–19.

7.   Adam Smith, *The Wealth of Nations* (Indianapolis: Liberty Classics, 1976), 1: 494–95.

8.   Ibid.

9.   Edmund Burke, *The Works of the Right Honorable Edmund Burke*, 1: 371, cited in Jonathan Haslam, *No Virtue Like Necessity: Realist Thought in International Relations since Machiavelli* (New Haven, Conn.: Yale University Press, 2002), 141.

10.   Ha-Joon Chang, *Kicking Away the Ladder: Development Strategy in Historical Perspective* (London: Anthem Press, 2002), 52.

11.   Ibid.

12.   Alex Roberto Hybel, *Made by the USA: The International System* (New York: Palgrave, 2001), 15.

13.   Adam Smith, *An Inquiry into the Nature and Causes of the Wealth of Nations* (New York: Random House, 1937 [1776]), 347–48.

14.   The story is told in Pat Choate, *Hot Property: The Stealing of Ideas in an Age of Globalization* (New York: Alfred A. Knopf, 2005), 30–31.

15.   Allen C. Guelzo, *Abraham Lincoln: Redeemer President* (Grand Rapids, Mich.: Wm. B. Eerdmans, 2003), 134.

16.   Henry Clay, *The Works of Henry Clay Comprising His Life, Correspondence and Speeches*, ed. Calvin Colton, Federal Edition, 10 vols. (New York: G. P. Putnam's Sons, 1904), 6: 98.

17.   See, generally, Michael Lind, *Hamilton's Republic: Readings in American Democratic Nationalism* (New York: The Free Press, 1997).

18.   Heather Cox Richardson, *The Greatest Nation of Earth: Republican Economic Policies during the Civil War* (Cambridge, Mass.: Harvard University Press, 1997), 19. See also Michael Lind, *What Lincoln Believed: The Values and Convictions of America's Greatest President* (New York: Doubleday, 2005); idem, *Hamilton's Republic*.

19.   Paul Leicester Ford, ed., *The Works of Thomas Jefferson* (New York: G. P. Putnam's Sons, 1904), 11: 504–5.

20.   James Madison, "Seventh Annual Message to Congress, December 5, 1815," *State of the Union Addresses* (New York: Kessinger Publishing, 2004), 38–45.

21.   Quoted in Alfred E. Eckes, Jr., *Opening America's Markets: U.S. Foreign Trade Policy Since 1776* (Chapel Hill: University of North Carolina Press, 1995), 20.

22.   See Lind, *Hamilton's Republic*; Eckes, *Opening America's Market*; Daniel Walker Howe, *The Political Culture of the American Whigs* (Chicago: University of Chicago Press,

1979); Heather Cox Richardson, *The Greatest Nation of the Earth: Republican Economic Policies during the Civil War* (Cambridge, Mass.: Harvard University Press, 1997); Gabor S. Boritt, *Lincoln and the Economics and the American Dream* (Chicago: University of Illinois Press, 1978).

23. W. Henderson, *Friedrich List—Economist and Visionary, 1789–1846* (London: Frank Cass, 1983); Friedrich List, *National System of Political Economy*, trans. Sampson S. Lloyd, 3 vols. (Roseville, Calif.: Dry Bones Press, 1999–2000 [1885]).

24. Yukichi Fukuzawa, *An Outline of a Theory of Civilization*, trans. David A. Dilworth and G. Cameron Hurst (Tokyo: Sophia University Press, 1973), 192, cited in Richard J. Samuels, *"Rich Nation, Strong Army": National Security and the Technological Transformation of Japan* (Ithaca, N.Y.: Cornell University Press, 1994), 43.

25. Edward Hallett Carr, *The Twenty Years' Crisis, 1919–1939: An Introduction to the Study of International Relations* (London: Macmillan, 1939), 75.

26. Clyde Prestowitz, *Three Billion New Capitalists: The Great Shift of Wealth and Power to the East* (New York: Basic Books, 2005), 111.

27. Ibid., 112.

28. "The Internet and the WWW: A History and Introduction," www.albany.edu/ltl/using/history.html.

29. "Fastest Growing Occupations 2002–2012," *U.S. Bureau of Labor Statistics* (February 2004): www.accd.edu/sac/students/cpc/pdf/occupations.pdf.

30. Klans Schwab, "Global Competitiveness Report: 2004–2005." Growth Competitiveness Index Rankings and 2003 Comparisons. *World Economic Forum* (New York: Palgrave Macmillan, forthcoming).

31. Jacob S. Hacker, *The Divided Welfare State: The Battle Over Public and Private Social Benefits in the United States* (Cambridge, UK: Cambridge University Press, 2002).

32. See Barry Lynn, *End of the Line: The Rise and Coming Fall of the Global Corporation* (New York: Doubleday, 2005); idem, "War, Trade and Utopia," *The National Interest* 82 (winter 2005/06): 31–38.

33. Charles P. Kindleberger, *The World in Depression, 1929–1939* (Berkeley: University of California Press, 1986); Helen Milner, "International Political Economy: Beyond Hegemonic Stability," *Foreign Policy*, no. 110 (spring 1998); G. John Ikenberry, "Getting Hegemony Right," *The National Interest* 63 (spring 2001): 17–24.

34. Aaron L. Friedberg, *In the Shadow of the Garrison State: America's Anti-Statism and Its Cold War Strategy* (Princeton, N.J.: Princeton University Press, 2000), 250.

35. Ibid.

36. David M. Lampton, "Paradigm Lost: The Demise of 'Weak China,'" *The National Interest* 81 (fall 2005): 75.

37. George Washington, "First Address to Congress, January 8, 1790," in John C. Fitzpatrick, ed., *The Writings of George Washington from the Original Manuscript Sources, 1745–1799*, vol. 30, June 20, 1788–January 21, 1790 (Washington, D.C.: U.S. Government Printing Office, 1939), 491–94.

Chapter 14

1. John F. Kennedy, "Inaugural Address, January 20, 1961," in Theodore C. Sorensen, ed., *Let the Word Go Forth: The Speeches, Statements, and Writings of John F. Kennedy* (New York: Delacorte Press, 1988), 12.

2. Hans J. Morgenthau, *In Defense of the National Interest: A Critical Examination of American Foreign Policy* (New York: Alfred A. Knopf, 1952), 3–4.

3. Woodrow Wilson, "Address of the President of the United States to the U.S. Senate, January 22, 1917," in *A Day of Dedication: The Essential Writings and Speeches of Woodrow Wilson*, ed. Albert Fried (New York: Macmillan, 1965), 281–87.

Index